# Dos, Don'ts & Maybes of English Usage

# Dos, Don'ts & Maybes of English Usage

## Theodore M. Bernstein

### with the assistance of
### Marylea Meyersohn and Bertram Lippman

Times
BOOKS

Published by TIMES BOOKS, a division of
Quadrangle/The New York Times Book Co., Inc.
Three Park Avenue, New York, N.Y. 10016

Published simultaneously in Canada by
Fitzhenry & Whiteside, Ltd., Toronto

**Library of Congress Cataloging in Publication Data**

Bernstein, Theodore Menline, 1904-1977
   Dos, don'ts and maybes of English usage.

   1. English language—Usage.   I. Meyersohn, Marylea,
joint author.  II. Title.
PE1460.B4618     428       77-4293
ISBN 0-8129-0695-0 (hardcover)
ISBN 0-8129-6321-0 (paper)

Manufactured in the United States of America

10 9 8 7 6 5 4 3 2 1

# Read This First

Usually I act at my readers' bidding (provided the bid isn't too high) and that is what I have been doing in putting together this book. Readers of my column sent me a flood of mail asking whether the column could be had between covers or whether it was ultimately going to be put out in book form and I finally decided that rather than answer those four letters it would be easier to get out a book. So here it is.

*Dos, Don'ts and Maybes of English Usage* draws its material almost entirely from the column and a good deal of the column consists of answers to readers' questions. Inevitably some of the answers embrace material that I wrote about in *The Careful Writer*, but most do not. The column, by the way, is a thrice-weekly, nationally syndicated production called "Bernstein on Words." That title wasn't my idea; to me it sounds immodest. It was the idea of John Osenenko, manager of the Special Features syndicate of *The New York Times*, who, with a minimum of argument, persuaded me (he convinced me, too) that it was a good idea. After all, he said, did anyone ever ask you, "Did you read 'Words Worth and Tennis Anyone' today? Hell, no; they ask you, 'Did you read Art Bookwood' today?" So I gave in.

Nobody had to persuade me to write the column. Of course, I thought it would help me, but, more importantly, I thought it would help users and readers of English everywhere. And without doubt many of them—too many of them—need help. Just read your average newspaper, listen to interviews and talk shows on television or study your daily mail and you will find that English usage is becoming English loosage: bad grammar, an excess of slang, too many words to express something simple, pomposity and pretentiousness and lack of clarity.

But I think I detect some signs of change; the cause is not hopeless. There is evidence that more people have become aware of what is wrong and are interested in making things better. Schools and colleges are giving more attention to remedial courses. And that means that more teachers will intensify their efforts to give good instruction. I think I even discern tiny signs that today's younger generation is getting away from the I-could-care-less attitude of yesterday's younger generation. I don't expect any overnight revolution, but I do hope for a slow and constant reform.

It is not necessary or advisable to ram every one of Miss Thistlebottom's grammatical rules down people's throats. Rules have changed and will continue to change, and if the changes make sense and are not destructive of words or of clear syntax, we should be willing to accept them. Let's be neither radical nor reactionary; let's be liberal. That is the position that I hope and think is mine in the pages that follow.

*

## ACKNOWLEDGMENTS

My collaborator in putting this book together was Marylea Meyersohn, deputy chairman of the English Department of The City College of the City University of New York. Studying more than 2,000 items in over 700 of my columns, she skillfully selected, organized and edited the items that are here published.

Another big help was (and is) Bertram Lippman, who was a member of the English Department of Bayside High School, New York City, and more recently a senior member of the Queens College (N.Y.) staff teaching English to the foreign-born. Mr. Lippman goes over every column I write, checking in advance of publication for boo-boos and rah-rahs. He is indispensable.

# Dos, Don'ts & Maybes of English Usage

# A

**A, AN**
*See* ARTICLE USE.

**ABSENT**
(Makes the mind go wander.) Here is a sentence that poses a tough question: *"Absent* any instructions, the jury might have gone wrong on the question of perjury." Used in that sentence as an adjective meaning "lacking," how can the adjective take an object? It is true that every dictionary lists *absent* as an adjective or a verb. But one—Webster's unabridged, third edition—in addition lists it as a preposition, giving this example of its prepositional use: ". . . *absent* any other facts, there arises an implied contract." That makes sense. And if you have trouble conceiving of *absent* as a preposition, don't think of it as meaning "lacking," but rather as meaning "without." An exactly parallel word is *given,* which is used in the same way, as in, "Given the present inflation, the country's economic future poses some problems." In that example think of *given* as meaning "with." Apparently Webster's unabridged didn't think of it that way because it does not list *given* as a preposition as it does the similarly used word *absent.* Maybe it will in the fourth edition. Then there is the word *granted,* which is similarly used: *"Granted* the defendant was intoxicated, he was nonetheless at fault." That use of *granted* does not appear in that dictionary and one wonders what part of speech the dictionary would assign to that. The significant thing in each of the foregoing instances is not to find a part-of-speech label but rather to be aware that each use involves an ellipsis:

if unforeseen events are *absent;* if we are *given* the present situation; if it be *granted.*

## ACCESS
*See* EXCESS.

## ACCESSIONED
If a library received some books in a bequest, you'd think the books were *acquired* or *obtained.* That's what you'd think. But libraries think they were *accessioned.* Which proves, apparently, that every field of human endeavor has to have its own jargon. Professor O. G. Ludwig of Villanova University writes that he finds the verb *accessioned,* which has been in use for well over four decades, infelicitous-sounding. But he was horrified to read in the press that New York's Metropolitan Museum of Art had *de-accessioned* some of its holdings, and you can hardly blame him. It's true that the prefix *de-,* according to Webster's unabridged dictionary, second edition, is now "freely used as a living prefix" to form words that mean the undoing or reversing of an action. But why attach a negative prefix to a positive verb to form a clumsy word, when it is quite possible to use a simple, direct word and say that the museum *sold* the holdings or *traded* them or, if it is wished to cover both ideas, *disposed* of them? *De-accession* sounds like a word that should be *de-accessioned.* (*See* JARGON.)

## ACCOMPLICE
*See* CONFEDERATE.

## ACCUSED
*See* ALLEGED.

## ACCUSED (OF)
"I stand before you *accused with* not cooperating with an investigating committee." Thus spoke, believe it or not, a professor of medieval history with a Ph.D. from Princeton. A person may be *charged with* an offense, but if the verb is *accused* the preposition should be *of.*

## ACRONYM
That word *acronym* is a relatively recent coinage, not more than three or four decades old. It derives from the Greek *acro-* or *akros,* meaning highest or topmost, hence first, and *onyma,* name. The first letters or syllables of words make up a *name.* Acronyms flourished during and since World War II, though some antedated that period.

## ACRONYMOMANIA
At the rate at which words formed from the initials of organizations or movements are appearing, there is an overabundance of acronyms. Here are some that have appeared in the press fairly recently:

ACRONYM—Allied Citizens Representing Other New York Minorities.
C.H.I.P.—Community Housing Improvement Program.
COYOTE—Call Off Your Old Tired Ethics.
PRIME—Productivity Improvement by Managers and Executives.
SCAMP—Senior Citizens Activities and Meals Program.
SWAT—Special Weapons and Tactics.
V.I.T.A.L.—Volunteers to Improve Third Avenue and Lexington.

To which we might add: APPALLING—Acronym Production, Particularly At Lavish Level, Is No Good.

## ADDITIONALLY, IN ADDITION
(And what's more . . . ) Let's say we have a sentence that reads, "He can swim, play football, read Greek, and, *in addition to* all that, write poetry." Is it correct to use *additionally* in such a sentence so that it reads, *"additionally* write poetry"? *Additionally* means moreover or besides. Therefore the word is appropriate in its meaning and additionally it is more economical. Yes, it is perfectly proper.

## ADJECTIVES VS. ADVERBS
*How do you feel?* Those who would reply to the foregoing question by saying, "I feel *badly,"* would be guilty of overrefinement, as would be the dinner guest who tried to eat an olive with a fork. The word *feel* in the question is equivalent to *are*—"How *are* you?" Both are what are called copulative, or linking, verbs,

which are properly followed in this example by adjectives *(bad* or *good)*. The adverb *badly* would be used only to express a defect in the sense of touch or to express degree rather than quality, as in "I feel *badly* (i.e., *intensely*) the need for more discussion of this issue." And don't be misled by the fact that it is proper to say, "I feel *well.*" In this context *well* is an adjective meaning in sound health, not an adverb meaning excellently or favorably.

Another adverb problem was handed to me by this question: "Which usage is correct: He walks *slow* or he walks *slowly?*" The answer is that either one is correct because both words are adverbs, though *slowly* is the more commonly used. The inquirer then went on: "If we say *slow,* then the opposite would be *fast,* which sounds right to me. But if *slowly* is used, we'd need to use *fastly* for the opposite, wouldn't we? And that sounds off the track to me." And well it might. Once, centuries ago, there was an adverb *fastly,* but it is now archaic. However, adverbs don't have to end with *-ly* and it doesn't sound out of line to say, "Sometimes he walks *slowly* and other times *fast,*" does it?

## ADMISSION, ADMITTANCE

Is there any difference between these two words? One difference is that *admittance* is by far the less commonly used of the two. Another is that *admittance* is restricted to the literal meaning of allowing entry, whereas *admission* can convey not only that sense but also the sense of making available certain privileges. A moviegoer may gain *admission* to a theater and then find a sign on the theater owner's door that says, "No *admittance.*" In addition, *admission* has another meaning—a confession or a conceding, as in an *admission* of guilt.

## ADMIT

A prisoner can *confess* a crime or *confess to* it. But idiom, which often acts illogically, does not permit the same constructions to be used after *admit.* That prisoner could *admit* a crime, but the strict idiom watchdogs would not allow him to *admit to* a crime. However, *admit* may be teamed up with the preposition *of* to mean allow or leave room for, as in, "The President's statement *admits of* two interpretations." When used in this way the phrase should not apply to persons but rather to impersonal nouns or abstractions. It would not be proper, for instance, to say, "The President *admitted of* differences of opinion."

## ADOPTED, ADOPTIVE
A child who is adopted is an *adopted* child, but the couple who do the adopting are not *adopted* parents; they are *adoptive* parents. *Adoptive* is not always used when it should be, perhaps because it has too proper a sound. As I said on another occasion, words that are too proper, like girls who are too proper, are not easily embraced.

## ADVERB, EVERYDAY VARIETY
A sentence read, "It seems worse *mornings,*" and that prompts one to ask whether such use of *mornings* is ungrammatical. The answer is no. *Mornings* is an adverb in perfectly good standing, and so are *nights* and *evenings.* They appear as such in just about every dictionary.

## ADVERB PLACEMENT
(We're only trying to help.) Normally the placement of *only* next to the word it qualifies is best. But there are exceptions to that "rule." One is a sentence in which idiom calls for a different placement. Example: "What is happening in foreign exchange markets can *only* be termed a disaster." The "normal" positioning of *only* would be ahead of "a disaster," but that would be unidiomatic and might even suggest a different meaning.

A second seeming exception comes about when *only* is what is called a sentence adverb, qualifying the entire thought rather than a part of it: "I *only* thought I was being helpful."

A third exception occurs when the writer wishes to signal the reader early in the sentence that there is a qualification attached to the statement. "Normal" placement would produce this sentence: "Cars will be permitted to park on the avenue between 9 A.M. and 6 P.M. only if drivers remain at the wheel." That's all right, but it would be preferable to place the *only* ahead of "be permitted" so that the reader would learn early in the sentence that there was a string attached to the thought.

The moral of all this is that sometimes it is best not to be too sticky about rules.

(Out of place.) The following sentence illustrates a fairly common misplacement of an adverb: "The period from mid-March to April 6 is believed to have been the time of the heaviest and *most potentially controversial* Republican contributions." The *most* doesn't modify *potentially,* as this placement suggests, but rather *controversial.* Therefore, proper placement would make it read, "potentially the most controversial." (*See* MODIFIERS.)


## ADVERBS

(Reluctant ones.) A sentence read, "The appeal was dismissed on the ground that it was *untimely* filed." Although *untimely* doesn't sound like an adverb, it is one. Still, some words ending in *y* seem to fight off being turned into adverbs. Although *happy* is happy to help out in a sentence such as "He sang *happily,*" the word *ugly* screams and squawks when it has to play an adverbial role, as in "He behaved *uglily,*" despite the fact that it has that adverbial form. Several other words—*friendly, masterly, funny, kindly*—are reluctant to appear in clumsy adverbial garb and so they are rarely used in that form. When such words rebel the thing to do is to give in and reword the sentence. That opening sentence above would have been more graceful if it had read, "The appeal was dismissed on the ground that its filing was *untimely.*"


## ADVERSE, AVERSE

(Two negative words.) A newspaper sentence said, "Holbrook would not be *adverse* to a regular TV series," and that prompted an inquiry concerning whether *adverse* should not have been *averse.* The words *adverse* and *averse* both have a negative connotation, but *adverse* has a considerably stronger meaning than *averse. Adverse* means opposed, antagonistic, hostile, and that was not what the quoted sentence intended to imply. *Averse* means disinclined, reluctant, loath, which was the intended meaning of that negatively expressed sentence.


## A FEW
*See* FEW.

## AFFECT, EFFECT

*Affect* means to influence ("Weather *affects* the farmer's income") whereas *effect* means to bring about or accomplish ("Congress is trying to *effect* an improvement in the farmer's income"). Although we know there is no foolproof way of teaching the distinction between them, we shall take a stab at it. Think of the first letter of each word—the *a* in *affect* and the *e* in *effect.* Then think of the *a* as standing for *alter* (which is not a synonym for *affect* but is close to the meaning) and the *e* as standing for *execute* (which ditto). Now recite the previous sentence 100 times, then proceed to the next item. (Hoping this will not confuse matters, we present here the noun *affect.* The word is confined to use in psychology and means, in general, a stimulus producing a mood, or, even more generally, an emotional response or lack thereof.)

## AFFINITY

(Mutual attraction.) An *affinity* denotes a sympathetic or close relationship marked by mutuality. That two-sidedness seems to have something to do with the choice of the preposition to use after *affinity.* Often the word *for* is used after it, but at least one dictionary frowns on that usage and says only *of, between* or *with* may be used. Follett's *Modern American Usage* suggests the reasoning behind the ban on *for* when it says that *"affinity* expresses a mutual relationship, not someone's attraction to a passive or insentient object—and it does not denote a propensity for doing or being something." On the other hand the less strict Webster unabridged dictionary, third edition, finds *for* acceptable in certain uses; for example: "The special *affinity* of a virus *for* the nervous system" or "Basic dyes have an *affinity for* wool and silk." The combination *affinity for* is widely used so the ban should not be taken too strictly.

## AGGRAVATE

(A condition worsened.) A widespread but inept use of a word appears in this sentence: "The rise in United States arms costs *aggravated* the Iranian general." A person can be irritated, but not *aggravated.* Most authorities contend that *aggravate* should apply to a troublesome existing condition. The word comes from a Latin term meaning to make heavier or worse. It is true that its application to a person has become quite common, but that does not make it proper and certainly it is not necessary when you consider the correct words that convey the intended meaning—words such as *irritate, vex, bother, inflame, annoy, arouse* and *exasperate.*

## AGREEMENT IN NUMBER

(Any.) A book publisher recently sent out an ad that asked this question: "Do any of these texts suit your course needs?" That might lead someone to ask whether *any* could be used as a plural. Is it time for purists to throw in the towel? The answer is that the towel has been lying in the ring since time immemorial. *Any* may be used as either a singular or a plural. Indeed, as a pronoun *any* is scarcely ever used as a singular; one authority calls that use archaic. But as a plural it is common and proper: "There are bright students in the class, but it is doubtful whether *any are* geniuses."

(One or more.) The phrase *one or more* puzzles some writers and speakers because they don't know whether it takes a singular verb or a plural verb. Thus, you will sometimes see a sentence like this: "Inside each folder *is one or more* sheets of information." The verb should be *are.* Like *one or two,* which means a few, *one or more* is an entity meaning some. Both phrases should be linked to plural verbs.

(You is?) The sentence in an ad read, "You, the educated consumer, is our best customer." The question is whether the verb of the sentence is governed by *consumer* and therefore is properly *is* or whether the verb is governed by *you* and therefore should be *are.* The word *consumer* is the one nearer to the verb, but it is not the subject of the sentence. The subject is *you.* The phrase "the educated consumer" is merely an appositive expression that describes or defines *you.* If the *you* is the grammatical subject followed by an interpolated phrase the verb has to be *are.*

(The word "number.") Quite often a type of sentence comes along in which the subject is singular on its face but plural in its meaning, and the question arises whether the verb should be singular or plural, as in this example: "A number of observations of the sun (was? were?) made during the eclipse." A general guide is that if the idea of oneness predominates, treat the subject as a singular; if the idea of more-than-oneness predominates, treat it as a plural. In the foregoing sentence *number* on its face is a singular noun, but its sense is *many;* therefore the verb should be *were.* In general, *a number* takes a plural verb and *the number* a singular.

(Multiple subject.) A common error is illustrated in the following sentence: "The Jones company, together with other manufacturers of plastic widgets, *have* been trying to reach an agreement with the union." The phrase *together with* does not add to the grammatical subject; it simply designates something that accompanies it. Hence, the verb should be singular: *has.* Other words that function this way are *as well as, in addition to, including, with* and *plus.* They may have the sense of *and,* but they don't have the same grammatical effect; they either are or serve as prepositions. To take a simple and clear example, surely you wouldn't say, "His salary, including all extras, *are* $200 a week." Let's hope not.

(Wrong number.) Incredible as it may seem, a full-page newspaper ad for CBS television contained two errors of elementary grammar. Speaking of the news anchorman Jim Jensen, the ad said, "Backing up Jensen *is* Stephen Bosh, Chris Borgen, Joe Witte, Pat Collins, Joel Siegel, Ron Swoboda—plus the most dedicated staff of professionals in broadcast journalism today." Three paragraphs later the ad said, "Leading the list of awards from fellow journalists *is* the National Headliners Award for Outstanding Achievement in Journalism and two New York Associated Press Broadcasters Awards for Excellence." The fact that in each instance the sentence is inverted, with the subject following the verb, does not excuse the errors of using a singular verb with a plural subject. Nor are they excusable if the argument is made that the ad writer was attempting—as so many of them often do attempt—to bend his language down to the level of the masses.

## AIN'T (BAD)
In *The Story of Language* Mario Pei says that *ain't* as a substitute for *am not* or *are not* was established in current usage by King Charles II. That would date it back some three centuries. When

it became substandard is difficult to learn. But Porter G. Perrin in *Writer's Guide and Index to English* says that "prejudice against it among educated people has been almost unanimous for the last half century or so." There can be no doubt that *ain't I* is easier to say than *aren't I* or *amn't I* and sounds less stilted than *am I not*. Nevertheless, what should be not always is. Incidentally, Webster's New International Dictionary, third edition, says that *ain't* is "used orally in most parts of the U.S. by many cultivated speakers esp. in the phrase *ain't I,*" a statement that is open to serious doubt.

## ALBEIT

(So be it.) Not so many years ago the word *albeit* was on the way to being classed as archaic, but it has survived though its legs are shaky. It originally was a compound of *all, be* and *it* in the sense of "let it all be (whatever)." It had, and has, the meaning of although. One caution about how not to use it is exemplified by this sentence: "We are presently witnessing the banal but *albeit* tragic spectacle of a world community idly watching the wanton murder of innocents by fanatic organizations." The use of *but* ahead of *albeit* creates a redundancy. You could—and should— delete either the *but* or the *albeit.* Just as you wouldn't say "but although," so you shouldn't say *"but albeit."*

## ALL (OF)

(All of us wrong?) For generations some nit-pickers have argued against following *all* with *of.* They contend it is illogical and careless to say, *"All of* the pupils passed the exam." The words *"of* the pupils," they maintain, signify a part, whereas *all* signifies the total number, and thus *all of* is, in a way, self-contradictory. The argument is pure nonsense. If a pronoun follows the *all*, the *of* is mandatory to produce acceptable English; you cannot say *all them*, or *all us* or *all it.* If the nit-pickers' logic rules out *"all of* the pupils" and demands "all the pupils," the same logic should demand "all them." But it doesn't. The most that can be said on the nit-pickers' side is that except with pronouns, the *of* following *all* is superfluous and may be omitted, but its use is well established and cannot be opposed on any other ground.

## ALL THAT
(Not all that good.) A present-day colloquialism is illustrated by this sentence: "The garbage problem is a pressing one, but it should not be *all that* difficult to solve." (Sometimes the phrase is reversed and appears as *that all.*) *All* is a legitimate adverb, as in the phrases *all alone* and *all gone,* but it is superfluous as used in current conversation and some writing. In straightforward speech and writing it is best avoided.

## ALL/-RIGHT, -READY, -TOGETHER, -MOST
(Okay? Oh kay?) A phone company ad, observing that an obscene call is an upsetting experience, remarked, "But if you know how to handle it, it can turn out *alright.*" That last word is frowned upon by just about every authority, the characterizations ranging from "a common misspelling" to "a vulgarism." Defenders of *alright* point to such compounds as *already* and *altogether* as if they were pertinent precedents. But a moment's thought will disclose that *already* and *all ready* mean quite different things, as do *altogether* and *all together.* The only occasion on which *alright* and *all right* could have different meanings would be the relatively rare one exemplified by this sentence: "His answers to the five questions were *all right.*" On other occasions the two versions would have the same sense. And that raises the question, who needs *alright?* Forget it.

Parenthetically, this writer, in breaking in a new secretary, had brought home to him the distinction between *almost* and *all most.* A dictated letter was supposed to say, "Your comments are *all most* heartening." Guess how the secretary typed it.

## ALLEGED, ACCUSED
"*Alleged* murderer" has been in common use for years, but of late we have seen the term "*accused* murderer" and our feeling is that *accused* lacks some of the mitigating force of *alleged.* The term *alleged* refers to a declaration made without proof or to a statement perhaps improperly put forth. *Accused* usually involves a formal charge and thus is more forceful. It may be noted incidentally that a softer and safer way of expressing the thought involved in both terms is to say "*alleged* to be the murderer" or

*"accused* as the murderer," but headline space does not always permit such longer constructions.

## ALLITERATION
(Similar sounds.) *Alliteration* is the repetition of sounds at the beginnings of words or in accented syllables. Properly handled, it is a useful device in poetry. But here is how it was used by a Federal judge in a recent order issued in the case of an army lieutenant: "He was pummelled and pilloried by the press. He was taunted and tainted by television. He was reproached and ridiculed by radio. He was criticized and condemned by commentators. . . . His conviction was to be a cathartic to cleanse the national conscience and the impellent to improve the Army's image." How about that? Most stylists would agree that alliteration of that sort is so contrived, so unsubtle, and so inappropriate that it damages rather than adorns the prose into which it is introduced. Rather than write like that it would be better to leave alliteration to the ad men, who love it: "Bohunk's beer is the best beer."

## ALREADY
*See* ALL RIGHT.

## ALTERNATIVES
You have three alternatives: One is to confine the word *alternatives* to two options, the second is to use it to apply to more than two options, and the third is to strike the word from your vocabulary altogether, which would be ridiculous. Strict purists point to the Latin derivation of the word, which includes *alter,* meaning other (of two), and maintain that it can apply only to a choice between two possibilities. More liberal authorities call that position a fetish and point out that the word has been used reputably to apply to more than two possibilities since the middle of the last century. The advice here is not to be superstrict.

## ALTOGETHER
*See* ALL RIGHT.

**A.M., P.M.**
(The correct time.) If one minute before noon is written "11:59
A.M." and one minute after noon "12:01 P.M.," is 12 noon writ-
ten as "A.M." or "P.M."? Neither; you write it as either "12 noon"
or simply "noon." You could make it "12 M.," with the "M."
standing for the Latin *meridies* or noon, but that is not customary.
Midnight is written as either "midnight" or "12 P.M. midnight."
Incidentally, if you are speaking of one minute later than 11:59
P.M. Saturday, it's midnight Saturday, not midnight Sunday.
"Midnight" belongs to the expiring day, not the new one.

**AMERICA, AMERICAN**
Those two words refer to the United States and its citizens,
although some have asked if it isn't presumptuous usage. It is
true that *America* embraces more territory than the United States
and that technically *Americans* should apply to Chileans, Canadi-
ans, and American Indians as well as to United States citizens.
But the established fact is that in usage *America* means the
United States and *American* means one of its citizens or pertaining to that country. This use of *American* (and *America*) as relating
to the United States is not presumptuousness; it's simply common, established usage.

**AMONG**
  *See* BETWEEN.

**AMPERSAND**
The *ampersand* is a sign in writing or printing that means "and."
It looks like this: "&". Interestingly enough, the word *ampersand*
is a contraction of *and per se and,* which means literally "& by
itself (equals) and."

**ANACOLUTHON**
Here is a word you may never have heard before and there's no
reason why you should have. It means a sudden switch in the
same sentence from one grammatical construction to another.
(In the word the accent is on the *luth,* as in *luth conthtruction.*) An
example: "The preparation is one of those bits of bottled magic,
something you spread on your face before a good night's sleep
and wake up to find yourself glowing." Notice how the phrase

beginning with "and wake" goes off on a tangent; it has no grammatical connection with "something you spread on your face." Occasionally *anacoluthon* is used for rhetorical effect, but most often it is just a blunder. *Ana Coluthon* sounds like a nice girl, but she's not. Don't give her house room.

## AN (A) HISTORIC MATTER

In a message to Congress former President Ford spoke twice of *an historic* opportunity and once of *an historic* achievement. Should he have said *a historic?* In good usage on both sides of the Atlantic it should be *a historic.* In the earliest stages of the language there was no *a*, but only *an*. But it required too much effort to say "an great day" or "an balky horse" so everyday speech tended to slur over the *an* and say "a great day" or "a balky horse." Thus the article *a* came into being. The rule today is to use *a* before a consonant or a consonant sound and *an* before a vowel. But how, you may ask, does one determine whether a word begins with a consonant sound? The best way is to pronounce the word aloud. If you pronounce "historic" as *istoric* or "hotel" as *otel*, then you'd better say *an historic* and *an hotel*. But the rest of us will say *a historic* and *a hotel*. It should be noted that some words begin with vowels that are pronounced as consonants—*European* and *university*, for instance. Since those vowels are sounded like *y*, we say *a European* and *a university*.

## AND/OR

This combination, both a visual and a mental abomination, is a device much favored by lawyers, who are constantly trying to plug that last loophole. But in most instances a little thought will tell them that either *and* or *or* will do the trick. For instance, they will write that "there is no uniform assessment and/or tax rate in the region," whereas *or* by itself would take care of all possibilities. One situation that comes to mind in which choosing one conjunction or the other will not do the trick is this sentence: "The law provides a $25 fine *and/or* 30 days in jail." But even here the sentence could be put into plain English at the cost of only one word: "a $25 fine or 30 days in jail or both." In ordinary nonlegal writing there is no excuse for the awkward *and/or* gadget. (*See* LEGAL LINGO.)

## ANECDOTE, ANTIDOTE
(Funny story.) An article that appeared in *The National Tattler* spoke of accidental poisonings of children and then said, "So why not have a universal *anecdote* readily available and easy to use if such a tragedy occurs in your home?" A typographical error? Hardly, because the headline on the article read, "Keep *Anecdote* for Poisonings Close at Hand." There should be an *antidote* handy for poor editing of that sort.

## ANSWER, REPLY, RETORT
Apparently there are more Miss Thistlebottoms teaching in schools than we thought. In a note we wrote recently, we asked forgiveness for delay in replying to a letter. In a pleasant second letter our correspondent said we must have skipped school the day Miss Prim (that's an alias for Thistlebottom) taught about the difference between *answer* and *reply;* you *answer* a letter, said he, and you *reply* to a charge. Those definitions are far too confining. The American Heritage Dictionary, in its discussion of synonyms, says that *"answer,* the most general, refers to any act that completes a process initiated by another" and that *reply* "means to answer in speech or writing to a direct question." We did indeed *reply* to that first letter. A *retort,* on the third hand, is a reply in a quick, direct manner.

## ANXIOUS, EAGER
To the average person these words mean about the same thing. He will say, "I'm *anxious* to see what my tax is going to be," and in the next breath say, "I'm *anxious* to see the Expos play tomorrow." In careful usage, though, one of those is not quite correct. Both *eager* and *anxious* convey the idea of desire, but *anxious* has a slight connotation of apprehension or uneasiness. For some reason—perhaps because it sounds a little flossy—*eager* is not used very often in spoken language. In the more precise form of language—writing—it is well to reserve *anxious* for situations in which some anxiety is involved.

## ANY
*See* AGREEMENT.

## ANY (OTHER)

(Be other-wise.) An example of improper usage appeared in this ad: "This refrigerator-freezer uses less energy than any refrigerator-freezer available today." What is required is the word *other* after the *any.* The intent of the statement is to take the advertised refrigerator out of the class of which it is a part, and to accomplish this the word *other* is required. A general guide that should be observed is this: When a thing is being compared with others of its own class it must be set apart from the others; to do this the word *other* is needed. (*See* COMPARATIVES.)

## ANYMORE

A question is sometimes raised about the following usage: "We haven't *anymore* candy." That word is not correct if what you are thinking of is the compound term *anymore,* which means now or hereafter or further. The intent in that quoted sentence is to say that "of more candy we haven't any"—that is, *any* and *more* are being used as separate words, just as *any additional* would be. Another related question concerns a sentence such as, "We don't go to the movies often *anymore* the way we used to." That use is correct; there the meaning of *anymore* is now. It should be noted that *anymore* is properly used with a flatly negative statement ("The movies are no good *anymore*") or with a statement that has a negative connotation ("Movies are hardly worth bothering with *anymore*") or sometimes with a question ("Are movies any good *anymore?*"). The term is not properly used with an out-and-out affirmative statement ("Movies are such a bore anymore"). (P.S. We have nothing against the movies.)

## ANYONE

*See* ONE WORD, TWO WORDS.

## ANYWHERE

A news article contained this sentence: "A spokesman for Public Service Electric & Gas said, 'Service was interrupted *anywhere* from a few minutes to four hours.' " Some may find this use of *anywhere* awkward and unnecessary. But to take another instance, "The price of the stock rose from $20 to $30" says something quite different from, "The price of the stock rose *anywhere* from $20 to $30." As to the question about usage, most dictionaries accept the *anywhere* as proper, though one dictionary labels it colloquial, which does not necessarily mean it is substandard. What most authorities do consider substandard, however, is the word *anywheres*.

## APHESIS
*See* LACKADAISICAL.

## APOSTROPHES
(Cute 'n' wrong.) In a supermarket ad in a New York newspaper recently one item read Quick *'n* Easy cookies and another item directly below it read Light *n'* Lively low fat milk, while in an adjoining ad a store was pushing Light-N-Lively ice milk. Let's forget the hyphens in that last one and focus on the apostrophes in the others. An apostrophe is used to replace an omitted letter. Therefore, if you are substituting *n* for *and,* you are omitting two letters, so that the only proper rendition of the contraction is 'n'. That punctuation rule is ignored most of the time by advertisers, but it is tried 'n' true.

(Joint possession of joint.) Let's say you know a couple named Mollie and Joe Jones and you want to talk about the place where they live. If you say, "Mollie and Joe Jones's home," there is no problem. But some people find it a problem when the name common to both of them is omitted and the first names alone are used; the question concerns where the apostrophe is to be placed. The answer is that the sign of possessive is placed after the second name (or the last of the names if more than two are involved). Thus you would write, "Mollie and Joe's home" (or "Adam, Smith and Robinson's book"). (*See* POSSESSIVES.)

(Purposes of apostrophe.) People unaccustomed to writing sometimes tend to drop in an apostrophe at the drop of a hat. One ad touts *azalea's;* another speaks of a closeout of *diamond's;* and still another says it is time to select your *sandle's* (by which is supposedly meant *sandals*). In each instance the apostrophe is not only superfluous, but also wrong. The apostrophe is used for three purposes: to indicate the omission of one or more letters *(can't, don't)* or figures (the spirit of *'76*); to indicate the possessive case (*Tom's* dog); and to indicate the plurals of letters (there are two *m's* in accommodate), figures *(B-52's)* and sometimes words.

That foregoing phrase "sometimes words" needs a little explanation. Plurals of words cited as words rather than as ideas or concepts are indicated by 's: "There are too many and's in your sentence." However, if it is the meanings or the senses of the words rather than merely the words as groups of letters that are meant, no apostrophe is used: "There are too many ifs in your proposal." Or, to come closer to home, "this book is entitled, *Dos, Don'ts and Maybes of English Usage.*"

## APPARENTLY

(Ambiguous word.) Two distinct, almost opposite, meanings are lodged in the word *apparently.* On the one hand, *apparently* can mean not hidden, obvious, evident: "Quite *apparently* the accountant had violated the law in the action that caused his conviction." On the other hand, *apparently* can mean seemingly but not necessarily true: "Apparently the prisoner had evidence indicating his innocence." To convey the first meaning the *apparently* almost always must be modified by an intensifying adverb such as *quite* or *very.* The word *apparent* does not require that kind of differentiation. The meanings are clear in the following sentence: "It is *apparent* that the city will have to increase taxes to meet the *apparent* deficit." Nevertheless, writers would be well advised to give close attention to those words.

## APROPOS

The naturalized English word *apropos* comes from the French *à propos,* meaning to the purpose. As an adjective it means fitting or pertinent, as in, "The minister made an *apropos* oration at the funeral." As an adverb the word means with regard to or suitably or opportunely, as in, *"Apropos* of the minister's remarks, he made one minor error." One slight word of caution should be made about the adverb: Use the preposition *of* with it or no preposition at all, but not the preposition *to.*

## APT

*See* LIKELY.

**ARSE**
(Word changes.) The English language changes, and some of the change occurs in the area of slang. Words once considered vulgar have become acceptable—*nuts,* for example. Others that once were standard English have become vulgar. An example of one of these came up in the White House transcripts that figured in the Watergate case. As published by *The New York Times* and some other newspapers, John W. Dean 3d, counsel to former President Nixon, was quoted as saying, "How do I protect my *ass?*" That word developed out of *arse,* meaning the buttocks or posterior, and both are considered vulgar today. But until the middle of the seventeenth century *arse* was a standard English word used in polite society. Times do change and so does the speech of the people.

**ARTICLE USE**
(Number puzzler.) A recent news report talked about "an estimated 2,000 political prisoners," and a Congressional resolution began with "an estimated 460 million persons. . . ." Is the use of the article *an* in such cases correct? If so, what does it agree with in each case? Some years back we were struck by the incongruity between the singular article *an* and a plural noun phrase such as *2,000 prisoners,* and we insisted that the word *total* should be inserted to make it read *an estimated total of 2,000 prisoners.* Without question that made grammatical sense. However, some time later we discovered in *A Modern English Grammar,* by Otto Jespersen, who was probably the foremost authority on the language, that he accepted similar "incongruous" constructions. They were similar but not identical because almost all the examples he offered contained plural phrases normally regarded as making up a single unit rather than considered severally: "a delightful three weeks," "a good three-quarters of a mile away," "another ten days." Even if the phrases are not ones that are normally regarded as units, we can think of the word *total* as being understood in the construction and accept it. We should accept it in any case because it is idiomatic and an estimated three-quarters of the population have been using it for years.

**AS**
*See* LIKE.


## AS A MATTER OF FACT

Nine times out of ten the expression *as a matter of fact* is mere embellishment; if a statement is a fact it need not be so labeled. But on some occasions the words are not intended to be taken literally as pointing out that a statement is factual. Rather they lend a flavor to what is being stated. Suppose you ask someone whether he has ever attended a basketball game and he replies, "I'm going to one tonight." It's a simple, rather flat response. But if he replies, *"As a matter of fact,* I'm going to one tonight," it could suggest that he's going for the first time or that it was quite a coincidence that you asked at this time or that he has been going to games for years, all depending on the intonation and facial expression. The words of the expression may not have much meaning, but they do on such rare occasions provide a light vehicle on which a tone or a sense can be conveyed.


## AS . . . AS, SO . . . AS

There are those grammarians who assert that *as . . . as* should be used in affirmative statements ("Frank is *as* smart *as* Einstein") and *so . . . as* in negative statements ("His brother is not *so* smart *as* Frank"). The truth is that no distinction between the phrases need be made and most often none is made by good writers and speakers. Follett's *Modern American Usage* says that Americans tend to shift to the *so* for negative statements whereas the English use *as* either way. The English part of that assertion is dubious. Eric Partridge, an English authority on usage, does draw some distinction by declaring that *as . . . as* is "neutral, colourless," whereas *so . . . as* is "emphatic." It is true that in certain situations the *so* version is emphatic. Partridge gives the example "They were *so* clumsy *as* to be dangerous to their companions." But it should be noted, first, that is not a negative statement; second, that it puts emphasis on degree; and third, that *as* could not be substituted for *so* in any event. In general, you will be safe if you use *as . . . as* for both positive and negative statements. There is no rule.

## AS BEST AS

It is perfectly proper to say, "He did the job *as best* he could."
The *as* in that sentence means in the manner. However, it is not
proper to say, "He did the job *as best as* he could." There the
*as . . . as* indicates degree, but the question of degree is already
answered in the word *best,* which is superlative—that is, it indicates the highest degree. The sentence is as erroneous as, "They
are *as thickest as* thieves." Just as you can properly say, *"as thick
as* thieves," so you can properly say, *"as well as* he could," but
not *"as best as* he could."

## AS FAR AS

(So far no good.) The phrase *as far as* (or *so far as*) leads many
speakers and writers into error. Example: *"As far as* the scientific
research into the causes of the common cold, very little new has
been turned up." Used in this way, the phrase constitutes a
conjunction and a conjunction introduces a clause, which is
required to contain a verb. In the foregoing example, as in nine
out of ten similar constructions, the required verb is "is concerned." To omit the "is (or are) concerned" is a serious solecism. Of course, sometimes *as far as* is used as a preposition
meaning *to* or denoting the extent of an action and then no verb
is required: "He went *as far as* the corner drug store, then turned
back." But the example given at the beginning of this item
should read, *"As far as* the scientific research into the causes of
the common cold *is concerned,* etc." (*See* SO FAR AS.)

## AS IF, AS THOUGH

Often you will hear people say something like this: "He was so
angry he looked *as if* he *was* going to explode." It is not a correct
locution; the *was* should be *were.* The reason is that the sentence
sets up a hypothetical situation; the *as if* shows that the statement is not factual. The sentence may be thought of as an
elliptical version of a fuller statement that would read, "He
looked *as* he would look *if* he *were* going to explode." Hypothetical or unfactual statements of that kind call for the subjunctive
mood and that is what the *would* and the *were* provide. Naturally,
the same rule applies to *as though,* which has the same meaning
as *as if.*

At this point some nit-picker is sure to be on the verge of

questioning the phrase *as though* on the ground it is illogical. Filling out the ellipsis of the sentence, "He looks *as though* he were crazy," the nit-picker is thinking, would make, "He looks *as* he would look *though* he were crazy." *Though* does not make any sense in that context, the nit-picker contends. True enough, with the present-day meaning of *though* the phrase does not seem to make any sense. But an ancient meaning of *though* is *if,* which is now obsolete except in the phrase *as though.*

## AS YET
*See* YET.

## ASSASSIN
Ten years and more ago the man who shot and wounded Governor Wallace would have been called an *assassin.* The word was defined then as meaning one who treacherously kills *or attempts to kill* another person, especially a public figure. All the new dictionaries, however, have dropped that alternative of attempting to kill, presumably because in popular usage *assassin* means only one thing—a person who succeeds in killing. The word has an interesting background. It derives from the Arabic *hashshashin,* meaning persons addicted to hashish. Originally they were members of a Mohammedan sect who, under the influence of hashish, secretly murdered Christians during the Crusades. Those, of course, were the bygone days of violence.

## AUTONOMOUS
(Independent word.) A newspaper article said, "Congressional sources noted that the Federal Reserve system is autonomous from the President." That is an error in usage. Though it means about the same thing as *independent,* the word *autonomous* is independent; it doesn't take a preposition as a follower.

## AVERSE
*See* ADVERSE.

## AWAKE, AWAKEN
(End sleep.) *Wake* is, in the words of H. W. Fowler, the ordinary working verb: "It's time to *wake* Johnny," "Thunder *woke* me last night," "He wants to be *waked* (up) early tomorrow." Ac-

cording to Fowler, *awake* and *awaken* are preferred to the others in figurative senses: "The citizens *awoke* (or *awakened*) to the long-term energy crisis," "The indictment *awakened* a feeling that something was wrong." *Awake* and *awaken* are not followed by *up*. Other subtleties are attached to these words, but to go into them would probably put you to sleep. (*See* WAKE.)

## AWFUL, AWFULLY
The adjective *awful* in proper use means causing awe or fear or being impressive. But the word is often used as if it were an adverb and in a sense that is completely different from what the speaker or writer really has in mind. Such uses produce phrases like *"awful* pretty," *"awful* cute," *"awful* good," *"awful* talented." Phrases of that kind are, strictly speaking, self-contradictory, but, still worse, they are colloquial and substandard. What the user means and should say is *very, highly,* or *extremely.*

## AWHILE
The errors made in the use of this word are, to put it mildly, numerous. The reader of a California newspaper complained about the frequency of the appearance of the word *détente,* and the paper replied, "It is a word that, if we are lucky, will be with us for *awhile."* The meaning of *awhile,* which is an adverb, is for a period; the *for* sense is built into the word. Therefore it is redundant to write "for *awhile."* However, there is a word *while,* which is a noun meaning a period of time. Therefore you can put an article in front of it (but not attached to it) and you can let a preposition govern it. Thus it would be proper to write, "The word will be with us *for a while."*

Another misuse of *awhile* should be mentioned. A comic strip spoke of a woman getting out of the house *once and awhile.* It should, of course, be *once in a while.* The error quite obviously arises from a mistranslation of the heard words into written words. (*See* ONE WORD, TWO WORDS.)

# B

## BACK CLIPPING
(Are you in tune with this one?) By a process known as back clipping, the word *synchronization* has for some time been shortened to *sync* in colloquial language. It refers to the fitting together of picture and sound in a movie or of flash gun and shutter in a camera or of any other mechanical harmonization. But more recently the word has been embedded in a broader, more abstract phrase: *out of sync*. You will see it used this way: "Mr. Wilson is totally *out of sync* with modern impulses." That means, of course, that he is out of touch, not plugged in, not with it. Back clipping, by the way, is not at all uncommon; we see it in such words as *math* (from *mathematics*), *taxi (taxicab)*, *exam (examination)*, *mike (microphone)*, *natch (naturally)* and a host of others. The process is not *sensaysh*, but neither is it *ridic*.


## BACK-FORMATION
An *editor* is a fellow who gives out with the news or with articles or books. The word comes from the Latin *edere*, to give out. It's that simple. But the word *edit* is what is called a back-formation from *editor*. Some people thought that what an *editor* did was *edit*, though there was no such word at the time. A back-formation is a word coined on the erroneous supposition that a normal word was derived from it, as *enthuse* from *enthusiasm*, *peddle* from *peddler* and *edit* from *editor*.

## BAD
*See* ADJECTIVES AND ADVERBS.

## BARBECUE
Every suburbanite knows the meaning of *barbecue,* and even city dwellers have a pretty good idea of its meaning. Derived from the Spanish, it refers to meat broiled over a rotating spit. But how many people know the word's meaning as a space age term? It denotes the rolling of a spacecraft in orbit to take advantage of or to avoid the sun's heat. Thus do words take on new meanings and thus does the language grow.

## BASEBALL TALK
With baseball in the news most of the year by now, it might be well to examine some of the lingo of the diamond. Not that you aren't familiar with it, but rather that most of us are so familiar with it that we scarcely notice its strange deviations from normal English.

For instance, who ever heard of the past tense of *fly* being *flied?* But you wouldn't dream of saying that "Johnny Jones *flew* out to left field." And then there's the noun *fly.* Most commonly it's an insect, but to the fanatics of the national pastime it's a ball hit high into the air. If it's high and slow and easy to catch, it's a *can of corn.* If it's high and within reach of the infielders, it's a *pop-up.* On some occasions the TV announcers will tell you that the infield is *defensing* against the possibility of a bunt. (Ever hear *defensing* used in any normal, nonsports context?) Then if an infielder bobbles the bunt, the announcer is likely to say that the batter *reached* on an error—not *reached* first base, but plain, old *reached.* If the batter hits a *grounder* and a fielder snares it immediately after a bounce, the announcer will say that he *trapped* it or *short-hopped* it or got it on the *pickup.*

Pitchers, of course, throw a variety of slang terms: a *fastball* (that's one with a lot of smoke on it), a *change-up* or *change of pace* (one delivered with the same motion as a *fastball* but with less *smoke* on it), a *knuckler, knuckle ball* or *blooper* (a slow pitch thrown with the knuckles rather than the fingertips on the ball), a sinker (formerly known as a *drop*), a *curve* (a pitch that swerves to a right-handed pitcher's left and a left-handed pitcher's right), a *screwball* (one that swerves in the opposite direction of a *curve*), and a *slider* (which Frankie Frisch used to define as a five-cent curve ball). (*See* FUNGO.)

## BEG THE QUESTION

What we have here is a fallacy in logic. *To beg the question* is to base a conclusion on a premise that needs proof as much as the conclusion does or on a premise that says substantially the same thing as the conclusion but in different words. Here is an example from Brewer's *Dictionary of Phrase and Fable:* "Parallel lines will never meet because they are parallel." In that example one is assuming as fact the very thing he is professing to prove. Another example: "Everybody believes in justice. Therefore the belief in justice is universal." The two sentences do not prove anything; they merely say the same thing in different words. There is a Latin phrase for this type of fallacy. It is *petitio principii,* which means a begging of the question.

## BEHALF (OF)

What is the distinction between *in behalf of* and *on behalf of?* Although many good writers and readers don't insist on any distinction at all, more do make one. They maintain that *in behalf of* means for the benefit of or as a champion or friend: "A large sum was raised by the women's society *in behalf of* ailing Mexican children." *On behalf of,* under this distinction, means as the agent of or in place of: "The lawyer entered a not guilty plea *on behalf of* the defendant." Now that you have seen the distinction exhibited in examples, doesn't it seem natural and worthwhile? (The word *behalf* was used in the Middle English phrase *on mi behalfe* based on the Old English *be healfe,* meaning by the side, half, or part.)

## BEMUSED MISUSED

Because of the sound of it, *bemused* is sometimes used as if it meant *amused,* but it means nothing like that, though there is an etymological connection between the two words. You will occasionally see a sentence such as this: "The parents were *bemused* by Johnny's antics and broke into laughter." What *bemused* really denotes is being puzzled or muddled or in a daze or in deep revery.

## BETWEEN, AMONG

When Miss Thistlebottom taught you in grammar school that
*between* applies only to two things and *among* to more than two,
she was for the most part correct. *Between* essentially does apply
to only two, but sometimes the "two" relationship is present
when more than two elements are involved. For example, it
would be proper to say that "The President was trying to start
negotiations *between* Israel, Egypt, Syria and Jordan" if what was
contemplated was not a round-table conference but separate
talks involving Israel and each of the three other nations. *Among*
would not be improper in that context, but it would be vaguer
and less exact. Likewise it would be proper to say that a triangle
lies *between* points A, B, and C and less proper to say that it lies
*among* them.

## BETWEEN EACH

The sentence that follows is from a news magazine: "Electronically coordinated with the action of the heart, the balloon in-
flates *between each* heartbeat and gives an extra boost to send
blood through the patient's body." It is possible to say that the
*between each* construction is not uncommon and it is even possible to cite some distinguished writers who have used it. Nevertheless, the facts remain that (a) the idea of two is the very
essence of the word *between,* as it is of *twin* and *twain,* and (b) the
idea of singleness or oneness is the very essence of the word
*each.* Obviously, then, if you are speaking or writing with precision, you can't say something is *between* one thing. Correct the
quoted sentence to read, "between each heartbeat and the
next," or, "between every two heartbeats," or, "between heartbeats," or *"after* each heartbeat."

## BISTRO

Most dictionaries will tell you that the word *bistro,* meaning a
little wine shop or restaurant, comes from the French, and then
they drop the subject, usually not telling you what the French
ancestor was. However, Albert Parry, an expert on Russia and
a professor emeritus at Colgate University, has a fuller and quite
plausible theory. In a letter to *The New York Times* he said the
word came from the Russian *bystro,* meaning quick. In 1814
when the troops of Czar Alexander I occupied Paris, he says,

some parts of the city containing drinking places were put out of bounds to Russian soldiers by their commanders. Nevertheless, Russians sneaked into taverns, pointed to bottles and shouted to the proprietors, *"Bystro! Bystro!"* so that they could make quick purchases and get out before any patrols could catch them. And so, the professor says, taverns became *bistros.* We'll drink to that.

## BITE THE BULLET

(Traumatic experience.) In the Watergate scandal many notables had to *bite the bullet,* that is, face up to or accept a painful experience. The meaning of the phrase is well known, but its origin brings us to one of the most astonishing lexicographical lapses of all time. Here we have a common phrase and, believe it or not, it appears in only one general dictionary and not in a single phrase book—indeed, only one of more than fifteen reference works consulted contained anything at all about it. Not to keep you in suspense any longer, *bite the bullet* dates at least to the nineteenth century and perhaps to the sixteenth and has a battlefield origin. Anesthetics were not available and so, to distract a wounded soldier while he was undergoing some painful treatment, the medics of those days told him to bite a bullet. Supposedly that helped him to bear the suffering.

## BLEND WORDS

Words made up of parts of other words are called *blend words* or *portmanteau words.* The *portmanteau* term was coined by Lewis Carroll to designate a word like his *slithy* (a combination of *slimy* and *lithe*). As he said in *Through the Looking Glass,* by way of explanation of the term, "You see it's like a *portmanteau* . . . there are two meanings packed up into one word." Carroll originated the term, but he didn't originate blend words. Long before him there were words such as *splutter* (a combination of *splash* and *sputter*) and, on this side of the ocean, *gerrymander* (a combination in 1812 of *Gerry* and *salamander*). In more recent times Walter Winchell gave us such coinages as *infanticipating* and a nameless somebody gave us *smog (smoke* plus *fog).* In Carroll's day everyone knew what a *portmanteau* was—a leather traveling bag with two compartments—but how many people know it today? Very few, and for that reason I coined the term *centaur word* a few years ago to describe *blends*. A *centaur*, as you of course know, was a mythological beast, part man and part horse. So there is an analogy in that word. In 50 years or so the term will catch on, but that's just a guesstimate.

## BOTH

The word *both* tempts people into redundancies. It is superfluous in a sentence like this: "The two sisters *both* look alike." Another example: "The two friends *both* work together at the library." In both cases the *both* should be omitted. One of the meanings of *both* is not only this, but the other *as well.* Therefore, it is repetitive in a sentence like the following: "The speeches should produce good feeling *both* in the United States as well as in the Soviet Union." Either strike out *both* or change *as well as* to *and.* As must be obvious by this time, *both* applies to two and only two. It is incorrect to say, "His remarks were *both* improper, ill-timed and untrue."

## BOTH (AND)

Sloppiness often creeps into writing through the improper placement of *both* together with *and.* This may be taken as a general rule: Whatever appears after the *both* must be exactly paralleled grammatically by what appears after the *and*—a noun after the *both* must be matched by a noun after the *and,* a verb must be matched by a verb, a prepositional phrase by a prepositional phrase. An example of a misuse should make clear the requirement of the rule: "The Senator said that *both* from the viewpoint of economics and morality the nation must practice self-denial." Here the *both* is followed by a prepositional phrase, but the *and* is followed by a noun. The sentence may be corrected in one of two ways: either by placing the *both* ahead of *economics* (then a noun follows *both* and *and*) or by making it "the viewpoint *both* of economics *and* of morality" (a prepositional phrase follows each word). Logical tidiness is always an asset in the use of language.

## BOWDLERIZE

Whence cometh the word *bowdlerize?* The word derives from the name of Thomas Bowdler, an English editor who was born in 1754 and died in 1825 and who in 1818 issued an expurgated edition of Shakespeare "in which those words and expressions are omitted which cannot with propriety be read aloud in a family." In other words, the 1818 version of the "expletive deleted" process.

## BRING, TAKE

If a boss were to say to his secretary, *"Bring* this up to Mr. Jones on the fifth floor," he would be guilty of bad usage. On the other hand, if he were to say to her, *"Bring* me a chicken salad sandwich, no mayo, and be quick about it," he would be correct (but would also probably be a chauvinist pig). *Bring* and *take* both involve direction when they denote physical movement: *bring* means movement in the direction of the speaker or writer, *take* means movement away from the speaker or writer. The mistakes that occur are almost entirely the misuse of *bring* when the proper word should be *take,* as in the boss's first sentence above. When no physical movement is involved, *bring* may properly be used in the sense of produce as a result: "The President's message is expected to *bring* the whole issue to a climax."

## BRITISHISMS

(For the motorist.) If you are planning to drive a car in Great Britain, you may need a little dictionary to help you understand what the road signs mean. Elliott L. Biskind, who writes a column in the *New York Law Journal,* has assembled a few terms for us ignorant North Americans. For instance, an emergency parking area on our highways the British call a *lay-by;* instead of our "men working" or "construction ahead" they say *road up*; a warning of falling rock they term *loose slippings;* a circle of intersecting highways they designate a *roundabout* (unless it's in an urban area, in which case it's a *circus*); "no parking" they translate into *clear way;* and "slow" they emphasize by using a sign that says *dead slow.* And if your car won't start, just look under the *bonnet* and maybe you'll find out what's wrong.

(River Names.) Why do we read "the River Jordan"? We never say "the River Delaware." It is the opinion here that the answer to the puzzle lies in British custom and influence. The British, with few exceptions, put the name after the geographical word —they speak of the River Thames, the River Mersey, the River

Dee. Most other countries reverse the order—they speak of the
Mississippi River, the St. Lawrence River, the Amazon River.
There are, of course, exceptions on both sides, but those seem
to be the general rules. What is now Jordan was under British
tutelage for a period after World War I. If the point is made that
"River Jordan" goes back to Biblical times, it may be noted that
the Bible that has predominated for centuries is the English
King James version. The question that all this leaves unan-
swered is: Why do the English prefer putting the geographical
word first? Well, why do the English like fish and chips?

## BRAND NAMES

(Success headaches.) Recently the Xerox Corporation sent to
stockholders a pamphlet pointing out that aspirin was once a
brand name but people used it as if it were synonymous with
headache pill and soon it became part of the language. The
point of the pamphlet was that the same sort of thing could
happen to *Xerox* if people used the word as if it were a synonym
for *copy* or *copier.* The situation is not at all unusual. Other brand
names that either have become or are in danger of becoming
generic words are Nylon, Band-Aid, Scotch Tape, Frigidaire,
Levi's and Linotype. The irony of the whole thing is that companies spend huge sums building up their products and brand
names to the point where the names sometimes become so well
known and so widely used that the companies then have to
spend huge sums to protect them. They run ads in trade and
media publications, send letters to editors and broadcasters at
the mere drop of a Levi and issue pamphlets to stockholders.
They have to do this because if a company sues a competitor for
using its brand name, it must prove in court that it has energeti-
cally done whatever it could to protect the brand name. And so
the company pleads, "Copy things, don't 'Xerox' them." Sometimes the effort is even successful.

Strangely enough, there is no noun that describes these common words that have lost their trademark protection. There is
an adjective—*generic.* Why not turn generic into a noun (plural:
generics) so that instead of having to say that aspirin has become a *generic word* we will be able to say aspirin has become a
*generic?*

## BROADCAST
*See* FORECAST.

## BURGLE, BURGLARIZE
A word that bothers some people is *burglarize.* They maintain that a house is not *burglarized,* but rather is *burgled.* Painters do not painterize, nor do farmers farmerize. But patrons patronize and theorists theorize, do they not? Actually, most dictionaries list both *burgle* and *burglarize* as informal. The Merriam-Webster, second edition, even labels *burgle* as humorous.

## BURN UP, BURN DOWN
(Not all burned up.) Some things *burn up* and others *burn down.* Why is that? It has been suggested that large objects, such as houses, *burn down* and smaller objects, such as cars or piles of paper, *burn up.* But there seem to be some exceptions to the theory. Think of a barn and a garbage pile of the same size. The barn would *burn down,* but the garbage pile would *burn up.* Perhaps a distinction lies in whether the object is permanently or at least temporarily attached to the ground or is not. Thus, a barn or a circus tent would *burn down* though an airplane would *burn up.* (*See* VERBS WITH TAILS.)

## BUT
The expression, "I will not be *but* a minute," is fairly common, but it is not correct. The sentence is the equivalent of a double negative. In older English the negative *ne* frequently preceded the verb. If the verb was *is,* the two words were run together as *nis,* so that a sentence might read, "She *nis* but 6 years old." Later the *nis* was omitted, so that *but* took on the meaning of *nothing but* or *only,* and that is where it stands today. Therefore it should not be preceded by a negative.

(A problem.) A newspaper sentence read, "Probably no one *but he* knows when or why he developed an interest in Governor Wallace." Should it be *but him?* Maybe yes, maybe no; the authorities differ. Some regard *but* in a sentence like that as a conjunction introducing a hidden clause such as "but he does." Others regard it as a preposition equivalent to *except,* which would be followed by an objective pronoun: *him.* Two guides will be offered here. First, if the pronoun comes at the end of the sentence (where a noun or pronoun is normally in the objective case) make it objective: "The fact is known to no one but *him.*" If the pronoun appears elsewhere in the sentence, put it in the same case as the noun to which it is linked by *but:* "It is known to no one (objective) but *him* (objective) how he developed that interest"; "No one (nominative) but *he* (nominative) knows how he developed that interest." This probably sounds complicated to a chap who flunked grammar in school but it's fairly simple to everyone *but him.*

## BYZANTINE
Senator Gaylord Nelson pointed out to a *New York Times* correspondent recently what is not so much a word oddity as a dictionary oddity. Not one of his dictionaries, he said, contains a definition of *Byzantine* as the word is most commonly used—that is, implying underhanded maneuvering or crookedness. Actually, one standard dictionary, the Funk and Wagnalls desk edition, does have a brief such definition, but none of the big dictionaries do. The only other book I have discovered that contains such a definition is the Barnhart Dictionary of New English Since 1963. It gives one meaning of *Byzantine* as "characterized by much scheming and intrigue; Machiavellian." Maybe the dictionaries should pay closer attention to Byzaness.

# C

---

## CAMP

Originally *camp* was a piece of homosexual jargon, but it is not that now. As popularized by the critic Susan Sontag, it connotes something that is so banal and so passé that it is amusing to sophisticates. There are two kinds of *camp*. *High camp* refers to the deliberate use of something artistically mediocre for its amusing effect. *Low camp* refers to the unconscious use of something amusingly out-of-date and mediocre.

## CAPITAL, CAPITOL

The New York City Bicentennial Corporation issued a medallion inscribed, "New York City. First Capital of the United States of America." A New Yorker, who is a lawyer, no less, sent a letter to the corporation deploring "the state of education" in the city and asserting that the medallion is "hardly literate" because, says he, the word should be *capitol* not *capital*. With the intent of clarifying matters he explains that *capital* is a term in political economy. However, the counselor's contention is wrong. A *capitol* is a building in which a legislative body meets. A *capital* is a city or town that is a seat of government, and New York was indeed the first *capital* of the United States. The economic term is something else again.

## CARAT, KARAT

(Not always pure gold.) The normal word for measuring the fineness of gold, so the books tell us, is *carat*. Why, then, is the form *karat* used? Probably because, for one thing, *karat* applies

**36**

to gold alone whereas *carat* is a measure used for pearls and precious stones as well as gold and thus it could conceivably cause some ambiguity. For another thing, there is a third similar word, *caret,* which refers to a mark in the shape of an inverted *v* used in printing or writing to indicate where something is to be inserted. That probably couldn't cause ambiguity, but it might cause confusion in some rare instances. That's enough. We are not going to go into carrots.

## CAVALIER
The word *cavalier* keeps you guessing because it has a couple of quite different meanings. On some occasions it means debonair, jaunty, carefree. On many more occasions it means arrogant or haughty or having no regard for the views or feelings of others. Considering that a cavalier was originally a courteous, knightlike fellow, you may find that some of those meanings are surprising.

## CENTAUR WORDS
*See* BLEND WORDS.

## CENTENNIAL
In 1876 we celebrated the centennial (100th anniversary) of American independence, in 1926 we celebrated the sesquicentennial (150th anniversary), and in 1976 we celebrated the bicentennial (200th anniversary). What will we call the 250th anniversary in 2026? Apparently there is no term for such an anniversary, so we will have to coin one. How about *bi-sesquicentennial?* Or if that seems to suggest 300 years, how about *bi-plus-semicentennial?* Or if you don't like that one, consult me in 2026; my address will be Potter's Field. (*See* PREFIXES, BI-.)

## CERTAIN (AND SOME)
When, if ever, does *certain* equal *some?* How about the following sentence: "You must always allow a *certain* amount of time for the dregs to settle"? Used in that way, *certain* means *some,* though not very much. It gives the impression of being slightly more specific than *some.* Another example: "In any group of married couples a *certain* number will end up in divorce courts." There *certain* is more certain than *some* would be, though not greatly so. Presumably the statement is based on averages that have been

accumulated over a period of time, so that an approximation can be forecast, though the forecast will not be a certainty. In short, though most meanings of *certain* contain the sense of sureness or fixedness, some (not a certain number) have the loose sense of *some*. Is that all unclear?

## CHAUVINISM

Originally, *chauvinism* meant simply blind, militant patriotism. The word originated in the name of Nicolas Chauvin, a soldier who was blindly devoted to Napoleon. In recent years usage has broadened the word so that it now also denotes (in the words of Webster's New World Dictionary, 1970) "unreasoning devotion to one's race, sex, etc. with contempt for other races, the opposite sex, etc." Hence, we have these days *male chauvinist pigs*. The word *chauvinist* is not thus misused, though the label may sometimes be misapplied.

## CHORDS
*See* CORDS.

## CIAO

What is the etymology of *ciao*, which has become a form of salutation or farewell not only among teen-agers, but also among many adults. A couple of authorities say it is an Italian colloquialism for *schiavo* and means at your service or I am your slave. That is not improbable because the word *schiavo* denotes a slave or servant. The only thing certain about the word *ciao* is that it is pronounced chow.

## CLEANSE

In the liturgy of the Mass the celebrant prays, "Lord, wash away my iniquity and cleanse me *from* my sins." Sometimes it is said, "cleanse me *of* my sins." What is the difference?" There is no difference; either *from* or *of* may be used. The word *cleanse* (which is mostly used as a ceremonial term) means to rid of dirt or impurity or guilt and though either preposition may be used with it, *of* is the commoner.

## CLEAVE

When you stop to think about it (which, like it or not, you are about to do), *cleave* can have two almost directly opposite meanings. One is to split apart ("The ax *cleaved* the plank") and the other is to cling or stick to ("Her dress was rain-soaked and *cleaved* to her body"). Verily, a two-faced word. (*See* OVERSIGHT, SCAN, SANCTION.)

## CLICHES

(What a cliché is.) The word *cliché* comes from the French *clicher*, meaning to stereotype, that is, to make a printing plate from a matrix or mold taken from set type. The general idea is of a thing hard and fixed, and that describes some qualities of a *cliché*. Other qualities are triteness and bromidic, figurative language.

(Curdled clichés.) A reader of Roy H. Copperud's knowledgeable column on editing in *Editor & Publisher* asked him what was the "proper handle to attach to expressions such as, 'Anybody who would go to a psychiatrist ought to have his head examined.'" The columnist suggested "Irish bulls" or "Goldwynisms," both of which are forms of "malapropisms." Those terms would apply to the example cited above, but such examples are usually contrived. For the uncontrived variety, spoken by people who get their clichés confused, I used in the book *The Careful Writer* the phrase *curdled clichés* and cited more than thirty reallife examples. Now I have a few more: "I stuck my neck out on a limb," "I'm not going to do it, come heaven high water," and "The battle is over but for the shooting." Then there was a member of the New York Transit Authority who said that the problems of graffiti no longer had top priority, and added, "In fact, they have been relegated to the back of the burner." That must be the same fella who said, "I need some money to tidy me over."

My notes show a few more: "A consommé devoutly to be wished" or "It's a fragment of your imagination" or the one by an aide to the New York Governor: "The ball is in Louie's park now." Tennis court, anyone? Finally I don't want to forget the chap who said, "I've got a photo that's as pretty as a picture."

(Cliché tip.) A newspaper sentence read, "The finding of this unusual cancer was assumed to represent *just the tip of an iceberg* of an illness that may be widespread." Those icebergs seem to become more and more prevalent and they are making for a dangerous sea—that's C, for cliché. But they are expressive and not easy to replace. How else can you get that iceberg idea across? You could resort to an even more commonplace cliché: *there's more than meets the eye.* But what else? The only thing that this writer can think of to invent is *it's just the fin of the shark.* But then we would all still be at C.

## CLIOMETRICIAN
For a few years now we have had the word *econometrician,* referring to economists who use computers, mathematical data and economic theory to analyze the past and forecast the future. Now we have a subspecies of these analyzers who call themselves *cliometricians.* Instead of using the apparatus and theory to forecast the future, the *cliometricians* use such tools to try to figure out what economic activity was like back in the past. The word links Clio, the muse of history, to the idea of measurement.

## COCKAMAMIE
There is a slang word *cockamamie,* which means crazy, nutty, ridiculous or even, shall we say, lousy. It sprang from, but really hasn't much connection with, *decalcomania,* which is the name for pictures, designs or cartoons on specially prepared paper, which when moistened can be transferred to glass or wooden objects and even to children's arms. They are sometimes called *decals,* but the kids corrupted the real word into *cockamamies,* a word perhaps influenced, as Webster's New World Dictionary suggests, by *cock-a-nee-nee,* a nineteenth-century name for a cheap molasses candy. Anyway, it's a *cockamamie* word.

## COCKTAIL
You would expect that the etymology of the word *cocktail* would be as easy to get as a dry martini. But no; no one seems to know whence the word comes.

Mencken in *The American Language* lists seven guesses he encountered, which will here be reduced to three: that it is derived from *coquetel,* the name of a mixed drink known in the vicinity of Bordeaux; that it descends from *cock ale,* a mixture of ale and the essence of a boiled fowl (1648); that it is short for *cock tailings,* a mixture of tailings from various liquors thrown together in a common receptacle and sold at a low price. Appended to the list in the Mencken book is the comment "All are somewhat fishy." Amen.

According to a book entitled *Niagara Portage,* by Theodora Vinal, a tavern at Lewiston, New York, run by "an unforgettable couple," attracted a young midshipman who noticed that when the hostess served a mixed drink she put into the glass the tail feather of a cock. Soon the customers were asking for *cocktails.* The midshipman, who was named James Fenimore Cooper, put the couple and the *cocktails* into his book *The Spy.* Could be.

## COEQUAL
Talking about needless words, a wordmonger came across the following sentence the other day: "The candidate promised that women could have coequal status with men in the campaign." You look up *coequal* in a dictionary and whether the word is an adjective or a noun the definition is simply equal. Why, then, the *co-* word? And how has it managed to survive so long? Unbelievable as it may seem, the Oxford English Dictionary has a citation of *coequal* going back more than 500 years—to 1460, to be specific. (*See* REDUNDANCY.)

## COHORT
*See* CONFEDERATE.

## COLLECTIVE NOUNS
(Wrong number.) A news article began this way: "A quiet change is taking place on college campuses: Faculty *are* being held accountable, as never before, in how well *they* serve students, and there is a marked shift in the way faculty *are* being evaluated." Conceivably, but not certainly, that treatment of *faculty* as a plural noun would pass muster in British English; the British often use such words as *company, party, government* and *cabinet* as nouns of multitude and consider them to be plurals. But that treatment is infrequent on this side of the Atlantic. Over here "faculty are" sounds odd. It should be changed to either "faculties are" or "teachers are."

## COLON

When to put a colon after the words introducing a list sometimes presents a problem, but two guides may help to solve it:
1. Use a colon when the words *follow* or *following* are either
expressed or implied. (In the opening sentence of this item the
word *following* is implied—"the two *following* guides"—thus the
colon is used.) 2. Do not use a colon after *are* or *were* when the
items of the list come immediately after the verb. For instance,
"The colors of the American flag are (no colon) red, white and
blue."

## COLONEL

(A kernel about pronunciation.) A question everybody always
wants to ask but then forgets to ask is why *colonel* is pronounced
*curnel.* To begin with, the word originally denoted the leader of
a military column. The Italian word for *column* was *colonna* and
later *colonnello.* That latter word was a modification of *coronel,*
through a process known as dissimilation, which altered the two
*l* sounds to an *r . . . l* combination. In English the basic spelling
*colonel,* akin to *colonnello,* was kept, but the pronunciation with an
*r* in it was also retained. Confusing, isn't it?

## COMBINE

A noun that comes up frequently in discussions of financial and
economic matters, *combine* should be used with caution. Forget
about its designation of a harvesting machine; the discussion
here is concerned with its use to designate a group organized for
specific purposes. In casual usage, particularly in American casual usage, *combine* takes on the sense of a group with selfish,
unethical or illegal aims. Thus, it would be all right to speak of
a *combine* that was convicted of price-fixing, but it might not be
proper to speak of a *combine* to find more efficient ways of manufacturing widgets.

## COMMAS

(They can affect meaning.) The comma has played an important
part in changing the meaning of a document. Obviously we
aren't referring to something like Professor Maxwell Nurnberg's
pairs of sentences; e.g., "What's the latest dope?" and "What's
the latest, dope?" There is at least one instance of a seriously

erroneous comma, an instance cited in your host's book *The Careful Writer*. Michigan discovered in recent years that its state constitution inadvertently legalized slavery. Section 8, Article 2 read: "Neither slavery nor involuntary servitude, unless for the punishment of crime, shall ever be tolerated in this state." It was decided to shift the comma from its position after *servitude* to a position after *slavery*.

(Commas in series) Let's take a series such as "A, B and C." Some people are disturbed by the absence of a comma after B. Several reference works set forth a rule to use a comma before *and* in a series. But Porter G. Perrin's *Writer's Guide and Index to English* says, "Usage is divided over the use of a comma before the last item of such a series." And H. W. Fowler's classic *Modern English Usage* cites the series "French, German, Italian and Spanish" and says: "The commas between 'French' and 'German' and 'German' and 'Italian' take the place of 'and's'; there is no comma after 'Italian' because, with 'and,' it would be otiose." So we might say that the rule of a comma before *and* is honored in the breach almost as much as in the observance.

It is true that most school textbooks and publishing stylebooks insist that a comma be inserted before *and* in a series, yet many mass circulation newspapers and magazines omit it. The omitters do use a comma before the *and* if it is needed to avoid ambiguity, as it is in this sentence: "The cake consists of two layers and icing, and strawberries may be added." They also use a comma before *and* if the other elements in the series are separated by semicolons, as in, "Jones, the pitcher; Smith, the first baseman; Robinson, the catcher, and Zilch, the right fielder, got successive hits."

(Because, plus (or minus) a comma.) What about punctuation in certain situations involving the word *because*? Observe these two sentences:

1. I must have been tired because I had worked hard all day.
2. I must have been tired because I slept until noon.

Shouldn't a comma be inserted after *tired* in the second sentence? The answer is yes; otherwise it seems to say that the person involved became tired from sleeping too long. If we have to invent a guide to punctuation in this kind of sentence it would be this: When *because* introduces a second, even though closely related, thought it should be preceded by a comma. Here is another sentence to illustrate the distinction: "He did not go to the movie because he disliked the leading actress." As it stands the sentence could raise the question, if he didn't go for that reason, then what was the reason? However, a comma ahead of *because* would leave room for no ambiguity: It was his dislike for the actress that kept him away from the movie. The comma would indicate that a second, though closely related, thought was being introduced.

(Comma that rules out bigamy.) A group of newspapermen were embroiled in an argument over whether it should be "His wife Jane" (no comma) or "His wife, Jane" (with a comma). If the comma is omitted, the name is comparable to a defining or restrictive clause; you seem to be defining which wife you are referring to: his wife Jane, not his wife Alice. The comma, therefore, is mandatory unless the gentleman is a bigamist.

(Misplaced comma.) The point about to be made won't shake this planet to its innards, but it is worth making anyway. The following sentence is by no means atypical: "The question is whether the novel is behind, or ahead, of its time." A phrase embraced in commas that way is really an interpolation in the sentence; the rest of the sentence should read properly without the phrase. But does it here? Would you say, "the novel is behind of its time"? Obviously not. The comma should be inserted after "of."

(Commas between adjectives.) A question often arises concerning the use of commas with adjectives preceding a noun; here's an example: "a small honest unintentional mistake." The test for inserting commas is whether the adjectives are coordinate in meaning, more specifically whether you could insert an *and* between them. In this instance you could and so the proper punctuation would be "a small, honest, unintentional mistake." On the other hand, if one of the adjectives forms a compound with the noun—"roast beef," for example—you wouldn't put a comma after a preceding adjective. You wouldn't write "cold, roast beef"; you would make it "cold roast beef."

**COMMON**
  *See* MUTUAL.



**COMPARATIVES**
(Moister.) A television ad for a cake mix claimed that it produced a "moister" cake. To some people *moister* sounds awkward. They would favor *more moist.* H. W. Fowler in his *Modern English Usage* does not offer rules for forming such
comparatives, but gives some excellent advice, as follows:
"The adjectives regularly taking *-er* and *-est* in preference to
*more* and *most* are (a) all monosyllables (*hard, sage, shy,* etc.);
(b) disyllables in *-y* (*holy, lazy, likely,* etc.), in *-le* (*noble, subtle,*
etc.), in *-er* (*tender, clever,* etc.), in *-ow* (*narrow, sallow,* etc.); (c)
many disyllables with accent on the last (*polite, profound,* etc.)
. . . (d) trisyllabic negative forms of (b) and (c) words (*unholy,
ignoble,* etc.)" A simpler guide might be to consult your favorite dictionary. Some dictionaries give the comparative and
superlative forms of adjectives right after the entry word;
others do not give these forms if they follow the regular *-er*
and *-est* pattern, but do supply any irregular forms. Anyway,
*moister* is correct.

(Absolute comparatives.) Is the comparative degree passing out
as a device to appraise two things? Some ultrapurists cite sentences like these: "It is one of the *better* suspense movies," or
"This should be one of the *more* interesting days of the hearing,"
or "Barker is the *better* quality aspirin." There is nothing to be
afraid of here; constructions like these have been with us for
centuries and are called absolute comparatives. George O.
Curme in his authoritative book *Syntax* mentions (as examples)
"the *lower* classes," "*higher* education," "a *better*-class café," and
"the *more complex* problems of life." In each of these examples
there is an implied comparison: better suspense movies as
against poorer ones, for instance. What is objectionable today
in a similar category, however, is the advertising practice of
using the comparative degree when there is not even an implied
object of comparison: "the more healthful cereal," or "our
product is better for you."

## COMPARE TO, COMPARE WITH

(What's the word beyond compare?) When the sense of *compare* is likening one thing to another the proper preposition is *to*. For example: "He *compared* the computer *to* a human brain." When the sense of *compare* is examining two things to discover their likenesses and their differences, the proper preposition is *with*. For example: "The company's production was up but its earnings were down *compared with* last year's." The *with* senses are usually the more literal and the *to* senses the more abstract or figurative and so the *with's* greatly outnumber the *to's*.

If you were to take the Latin derivation of *compare* literally in defining today's usage of the word, you would have to scrap everything that has been said about the difference between the *with* and the *to* senses. The original Latin word, *comparare*, was made up of *com-*, with, and *par*, equal, and so meant originally to regard as equal to or similar to. But when you *compare* today's meaning *with* the original one you find today's is broader.


## COMPARISONS

(Incomplete alternative comparison.) That elaborate designation applies to a common fault in usage exemplified by this sentence: "The Russians apparently are trying to develop a giant rocket with lifting power *as great or greater than* the Saturn 5's." One of the alternatives is complete: *greater than the Saturn 5's*. But how about the other alternative; would you normally say *as great than the Saturn 5's?* Of course not. One way to correct the error is to change it to read *as great as or greater than*, which is unexceptionable but a bit on the prissy side. Another and more graceful way is to complete the *as great* immediately with an *as* and then tack *or greater* on at the end of the sentence. An equally graceful and shorter way out is to say lifting power *at least as great as* the Saturn 5's.

(Illogical comparisons.) The first requisite for good writing is clear thinking. But sometimes one gets the impression that a writer has not taken the trouble to think at all. Here is an example of a fairly prevalent use of *unlike* (and *like* is subject to the same mistreatment) in an illogical way: "Unlike six months ago, Chinese diplomats are now not very interested in such issues as most-favored-nation treatment." Here "six months ago" apparently is being compared with "Chinese diplomats," but of course that is not what the writer intended. One way to repair the sentence is to begin it, "Unlike what they thought six months ago . . ." Another way out is to begin it with a phrase such as, "Having changed their thinking in the last six months . . ." In any case, the thing to keep in mind is to avoid comparing or contrasting things that do not admit of such treatment.

## COMPENDIUM

Most people think of *compendium* as meaning a massive, all-inclusive work. Probably that is because its sound suggests *comprehensive*. Well, a *compendium* is indeed comprehensive, but it is brief, concise; it is an abstract or outline. The word derives from a Latin root meaning a weighing together, with the connotation of a gain or saving. The saving comes in not having to read the whole dreary business.

## COMPLETED

(Another straitjacket.) The letter said, "The enclosed form is *partially completed.*" If *complete* means entire or with no part lacking, some people say, can something be *partially complete?* The answer is yes. If, for example, a form contained 20 questions and 10 of them were filled in, it would be *half completed,* and if 18 of them were filled in, it would be *almost completed.* In general, some words are absolutes, but don't go around looking for words to add to the list.

## COMPLEX, COMPLICATED

(Not easy to understand—or explain.) Here's a simple explanation of the difference between *complex* and *complicated.* Let's first examine the sameness of the two words. Both refer to something that is a mass of interrelated parts so that the something is difficult to understand or operate. Now for the difference between them. *Complex* emphasizes the manyness of the parts; *complicated* emphasizes the intricacy of the relationship of the parts. To put it in simpler form, *complicated* is one step beyond *complex* in describing the difficulty of dealing with the assemblage of elements. Understand it?

## COMPLEXIONED, COMPLECTED

To speak of a dark-*complected* man is to use what amounts to a nonword. Probably *complected* is what is called a back formation —that is, a nonexistent word coined from an actual word supposed to be derived from it, as *burglary* is supposed to be derived from *burgle,* a coined word. Just as *reflection* is derived from *reflect* and *connection* from *connect,* some people assumed that *complexion* must be derived from *complect.* But no, there is no such word. *Complected* is not an approved term. Say a dark-*complexioned* man. (*See* BACK FORMATIONS.)

## COMPOUND NOUNS

(Disguised verbs.) A headline read, "Dinner will *Kickoff* '75 Charities Appeal." Had that been an isolated example we would not have been justified in being bothered, but here are four other similar items in which verbs and adverbs were for some mysterious reason tied together to look like nouns though not used as nouns: ". . . Drama Club to *Put-On* a New Play"; "Our truck will *pick-up* your old clothes"; "The contestants are beginning to *warm-up* before the start . . ."; "Bills Introduced to *Rollback* Electric Rates." All those compounds are in common use as nouns, but to use them as verbs is not only unacceptable, but pointless. In each instance the compound should be two words. If a single newspaperman had written them all you might almost think it was a put-on.

## COMPOUNDS

(But don't sit on the baby.) A new mother wanted to know which is correct: "I will *baby-sit* with Michael" or "I will *baby-sit* Michael"? The "with" version is correct. But the word *baby-sit* brings to mind some thoughts about such compounds. Normally when a preposition is an intimate part of a phrase that is being turned into a compound the preposition is not omitted from the new word. For instance, we do not speak of a *hip-shooter* (one who shoots *from* the hip) or of a *laurel-rester* (one who rests *on* his laurels). But *baby-sitter* was originated about 30 years ago and rapidly came into common use, so that it is now part of the language. By the way, is the past tense *baby-sat* or *baby-sitted?* Teen-agers use both.

## COMPRISE, INCLUDE

Often misused, *comprise* means to contain, embrace, comprehend. The whole *comprises* the parts, but not vice versa. Thus, it is proper to say, "The symphony *comprises* four movements," but it is not proper to say, "Four movements *comprise* the symphony." You would have to say that four movements *constitute, compose, form,* or *make up* the symphony. Shun also *comprised of.*

*Comprise* and *include* are synonyms, but there is a slight difference. *Include* normally suggests that the component items are not being mentioned in their entirety ("The Blitzville baseball team *includes* five high school dropouts"), whereas *comprise* normally suggests that all the component items are being mentioned ("The Blitzville baseball team *comprises* six right-handed batters and three left-handed batters"). In this sense *comprise* is rarely misused. *Include,* however, is often employed when all the items are being mentioned, but it is better not to use it that way.

## CONFEDERATE, COHORT, ETC.

(Partners in crime.) The question here laid before the house is why the words *confederate, accomplice* and *cohort* almost always are used in a pejorative sense. (One doubts that the negative use of *confederate* is related to the Civil War.) Although *confederate* can be used in an innocent sense, it most often is used to designate a partner in something unlawful, but that common use goes much farther back than the Civil War. The Oxford English Dictionary gives, among other citations, this quotation from 1680: "The very criminals themselves or their accessories and confederates." The word *accomplice,* however, has never had an innocent meaning; it has always designated an associate in crime.

*Cohort* might be called a neutral word; it may be used in speaking of either innocent or evil companions. But it is often misused in a different way. A *cohort* is not an individual, as is often supposed, but rather a band. The look of the word apparently deceives the misusers. They think of such words as *coauthor, costar,* and *coeducation,* in which the prefix *co-* means with and they jump to the conclusion that a *cohort* must be a *hort* who is *co* with another *hort.* But there is no such thing as a *hort;* therefore there is no such thing as a *co-hort.* The word comes from a Latin term meaning an enclosure and it was originally applied to a division in the Roman army. It now means a band or a company or a group. You could speak of "a *cohort* of Jones supporters," but you shouldn't speak of two of such supporters as "two Jones *cohorts.*"

## CONFESS
*See* ADMIT.

## CONJUNCTIONS
*See* CORRELATIVES.

## CONSENSUAL
A Supreme Court ruling upheld a Virginia law prohibiting *consensual sodomy* and that introduced a large part of the public to an unusual word: *consensual.* Joined to the word *sodomy,* the term probably produces a quick reaction that it is related to *sensual,* having to do with bodily pleasure. But that is not so. Actually at bottom it is related to *consensus* and has the meaning of mutual consent.

## CONSENSUS
(Matter of opinion.) Two booby traps flank the word *consensus* and both are avoidable if one keeps in mind the root of the word. It is a combination of the Latin *con,* together, and *sentire,* to think or feel. It means, therefore, a thinking together, a concord or general agreement. For that reason *consensus of opinion* is redundant or repetitive and is frowned on; *consensus* tells it all by itself. An error is often made in the spelling of the word and that, too, can be avoided by recalling the root idea of sense or opinion. The word has nothing to do with *census.* It has to do with a common sense and therefore is spelled *consensus.*

## CONTINUAL, CONTINUOUS
(Goings on.) The words *continuing, continual* and *continuous* have quite similar meanings. The first of the three words offers little trouble; its stress is on the absence of interruption or of cessation. The meanings of *continual* and *continuous* are closer together and are often confused. *Continual* means over and over again. *Continuous* means without any interruption. One way to remember the distinction between *continual* and *continuous* is to think that whereas both refer to a process of keeping up, the

"ous" in *continuous* may be regarded as standing for One Unin-
terrupted Sequence. To use all three words in one sentence, we
might write this one: "The tension on the Soviet-Chinese border has been *continuing* for several years with *continual* minor
outbreaks and *continuous* patrolling by both sides."

## CONVERSION

(Should nouns be verbed?) The answer is a restricted yes. The
process of what is called "conversion" has been going on since
the thirteenth century and has undoubtedly in many instances
made the language crisper and more precise. Isn't it more economical to say a man *gardens* than to have to say he tends a
garden? However, if conversions are made merely for the sake
of novelty, who needs them?

What triggered (and there's one for you) this discussion was
a sentence in a recent book about the Boston *Globe,* which spoke
of its "New York correspondent, officed in the World building."
Why *officed?* The word distractingly calls attention to itself and
incidentally is superfluous in the sentence. Similarly, why say
someone *authored* a book? He *wrote* it. It is too late to prevent
people from saying that Senator Hoodwink *chaired* the meeting,
although that usage is only a couple of decades old. The next
thing you know, when someone gets the floor at the meeting
we'll be saying he *floored* the meeting. A motion can be *tabled,* but
let's hope it never will be *committeed,* that is, sent to committee.

The upshot of all this is that conversions of nouns into verbs
are acceptable if they satisfy a need and if they are in general use
by educated people. If they are merely novelties, turn your back
on them.

## CONVINCE, PERSUADE

The distinction between these words is clear, but not to everyone. *Convince* means to get someone to believe something and
*persuade* means to get someone to do something. *Persuade* goes
beyond *convince* because it implies the bringing about of a shift
of position, usually with the implication of action to come. For
that reason *persuade* may be followed by an infinitive: "The police *persuaded* the robber *to drop* his gun." *Convince,* on the other
hand, should never be followed by an infinitive. It may be followed by an *of* phrase or a *that* clause: "The police *convinced* the

robber *of* the hopelessness of holding out" or "The police *convinced* the robber *that* his situation was hopeless." If you are *convinced of* the difference between these two words, perhaps you will be *persuaded* never *to use* an infinitive after *convince*.

## COP-OUT
The slang term *cop-out* is related to the earlier slang expression *cop a plea*. In that sense *cop* means to grab, take or seize and the whole phrase means to take or accept an accusation of guilt on a lesser charge to avoid a trial on a more serious one. A *cop-out* is a kind of surrender, a backdown, a phony excuse. Here's hoping that backdown doesn't get your back up.

## COPASETIC
The word *copasetic,* which is spelled in a variety of ways, means fine, great, topnotch. But where does it come from? The Dictionary of American Slang says it is "from the Yiddish," but that sounds a little unlikely since the word was for years in constant use by the great black entertainer and tap dancer Bojangles Bill Robinson, who, according to William and Mary Morris in their *Dictionary of Word and Phrase Origins,* may indeed have coined it. Then there is the British slang authority Eric Partridge, who says, "I provisionally accept the origin proposed by a witty and learned friend: 'able to *cope* and anti*septic.* '" That, too, sounds, and probably is intended to sound, unlikely. Finally there is this etymology presented (dreamed up?) by Funk & Wagnalls Standard College Dictionary: "From the Creole *coupesetique,* capable of being coped with." Actually, that sounds the likeliest of all. But who minted the word?

## COPS
*Cops* are, of course, policemen. The slang word is neither of recent derivation nor an Americanism. The Oxford English Dictionary records a quotation using the word *cop* that is dated 1704. The slang verb *cop* meant to catch or arrest and one who did that was a *copper*. Then *copper* was shortened to *cop*. One school of thought relates *copper* to the copper buttons once used on police uniforms. Anyway, the cops themselves would rather be called *officers*. But the word can be ambiguous because there

are officers in police forces—sergeants, lieutenants, captains—
who are above the rank-and-file policemen. Still, it's better not
to argue with a cop—er, an officer.

## COPY, REPLICA
(Copy catch.) The words *copy* and *replica* are not interchangeable. A *replica* is a facsimile or almost exact copy, with the additional meaning in the fine arts field of a copy made by the
original artist. Thus it would be ridiculous to say that "in the
center of the table there was a *replica* in chopped chicken liver
of the Governor's mansion." There are so many synonyms for
a mere copy—such as *model, reproduction, duplicate* and the like—
that it is best to restrict *replica* to its fine arts sense.

## CORDS, CHORDS
(Get the h out of here.) Perhaps through a typographical error,
a sentence by William Saroyan read this way in *The New York
Times:* "Voices on the telephone anywhere in the world and
especially in Paris are traditionally believed to come out of the
sound box and through the vocal *chords* of human beings."
Those musical combinations of three or more notes are *chords,*
but in American usage most of the other half-dozen meanings
of the same-sounding word are spelled *cord.* Thus, human beings have vocal *cords,* not *chords.*

## CORRELATIVES
(Not only . . . but.) The proper placement of the correlative
conjunctions *not only . . . but (also)* should be as simple as putting
on a pair of shoes that match. But, strangely enough, four times
out of five the conjunctions are misplaced. That is explainable
and excusable in spoken language because the speaker cannot
always look ahead and see how his sentence is going to be
composed. But there is little excuse for the error in written
language. Still the kind of thing one often sees in print is, "He
loved *not only* his parents, *but also* was a good husband." Logic
cries out for placing the *not only* ahead of *loved* or alternatively
making the second part of the sentence read, *"but also* his wife."
Why? Because correlative conjunctions should connect two of
the same kind of thing, they should link parallel grammatical
elements. If the sentence starts out, "He loved *not only* his par-

ents," the logical question that follows is, whom or what else did he love? Therefore, *"but also his wife."*

Here is a slight paraphrase of a real-life erroneous sentence: "Some old-time Democratic politicians think that their candidate will lose *not only* the Presidential election, *but also* hurt the Democratic party." After reading that he "will lose *not only* the Presidential election," anyone would be justified in thinking, what else will he lose? The remainder of the sentence doesn't answer that question. However, if the first part is changed to read "will *not only* lose," then the natural question is, what else will he do? The rest of the sentence properly answers that one.

There's nothing tricky about it. If a noun follows the *not only*, a noun should follow the *but also;* if a verb follows the *not only*, a verb should follow the *but also*. Never put on one black shoe and one brown shoe.

## COUNSELS
Some time ago a columnist wrote, "His various *counsels* have stressed a strict rather than a broad reading of the Constitution." Is *counsels* good English? One dictionary—the American Heritage—says it is; others indicate that both the singular noun and the plural are *counsel*. The big Oxford English Dictionary does cite one quotation using the plural *counsels*. By Thomas Jefferson of all people and dated 1789, it reads as follows: "They have charged . . . one of their ablest *counsels* with the preparation of a memoir to establish this." That sounds awkward, and the awkwardness derives from the extreme rarity of the word. Both the columnist quoted above and Mr. Jefferson would have been well advised to use *lawyers, attorneys* or *legal advisers* rather than *counsels*. On the other hand, a caption on a picture of a hearing of the House Judiciary Committee referred to half a dozen men representing different principals in this way: "At the table in the foreground are the *counsels."* Neither *counsel* nor one of the synonyms just mentioned would do the job in this unusual instance.

## COUPLE
(Sometimes coupled, sometimes uncoupled.) A strange characteristic of the word *couple* is that in some contexts it has the word *of* latched onto it and in other contexts it does not. For instance,

it is considered substandard usage to say, "Let's have a *couple* drinks"; the word *of* is required after *couple.* That is odd because the *of* is not required after some similar terms such as "a dozen" or "a few" or "many." On the other hand, the word *of* is omitted after *couple* when an adjective of degree is introduced. We don't say, "Let's have a *couple of* more drinks," or "No, we've had a *couple of* too many drinks already." Either idiom has played strange and unexplainable tricks with *couple* or we have had a couple too many drinks at this writing.

(A couple is or are.) Whether to regard *couple* as singular or plural is a question that returns again and again. Most writers prefer to treat the word as a plural most of the time. It is quite all right to say, "The Jones couple *was* the youngest at the party." But if you think the word must always be singular, you are likely to get into trouble with some sentences requiring a pronoun referring to your singular couple; for example: "The couple *was* uninjured when *its* car skidded off the road." The advice here is to favor the plural in nine cases out of ten.

## COUTH
*See* UNCOUTH.

## CREDIBLE, CREDITABLE
The Defense Secretary was being questioned at a hearing on armaments. According to one newspaper article, his questioner said that the United States wanted a national defense that assured us of a *credible* deterrent, then followed up with the statement, "But part of the *creditable* deterrent is more than just guns and tanks." Those two words have different meanings. *Credible* means believable and *creditable* means reputable or worthy of esteem. Oddly enough, however, at one time *creditable* meant the same thing as *credible,* but its use in that sense is now obsolete. Undoubtedly the word intended in both places cited above was *credible.*

## CREDIT
The word *credit,* in both its noun and verb senses, has a variety of meanings ranging from the idea of belief or trust to the notion of a kind of score for the satisfactory completion of a

course of study. A common meaning underlies half a dozen uses of the word in business contexts, such as dividends *credited* to an account, a deposit *credited* to a final bill or a *credit* toward the reduction of a debt. In all these senses the basic idea is a feeling or the evidence of faith or confidence; in fact, the word comes from the Latin *credere,* to trust or believe. Another meaning of the word *credit* is to give deserved praise for something, and this meaning sometimes leads a writer into error. For example, it is improper to say that "history *credits* Richard with the slaying of two young princes and other killings and crimes." Give *credit* only where *credit* is due.

**CRIMINAL CONVERSATION**
(You don't talk about this.) Away back when the White House tapes involved in the Watergate investigation were in the news a Congressman was being interviewed about the exchanges. "In my opinion," he said, "they amount to *criminal conversation.*" That phrase has nothing to do with what we normally regard as conversation. The phrase *criminal conversation* is a legal term for unlawful intercourse with a married woman—in other words, adultery. It's extremely unlikely that this is what the Congressman had in mind.

**CRIMINALIZE**
(New word currentized.) Not once, but twice within a week a district attorney of New York uttered a word that most people had never heard before: *criminalize.* "We feel," he said on one of these occasions, "that there is nothing now to *criminalize* what the Governor has done." The word does appear, albeit within doubt-casting quotation marks, in a passage cited in The Barnhart Dictionary of New English Since 1963. But one wonders whether the word is really necessitized. (*See* SUFFIXES.)

**CRITIQUE**
(On being critical.) The article read, ". . . he visited Miss Dottin's classroom and invited several of us to write poems which he promised to *critique.*" Other such uses of *critique* make one wonder if writers are trying to change the part of speech of the word from its usual noun function to that of a verb. *Critique* appears as a verb in a couple of new dictionaries. Without neces-

sarily approving the word, we can see the reasoning that lay behind the coinage: The normal verb *criticize*, though it essentially means to judge or appraise, often has the sense of disapproving or finding fault. (*See* CONVERSION.)

## CUCKOLD

"While happily celebrating my 45th wedding anniversary," an anonymous correspondent writes,"I am reminded that 40 years ago my wife had an affair of short duration. Was I or am I a cuckold?" At first I thought the letter writer had me confused with Dear Abby. The question was more up her alley than mine. The only thing that came to my mind was that juvenile jingle about, "How much wood would a woodchuck chuck if a woodchuck could chuck wood," with a variation something like, "Just how old is an olden cluck when an olden cuckold's he?" I thought that would not be very helpful, so I decided why not put it up to Abby and see what she has to say? I did and back came her prompt answer: "Dear Ted: If the wife has one affair, even briefly, her mate is a cuckold briefly. If she has another one a couple of months later, he's a cuckold for sure. If she has them on and off over the years, he's not a cuckold—quite the reverse: he's an old kook."

# D

## DANGLING PARTICIPLES
*See* MODIFIERS.

## DATA
As if it weren't enough that *data* may be pronounced three different ways—dayta, datta and dahta—the word also burdens us with a usage problem. Carlton F. Wells, professor emeritus of English at the University of Michigan, sent in a clipping that illustrates the problem. In an article in *The Wall Street Journal* one paragraph began, "Mr. Wattenberg's attitudinal *data suggests* . . ." and the next paragraph contains the phrase "the attitudinal *data suggest.*" *Data* is, of course, the plural of *datum,* meaning a piece of information or an assumed fact. *Datum* is scarcely ever used, however, so users of *data* often tend to regard it as a singular noun. That is more or less sanctioned, but the preference in good usage is to keep it a plural. In any event a writer should not change his mind between paragraphs. (*See* PLURALS, FOREIGN WORDS.)

## DEBRIEF
Undoubtedly we will never get rid of the word *debrief,* but it's a bad word and should never have been coined in the first place. When a person is *briefed* for a mission, information is given to him. What, then, happens when he is *debriefed?* Do the briefers, having changed their minds, take that information away from him? Of course not. It's hard to think of a substitute word, except something that sounds even sillier such as *outpump* or

*unload,* so we'll have to put up with *debrief,* just as for a far longer time we have put up with *disembark,* which means, when you stop to examine it, to unget-on a boat.

## DEBUT

(A word, but who needs it?) In a letter to the magazine *Editor & Publisher* an editor complained about the "obnoxious" use of *debut* as a verb in a headline that had appeared in the magazine: "24-Hour Tribune will *debut* with five editions." Darned if five pages later on in the same issue containing the letter the magazine didn't have a sentence that read, "As the Tribune Company *debutted* its format . . . displaced members of the Chicago Typographical Union local were bickering in court." *Debut* as an intransitive verb is bad enough since there are plenty of non-flossy words that say just about the same thing: *appear, begin, start, commence, come out.* As a transitive verb it is even worse because of its rarity and oddity. But as a past-tense verb (misspelled incidentally since it should be *debuted*) it is an atrocity—a mysterious-appearing pronunciation challenge. Let's have done with the verb *debut.* (*See* CONVERSION.)

## DECIBEL

There's a phone connection in the word *decibel.* The word, which refers to a measurement of sound, is made up of *deci-,* meaning one tenth, and *bel,* designating a unit in ratios of sound. The syllable *bel* springs from the name of Alexander Graham Bell, the inventor of the telephone.

## DECIMATE

Here is a word that has outgrown its primary meaning. The term *decimate* originally meant to do away with one tenth. In olden days, for example, in cases of mutiny or other crimes an army would choose by lot and kill one in every ten. Today we have gotten away from the literal one-tenth meaning and use the word to mean to destroy or kill a substantial part of. But the word should be used to designate something that can be reckoned in numbers. We should not say, as one newspaper did, "A gas explosion *decimated* a bar in the City Hall area."

## DENIGRATE

Here is a bit of unintentional paronomasia (that means accidental pun): "The month-long festival, which hopes to attract some 15,000 black artists and performers from around the world, is intended to be a catalyst to racial pride, not just by celebrating a heritage once *denigrated* by the West as 'primitive' . . ." One of the Latin roots of *denigrate* is *niger,* black, and the original meaning of the word was to blacken. Its common meaning today is, of course, to disparage or defame.

## DEPRECATE, DEPRECIATE

A newspaper editorial, speaking of the military spying on civilian officials, said, "Secretary of Defense Schlesinger *deprecates* its importance." Clearly what the editorial writer had in mind was that the Secretary belittled the importance of the affair, and therefore the word he wanted was *depreciates. Deprecate* derives from the Latin *precari,* pray, and means to pray against, to wish it would go away, to disapprove. *Depreciate,* on the other hand, derives from *pretiari,* value, and suggests a lowering of the value of something, belittling it or disparaging it. The newest dictionaries, surrendering to the frequent misuse of *deprecate,* accept it as synonymous with *depreciate.* But who needs two words that mean exactly the same thing—particularly when a useful distinction can be made between them?

## DÉTENTE

(Relaxation.) A word that has figured in the news is *détente,* a French term on long-term loan to English. The word began with the Latin *destendre,* meaning to slacken. The French made it into *destente,* at first a mechanism in a crossbow that released the taut string and later a trigger that released the projectile in a firearm. The ancestor *destendre* (from the Latin *dis,* equivalent to our modern *dis-,* and the French *tendre,* to stretch) is still evident in a general way in the modern word; the sense of slackening or relaxing has persisted. Today *détente* denotes an easing of tension, particularly in international relations.

## DIAGNOSE

(The ailment, not the patient.) A news article contained this sentence: "The boy was *diagnosed* as being severely retarded mentally." What the writer, like thousands of others, did not understand is that a physician diagnoses a condition, not a patient; in this instance the boy's mental condition, not the boy himself, was diagnosed. Likewise, if American economists are discovering what is wrong with business conditions, they are diagnosing the economy, not the United States.

## DICEY

In writing about Democratic campaign plans, a columnist called them "very *dicey.*" There is a word that has been around about 30 years, but it has come into common use only within the last few years. It apparently originated in World War II in the British Royal Air Force and was used to mean risky or perilous. Today *dicey* still means that, but it also has the connotation of chancy or tricky or unpredictable. Obviously the word derives from those bones one rolls. (*See* BRITISHISMS.)

## DIERESIS

(Those two little dots.) There is a diacritical mark that sometimes appears in such words as *coöperative* and *reënter.* Perhaps the mark originated with the need to distinguish the prefix in such words. But the need for the umlaut (as the mark is called in German) or the *dieresis* (as it is called in English) goes beyond merely distinguishing prefixes; it also serves to indicate that two adjacent vowels have separate pronunciations, as in *naïve,* for example. The umlaut, or *dieresis,* is not dying out, but its use is being held to a minimum. There could be three reasons for that. First, most of the words with prefixes ending in vowels are so familiar after all these centuries that attention does not need to be called to the prefix these days. Second, it is possible that as a result of two major wars there is an unconscious aversion to the umlaut, which has a German flavor associated with it. Third, as a practical consideration, all print shops—and this applies to many newspapers—do not always have letters with umlauts handy and so they either use a letter without that mark or use a hyphen to separate the prefix from the main word, making it, for instance, *re-enter* instead of *reënter.*

## DIFFER FROM, DIFFER WITH

It is not intended as either a slap or a pat when I say that I know you *differ from* me, but that I hope you don't *differ with* me too much. Everyone *differs from* me and from you, too, because no two persons are identical. The phrase *differ from* means to be unlike. On the other hand, *differ with* means to disagree with. It should be noted that *differ from* can also be used to mean disagreement if the ground for disagreement is specified: "Sally *differs from* Joan in her manner of raising children." But notice that here too *differs from* is equivalent to *is unlike*.

## DIFFERENT FROM (THAN?)

*Different* is normally followed by *from*, although exceptions may be made when a clause follows *different;* otherwise you might get such clumsy sentences as, "The book gripped me in a *different* way *from* the way in which it had ever done before." A simpler and better construction would be, "The book gripped me in a *different* way *than* it ever had before." But the intention here is not to give a green light to *different than* in all, or even in many, instances. Most often *different than* is improper. Here is a sentence in which that combination does not even convey the intended meaning: "The young reporters today are no *different than* their predecessors." If the implied clause in that sentence means anything at all, it means "than their predecessors were different," which makes no sense. Stick to *different from* unless there is an exceptionally good reason to depart from it.

## DINGBAT

Television is blamed, occasionally with justice, for flaws in English, but it had nothing to do with coining the word *dingbat* which was not a creation of Archie Bunker in "All in the Family." H. L. Mencken in *The American Language* says the word was formed as far back as 1861, though he offers no clue to what it meant. Eric Partridge in *A Dictionary of Slang and Unconventional English* dates the word to 1914 and says that in the Australian army it meant an officer's servant. A couple of other dictionaries rather uncertainly trace *dingbat* to the Middle English *dingen,* to strike or throw, and *bat,* a bat, and give as a primary meaning a small stone or article suitable for flinging. A more modern meaning refers to a thing, an article or a contrivance for which we cannot think of another name. There is in addition a more specific meaning: a printers' term for a typographical ornament. To a degree *dingbat* is a mysterious word.

## DIRECT, DIRECTLY
If a man says in a letter, "I will have Mr. Jones write to you *directly*," what does he mean? Does he mean that he will have Mr. Jones write immediately, or does he intend to say that there will be no intermediary? Perhaps the writer means *direct* not *directly*. Not that the letter writer is wrong, but rather that he is ambiguous. Probably what lurked in the back of his mind was that *direct*, without the *-ly*, did not sound like an adverb, which is what is required to modify the verb *write*. But both *direct* and *directly* are adverbs, so either would be grammatically proper. However, in this context *directly* is susceptible of two meanings—immediately or man to man—whereas *direct* can have only the no-intermediary meaning. Since the main purpose of language is to get a thought across clearly, the ambiguous word should always be ruled out.

## DIRT, SOIL
(Dirty words.) *Dirt* and *soil* are not dissimilar words. In general, *dirt* is the dirtier word of the two. It refers to anything unclean, foul or filthy, although it can also refer to the stuff that makes your garden grow. *Soil,* on the other hand, refers to the top layer of earth supporting plant life, or to one's native territory, his native *soil.* Still, let us not forget that there are some good kinds of dirt, too—for example, the kind in which we find gold or other minerals, that is, *pay dirt.*

## DISCOMFIT, DISCOMFORT
Discomfit and discomfort look somewhat alike and sound somewhat alike, but there the resemblance ends. To *discomfit* is to defeat completely, overthrow, rout. To *discomfort* is to make uncomfortable or uneasy. A similar distinction in meaning applies to the nouns *discomfiture* and *discomfort.*

## DISEMBARK
   *See* EMBARK.

## DISINTERESTED
*See* UNINTERESTED.

## DISSIMILAR (TO)
*Dissimilar* turned up in an article about a court case that said, "The lawyer remarked that the judge had a power not *dissimilar from* that of granting a pardon." Undoubtedly because of the related meanings of *dissimilar* and *different,* writers tend to give them the same preposition, *from.* But *dissimilar* takes the preposition *to,* just as *similar* does. *Dissimilar* contains a negative prefix, but dis- makes no difference.

## DONE
(Done ban is undone.) On a can of paint the label said, "As soon as you're *done* painting, wash out the brushes with water." Is *done* used that way atrocious grammar? Not exactly, but the authorities are not unanimous in sanctioning it. The usage panel of the American Heritage Dictionary split 53 to 47 percent in favor of that use of *done* to mean completed or finished. Webster's unabridged, second edition, labels it colloquial, but the third edition finds nothing wrong with it. Neither do Webster's New World, the Random House and the big Oxford English Dictionary. The verdict would seem to be that *done* in the sense of finished is well on the way to acceptability, if it has not already arrived. It is, of course, proper to say that the leg of lamb is done. That does not mean that it is finished but rather that it is sufficiently cooked.

## DOUBLE GENITIVE
Why do we say "a friend of Jack's," rather than "a friend of Jack"? The double genitive, as it is called, is idiomatic and of long standing and is by no means incorrect. Oddly enough, those who question the construction would not dream of questioning it if a pronoun rather than a noun were involved. They would not ever say "a friend of her" or "a friend of me." There are rare instances (though not ones that decide this) in which the double genitive has a different meaning from the single genitive. For example, "that picture of Jack's" means something quite different from "that picture of Jack."

## DOWN

(Take it easy.) As a noun *down* has two usual meanings: (1) soft, fine hair or feathers and (2) open grassy land. A third meaning is unusual because I made it up. In my meaning a *down* is a short period of lying down after each meal, a helpful way to recover from or prevent a heart attack. Humans often think that a good way to take off weight is to take vigorous exercise after every meal. But animals have more sense than humans. Notice what a dog or a cat or a tiger does after eating: it rests or, if possible, sleeps. So be sensible; stretch out horizontally and relax in privacy for ten or fifteen minutes after every meal. Enjoy a *down* three times a day if possible.

## DOWN EAST

Whence comes the expression *Down East?* There is no certain answer, but the speculation is that the *Down* was originally a borrowing from England. If we take a look at the word *up,* we find that it is used to designate the direction of a place of greater importance. To this day the English speak of going *up* to London, no matter in which direction they must travel. Conversely, when they leave London they go *down* to whatever destination they have in mind. On this side of the Atlantic Boston was the important place and New Englanders leaving that city went *Down East,* principally to Maine. The expression dates back at least to the early 1800's.

## DRUNK OR DRUNKEN?

A news article said, "Survivors of the bus accident said the driver had been *drunken.*" No. The adjectives *drunk* and *drunken* are fussy about where they should be placed. In the predicative position—that is, after the verb—the word to use is *drunk:* "The driver was *drunk.*" In the attributive position—ahead of the noun—the word to use is *drunken:* "A *drunken* driver caused the accident," "He was convicted of *drunken* driving." And a final note, one for the road, sho to shpeak: To call a person a *drunk* is generally considered slang; he should be called a *drunkard.* (*See* SPIFFLICATED.)

## DUE TO, OWING TO

(Over due.) If you were to write, "His debt was *due to* his spend-thrift ways," all grammarians would nod in approval. But if you were to write, "He owed everybody money *due to* his spendthrift ways," many of them would shake their heads negatively. How come? you may ask. The answer they would give you is that *due* is an adjective and is properly used when it modifies a noun—*debt* in the first sentence—but is improperly used when it introduces an adverbial phrase, as it does in the second sentence. All good and logical grammar. However, if you then ask them, "How about *owing to?*" they will tell you that is all right. If you pursue the subject further and say, "Well, *owing* is an adjective, too; why is that all right?" you will probably be met with either silence or hemming and hawing.

*Owing to* is far less common than *due to,* and that fact may be a clue in the mystery. Since it is less common and has a slightly more dignified air about it, *owing to* somehow seems more acceptable. Someday *due to* is going to overcome the disapproval by the sheer weight of its frequent use. Until then, however, you would be well advised not to employ it unless it modifies a noun lest you be convicted as a negligent writer.

## DUNK, DUCK

(Dippy item.) The world-shaking question in this item is whether you *duck* for apples or *dunk* for apples. Without a moment's hesitation the answer emerges here: You *duck* for apples. *Dunk* comes from the German word *tunken,* meaning to dip or soak. It is mainly used transitively, as to *dunk* a doughnut in coffee, though occasionally it becomes intransitive, which is the mood called for in this apple situation. In its German background it means to dip, dive or plunge, which is what you do for those apples.

## DUPLICITY

(Doubletalk?) A sports event was just getting under way in Montreal when a TV announcer said (unless a receiving set in New York played him dirt), "Montreal is a bilingual city; therefore the announcements are in two languages and you will notice a similar duplicity on the message board." Needless to say, there is no connection between a bilingual city and a dupli-city.

It is not too difficult to understand how that announcer came to use the word *duplicity* when he was thinking of two languages. When you think of *duplicate* and *duplex* and *double* and *duet* your mind is apt to be full of twosomes. The only trouble is that *duplicity* gives us the nasty side of twoness; it tells about double-dealing and deception. And that's not what that announcer was thinking of.

# E

## EACH (OTHER)
A newspaper sentence read as follows: "A key aide to the Secretary of State cautioned American newsmen not to expect that any decision will have been made to upgrade relations beyond the quasi-diplomatic liaison offices set up this year in *each other's capitals.*" In a later edition of the newspaper *capitals* was changed to *capital* and that was a boo-boo. *Each other* is regarded as a pronoun having a plural meaning. In the possessive case it is equivalent to *their.* Therefore *each other's capitals* was correct. If *each* was separated from *other* so that the sentence said that *each* was going to set up a liaison office in the *other's capital,* the singular noun would be correct.

## EACH OTHER, ONE ANOTHER
Quite possibly you were taught in school to restrict *each other* to two and *one another* to three or more, and if you follow that teaching you will never go wrong. Nevertheless, many good writers do not observe those rules strictly. They may not very often use *each other* for more more than two, but it does happen: "The four states promised to respect *each other's* rights to Delaware water." More common is the use of *one another* for only two: "In that family the husband and wife really love *one another.*" If you wish to stick to the rules you cannot be faulted, but you

should not insist that others stick to them; the rules are not that rigid.

## EACH SIDE, EITHER SIDE
*Each side* refers to an object with more than two sides whereas *either side* refers to something with two sides only, as in "Woods grew on *either side* of the road." But *each side* could refer to two ("Woods grew on *each side* of the road") or to more than two (*"Each side* of the equilateral triangle measures six inches").

## EAGER
*See* ANXIOUS.

## EFFECT
*See* AFFECT.

## EITHER
A question that is often raised concerns the use of *either* in the sense of *each*—that is, is it proper to say, "He can pitch with *either* hand," or, "The word is pronounced the same on *either* side of the Atlantic"? That use of *either* is acceptable. It is not wrong, but it is a little stilted. As to the pronunciation of the word, by the way, on the eastern side of the Atlantic eye-their has just about taken over completely, whereas on the western side ee-ther has a big edge.

## EKE OUT
The word *eke,* which has Anglo-Saxon roots meaning to augment or increase, is subject to a great deal of misuse. The misusers think it means to earn or make money, but it doesn't. What it means is to supplement or add to. A policeman might *eke out* his income by moonlighting as a taxi driver or a government might *eke out* its oil reserves by rationing or taxing. What is *eked out* is the original supply, not the thing that results. Thus, it would be improper to say, "After much seesawing the gold market *eked out* a small gain."

## ELECTRIC, ELECTRICAL, ELECTRONIC

(Current words.) Of the three words *electric, electrical* and *electronic* two are close relatives and the third is almost an outsider. *Electric* means carrying a charge or producing electricity or run by electricity. *Electrical* means all of those things and in addition is used to refer to a link with the science or use of electricity, as in an *electrical expert* or *electrical engineering.* The third word, *electronic,* is not so commonplace; it has to do with electrons, which are negatively charged particles that are in the make-up of all atoms.

## ELITE

(The elect.) A word that has both good and bad meanings is *elite,* from the French, derived from the Latin *eligere,* meaning choose or elect. Its normal and good meaning is a group that is the finest, the most distinguished or the strongest. But a bad meaning, a fad meaning, has come up these days in educational circles, where those who favor a strong academic program are criticized as being an *elite* composed of *elitists* who favor *elitism,* that is, the training of only the best. Advocates of good basic training in schools, such as the Council for Basic Education, resent being termed *elitists,* and there is much to be said on their side.

## ELLIPSIS SLIPS

A columnist writing in a paper addressed to lawyers produced this sentence: "I have not, nor do I now, advocate that law schools should teach elementary English." Notice that "advocate" fits with "nor do I now," but does not fit with "I have not"; you would not say, "I have not advocate." That construction illustrates a common error in ellipsis. In grammar, ellipsis permits the omission of a word in part of a sentence if it can be understood from a nearby part. Thus, it is permissible to say, "The day was long and the heat unbearable," where the second "was" can be readily supplied because of the first "was." But an ellipsis slip results when the word to be supplied would not be in the same form as the one from which it is supposed to be understood. It is improper, for example, to say, "The bases were loaded and Seaver pitching." The "were" does not carry over to the Seaver part of the sentence. Some authorities say that in a sentence with as simple a pattern as that the slip is forgivable. Be that as it may, the slip in the first sentence cited above is not forgivable. It would have to be redone to say, "I have not advocated, nor do I now advocate, that, etc."

The word *ellipsis* is akin to the word *ellipse* and that one comes from the Greek *elleipein,* meaning to fall short. An *ellipse* falls short of being a perfect circle; it is rather an oval. Similarly, an *ellipsis* falls short of being a complete grammatical construction. You might say it involves throwing the reader or listener a curve.

## ELSE'S
Do you say, "someone's else pencil" or "someone else's pencil"? Obviously it doesn't make much grammatical sense to say "someone else's pencil," but it is so natural—that is, so idiomatic—that nothing else is possible. In other words, you wouldn't expect a possessive indication ('s) to be attached to an adjective such as *else,* but in this instance it is not only expected, but also just about the only acceptable form. The two words are so closely coupled that they are thought of as a compound pronoun.

## EMBARK, DISEMBARK
(Un-get-on.) *Embark,* as everyone knows, means to get aboard a ship or perhaps an airplane. But the word for getting off such a craft is, in the most common usage, *disembark,* and that word construction—admittedly a piece of trivia—has always annoyed your host. In essence the word means to un-get-on the craft. Why, we have always wondered, wouldn't *debark* be simpler, more economical and at least as clear? The same situation arises with *disemplane,* when *deplane* would do the trick. And then there is that horrible word *de-escalate,* but the solution in that instance is not so simple. Anyway, now we have got the matter off our chest.

## EMINENT
*See* IMMINENT.

## END MARK: 30
Some newspapers still use *30* on news copy to indicate the end of a story. A question that has been prevalent for years is:

Whence came that symbol? A few years ago I tried to answer the question. In two separate columns I printed later there came from different sources seven different guesses as to the answer. Here they are in brief form:

1. During the Spanish-American War a correspondent, writing of a battle, was relating that 30 men had been killed or wounded and a bullet got him when he reached the number *30*.

2. Telegraph operators used *30* as the symbol for "good night."

3. The maximum length of a slug that can be set on a Linotype machine is said to be *30* picas, so when an operator reaches *30* picas, "he has gone as far as he can."

4. In the early days of the telegraph the operators, using longhand, put the symbol *XXX* at the end of correspondents' dispatches and the *XXX* quickly translated itself into *30*.

5. In the early days of the wire services member newspapers contracted for 30 stories. After the last of these the telegrapher sent *"30"* and if the member wanted more he paid extra.

6. In those same days, says a differing account, *30* was used to count the number of words in a message. Those under that limit were sent at a special rate.

7. An 1864 manual, *Wood's Plan of Telegraphic Instruction,* contains 30 "telegraphic numerals" ranging from "1—wait a moment" to "73—compliments to—." Included in the list is "30—finis."

Take your choice; we have now reached *30*.


## ENJOIN

In a now defunct library in Philadelphia, there was a sign that read, "Silence is *enjoined.*" Does *enjoin* apply to persons rather than actions? Not quite, although it is true that most often it is a person rather than an action that is *enjoined.* The American Heritage Dictionary gives the example, "The regulations *enjoin* the attendance of almost the entire ship's company," and the Random House Dictionary gives this one: "The doctor *enjoined* a strict diet." The oddness of the library sign really lies in the fact that *enjoin* means two contradictory things—to order something and to forbid something—and usually it denotes a prohibition, which the sign did not do.

## ENORMITY, ENORMOUSNESS
A newspaper columnist, writing about proposals for a four-day week, said, "The *enormity* of such a change in work habits on American life is only beginning to be considered." Did he mean the wickedness, the outrageousness, the monstrousness of such a change? Obviously not. But that's what *enormity* means. What he had in mind was the vastness, the great size of the change, and the word he should have had in mind was *enormousness.* It would be well for all of us to keep the difference in mind, lest another good word goes down the drain.

## ENSURE
*See* INSURE.

## ENTITLED (TO)
One man says, "I am now sixty-five. Can I ride the bus for half fare?" And his friend replies, "Sure. You're *entitled.*" Normally *entitled* is followed by a *to* phrase—"You're *entitled to half fare*"— but the omission of such a phrase, though not widespread, is heard with some frequency. It sounds as if it had a Yiddish background, but I have not been able to run down any such connection. The use of the word *cope* without its usual following phrase ("He doesn't make much money, but he is able to *cope*") is a similar innovation, though not of Yiddish origin. It has been advancing steadily toward general acceptance. In 1968 only 25 percent of the American Heritage Dictionary's usage panel approved it, but in 1972 the percentage was 40 and in 1975 it was 43. Whether *entitled* will follow a similar course is dubious because it doesn't seem to fill a need in the same way. (*See* VERBS WITH TAILS.)

## ENUMERATION
(Series out of control.) A proper series is A, B and C. But quite often writers give us A, B and Z. Example: "The vandal's attack on the sculpture broke off the Madonna's nose, her left arm and dented her left eye." The conjunction "and" should connect grammatical equivalents, but a "nose," an "arm" and "dented" are not equivalents. The series is out of control. It is what H. W. Fowler, the late British authority on usage, called bastard enumeration. The solution in this instance, as in many others, is to

insert another "and" after "nose." And don't let the repetition of that word bother you; it's far less objectionable than the out-of-whack series.

## ENVY, JEALOUSY

A former basketball star with the Boston Celtics, who is now a college coach, was quoted as saying that he was *"envious,* not *jealous"* of the money used by major colleges to recruit black basketball players. Unlike most people, the coach was aware that there is a difference between *envy* and *jealousy;* the only question is whether he drew the distinction properly. It looks as if he did. *Envy* means discontented longing for someone else's advantages, and it certainly appears that the coach was expressing that feeling. *Jealousy* means unpleasant suspicion of rivalship or apprehension of it, and there seems to be no indication that the coach felt that way. One tendency these days is to regard the two words as interchangeable, but an even stronger one is to discard *envy* and use only *jealousy.* It's too bad because the distinction between the words is useful.

## ETAOIN SHRDLU

Two words that are completely without meaning are *etaoin shrdlu.* What they convey to anyone who knows anything about typography is that some printer goofed. They are the sequences of letters in the two vertical left-hand rows on a Linotype keyboard. If the machine operator makes an error in setting a line of type, he often will run a finger down one or both of these rows of keys to fill out the line, which he intends to discard after it is cast into metal. But sometimes he forgets to throw the line away and thus, so long as Linotype machines are around, you may read in your newspaper:*"The President beruked etaoin shrdlu. . . ."*

## ETC.

The term *et cetera,* as well as its abbreviation *etc.,* means "and other things of the same kind." There is no objection to it in commercial or technical writing provided the sample items preceding it make clear what the "other things of the same kind" are. In what is intended to be good writing, however, the use of *etc.* suggests either laziness on the part of the writer or his ignorance of what the missing items are. Thus it is not approved for anyone who hopes to write well. Needless to say, the use of *and etc.* is definitely out; the *et* means *and,* so you don't say it twice. By the way, it is not pronounced *ex cetera.*

## ETHNICETIES

(New euphemism.) Some American citizens used to be called German-Americans or Italian-Americans or Lithuanian-Americans or even *hyphenated Americans.* But those terms seemed to make them appear too foreign or to suggest a divided loyalty. So, as is inevitable when something gives an impression of being too blunt, a euphemism was devised. Someone came up with the word *ethnic* to designate anyone who is not a white Anglo-Saxon Protestant (WASP). That word is still with us, but now a still softer euphemism has appeared. A cluster of hyphenated people is called a *heritage* group. What next?

(No change in hue.) The earliest and most scientific word to designate a dark-skinned person was *Negro.* Then in this country whites introduced the terms *darkies* and *colored people,* but those two were not popular among those to whom they were applied and they have dwindled in use. (Incidentally, *colored* is definitely in use in South Africa to describe anyone of racially mixed parentage.) In this country *Negro* was the common term for centuries until relatively recently. Then with the rise of the Civil Rights movement Negroes, as a kind of revolutionary gesture and a break with the past, seized upon the word *blacks* and brought it into general usage. There is also a movement to bring *Afro-American* into use, but any headline writer will predict for you that it is not likely to get anywhere.

The dark-skinned militants went a step beyond insisting on the use of the word *black.* They demanded that it be capitalized. And that caused a problem for newspaper and book publishers. They have never capitalized the racial designations for whites, yellows or reds, so to do so for blacks would introduce an inconsistency. And in printing style inconsistency is something normally not tolerated. One way out, you might think, would be to capitalize *whites.* Hardly any newspapers have taken that way out. As for capitalizing *blacks* only a minority have accepted that practice. What the future holds is anybody's guess.

(Introducing Mr. Booby Simpleton.) What follows has only the remotest connection with language, but it's something that should be said and this is as good a place to say it as any. The subject is ethnic jokes. Not, to be sure, the gravest question facing Western civilization or even the United States or even Canada. Still, ethnic jokes are considered by many to be a divisive element in our society, and divisions or differentiations, whether they be nationalistic, ethnic, religious or xenophobic, are believed to be a principal cause of hatred, conflict, even war. Every little thing we can do to prevent divisions, say these observers, advances the cause of harmony and perhaps of peace.

One little thing we can do, they believe, is try to abolish the ethnic joke—the joke that may be as funny as all get-out but that holds up a segment of society to ridicule and contempt. Most ethnic jokes, it so happens, can be just as funny if the ethnic element is removed. And that's where Booby Simpleton comes in. He doesn't mind being ridiculed and he makes a serviceable substitute for the Pole, the Italian, the Mexican, the Jew, the Irishman or the Arab who figures in the gags of this category. Take the case of a joke that has been going the rounds recently and see if it isn't just as funny without whoever it was that appeared in the original:

> Did you hear the latest about Booby Simpleton? He hijacked a submarine and demanded $300,000 ransom and a parachute.

Or the one that is somewhat older:

> They asked Booby Simpleton to screw in a new electric light bulb and he said it would take five men: one to stand on the table and four to turn it around.

Granted Booby Simpleton can't take over in every circumstance, but he is available for service whenever he can help the cause of human harmony. He's willing. Are you?

## EUPHEMISM
(The good word.) If you ask what a *euphemism* is, you are almost asking, What's the good word? *Euphemism* comes from the Greek *eu* (good) plus *pheme* (speak). The general idea of the word is an expression that softens reality or avoids harshness, distastefulness or bluntness. Examples of *euphemisms* are *passed away* instead of *died* and *underprivileged* instead of *poor*.

(The P.R. men take over.) Public relations men hate to call a spade a spade; they constantly deal in euphemisms. An Atlanta editor has noticed that what used to be called *house trailers* are now *mobile homes.* Then he goes on, *"House trailers* have gone the way of *saloons (cocktail lounges), bowling alleys (lanes)* and *pool halls (billiard lounges).* Even dirty-book stores are calling themselves *adult bookstores."* The first thing you know *garbage men* will become *sanitary engineers.*

(No more poor.) A United States interagency committee was reported to be considering doing away with the word *poverty* in government use. The committee wanted a less "value-laden" idea such as *income distribution* or *mean* or *median.* Of course, we no longer have any *poor;* we have only *disadvantaged* or *underprivileged.* And as far as the Census Bureau is concerned there is no *poverty,* only *low income level.* But dreaming up euphemisms won't do much good, because, as it almost says in the Bible, "ye have the ill-to-do always with you."


**EVER**
(Minor error.) Occasionally you will hear someone utter a sentence like this: "John *rarely ever* reads a book." He or she shouldn't. The *rarely* establishes the time element; it means infrequently. It is sufficient unto itself. Adding *ever* to it introduces another time element—*at any time*—a time element that is superfluous and perhaps even confusing. But obviously *rarely if ever* is perfectly acceptable when you examine what the words mean. Everything that has been said here about *rarely* applies also to *seldom.* Don't say *seldom ever,* but *seldom if ever* is quite all right. And so are *hardly ever* and *scarcely ever.*


**EVOKE, INVOKE**
What a difference a little prefix can make! A news story about a political candidate who took action against a Florida newspaper said three times that he had *evoked* an obscure 1913 Florida law. Three times the article was in error. The word that the reporter should have used was *invoked.* The verb *evoke* means to elicit, summon or call forth and none of those meanings have the sense he intended. *Invoke,* on the other hand, means to call

upon or resort to a source of authority, in this instance the 1913 law.

## EXCESS OF ACCESS
It sounds incredible, but a friend reports that he has recently heard *access* frequently used as a verb. For instance, he says, at a sales seminar a speaker said, "You can *access* the information if you dial 626," or, "It is now possible for you to *access* details of recent sales by calling Mr. Jones." It is not difficult to figure out the meaning of the verb: to gain access to, or to obtain or plain old to get. But who needs it?

## EXCUSE, ALIBI
If the controversial meaning of *alibi* was merely an excuse it would be a superfluous word and I would go along with its opponents. But it has a slightly different and useful meaning: an excuse, often an invented one, designed to shift the responsibility, to get out from under. No other word conveys quite that meaning. Furthermore, it will not impair the original meaning of the word, which is a legal term for a plea that the accused was not at the scene of a crime when it was committed. It is our belief that the two meanings will coexist happily.

# F

## FAD

Where does the word *fad* come from? It depends on which reference work you consult. Webster's unabridged, second edition, says it perhaps comes from the French *fadaise,* meaning trifle or silly thing, which in turn comes from the Provencal *fadeza,* which in turn comes from *fat,* meaning foolish. The Oxford Dictionary of English Etymology dismisses that explanation as "improbable" and suggests the word is of dialectal origin, probably from the second element of *fidfad,* a shortening of *fiddle-faddle,* meaning trifling talk. Webster's unabridged, third edition, has the most acceptable label: "origin unknown."

## FANNY

A letter writer who shall be nameless asked where the word *fanny,* meaning buttocks, originated. Most dictionaries list the word, but no dictionary or etymological book seems to have any idea of its derivation. That leaves the field wide open for a guess by this writer, a guess that probably can't be disputed but also one that should not be taken as authentic. The guess here is that *fanny* comes from *fantail,* which means a tail shaped like a fan or, among other things, a part of the rear or stern of a ship. With that etymological guess the dictionaries have gotten a little behind, haven't they? (*See* ARSE.)

## FARTHER, FURTHER

As is obvious from just looking at them, the words *farther* and *further* are related but are not identical twins. They even have different Middle English parents. *Further* is much more widely used than *farther*, partly because the contexts in which it is appropriate are much more common. The difference in meaning between the two words is summed up succinctly by Eric Partridge in *Usage and Abusage* as follows: "A rough distinction is this: *farther, farthest,* are applied to distance and nothing else; *further, furthest,* either to distance or to addition ('a *further* question')." As the present writer remarked elsewhere, fifty years hence writers probably will not have to worry about that distinction, because it looks as if *farther* is going to be mowed down by the scythe of Old Further Time.

## FECKLESS

The word *feckless* means ineffective or feeble. It derives from *feck*, a Scottish version of *effect*, plus *-less*. The Scots, thrifty as ever, apparently decided that the first sound in *effect* was useless and wasteful and so they dropped it. Eliminating a short unaccented vowel or syllable at the start of a word is an etymological process known as *apheresis* (also spelled *aphaeresis*). That process gave us such things as *though* as a substitute for *although* and *squire* for *esquire*.

## FEET (AND FOOT)

We commonly say, "He is a six-foot man," not "a six-feet man," despite the fact that feet is the plural. In Old English there was no distinctive plural sign; at least in the nominative and accusative cases the words were the same. This lack of distinctiveness has survived with nouns referring to measurement and so we say *two-hour show, ten-mile drive* and *six-foot man*. But this use of the singular as if it were the plural is proper only when it qualifies a following noun. If the noun comes first, the modern plural is used, as in a show two *hours* long or a man six *feet* tall.

## FEW, A FEW

(The curious few.) The word *few* has some peculiarities. Used by itself, the word has a negative connotation: "He had *few* regrets about leaving the city." But preceded by *a*, it takes on a positive connotation: "He had *a few* regrets about leaving the city." The word becomes even more positive if the negative word *not* is placed ahead of it: "He had *not a few* regrets about leaving the city." (But that sort of thing is not uncommon; it is a rhetorical figure called *litotes,* an understatement in which an affirmative is expressed by using the negative of the opposite.) And, of course, *quite a few* makes the word still more positive. Another peculiarity of *few* is that when it is preceded by the singular article *a,* it nevertheless takes a plural verb: "Only *a few were* on hand for the ceremonies." Confewsing, isn't it?

**FEWER**
   *See* LESS.

**FIB**
A *fib,* as everyone knows, is a minor falsehood. But what no one knows definitely is where the word comes from. The general supposition, however, is that it is related to *fable,* a fictitious story. Three or four centuries ago *fable* had a reduplicated form: *fible-fable.* (*Reduplication* is the process whereby a word is modified by combining with it a sound-alike element: *chitchat, fiddle-faddle, dilly-dally* and the like.) Then, the supposition goes, *fible-fable* (the *i* pronounced as in *fit*) was clipped back to *fib.* That account of the word's origin may be a fable, but it's not a fib.

**FIGURATIVELY**
   *See* LITERALLY.

**FILL IN, FILL OUT**
(Ancient question.) Is it correct to *fill in* a form or is it better to *fill out* a form? Either is good idiomatic English. Which you use may depend upon what you have in mind at the moment. You may be thinking of the blanks that require *filling in* or of the entire form, which needs completion—that is, *filling out.* Or you may be thinking of neither and that should not cause you unhappiness. *See* VERBS WITH TAILS.

**FISH, FISHES**
The proper plural of the word *fish* troubles writers. In general the plural *fishes* is restricted to reference to different species. In other instances *fish* is the proper plural.

## FIT, FITTED

(Not *fit*.) In the careful use of English *fitted* is preferred as the past tense of *fit:* "He exactly *fitted* the requirements of the job." And the same goes for *befit* and *outfit*. When the meaning is to cause to fit, the past tense form *fitted* is not only preferable, but is just about mandatory: "He was *fitted* for a new pair of jeans" or "Her upbringing *fitted* her for the task of social worker."

## FIX, FIXING

(Word fixation.) Imprecise users of English tend to *fix* everything from their hair to the club's next meeting date. Strictly speaking, one can *fix* something only if it requires repairing. But scarcely anyone these days speaks that strictly, nor should anyone be required to. The word has many common meanings based on the sense of to fasten, to say nothing of meanings suggesting illegal arrangements. A good course to follow is not to use the word if there is a more precise word to express the meaning. But that is a good course to follow in writing in general or speaking in general.

## FLACK

Public Relations men are sometimes called *flacks,* and the origin of that word is a real puzzler. One suggestion is that the word originated in the theatrical publication *Variety* and derives from an obsolete English word of the same spelling meaning to flap, flutter or throb. Maybe. Another theory is that it comes from a Greek slang word *vlakus,* meaning a fool or a loud-mouth. Maybe. This corner's pet theory is that the word, originally spelled *flak,* was an acronym for the German term *Fl*ieger-*a*bwehr*k*anone, meaning antiaircraft gun. By extension the word came to mean antiaircraft fire, by a further extension it denoted a barrage of words and by a still further extension it came to mean press agentry or a press agent. That's a lot of *flack* over very little.

## FLAMMABLE, INFLAMMABLE

*Flammable* means the same thing as *inflammable*—that is, readily ignited—but it is not, as one authority seems to suggest, a late coinage; the Oxford English Dictionary records its use as far back as 1813. What is fairly recent is its promotion by fire under-writers as the better word for labeling such things as gasoline and cleaning fluid. The underwriters discovered that many peo-ple thought that the prefix *in-* of *inflammable* meant not—as it does in such words as *inactive, ineffectual, incapable.* But that's not the meaning here; it is in or into. *Inflammable* means roughly capable of going up *in flame.* However, since most people are not philologists, it was thought that *flammable* was the clearer word and thus the safer. Probably it is.

## FLAUNT, FLOUT
Scarcely anyone misuses *flout,* but an abundance of people use *flaunt* when they mean *flout.* One weak-kneed dictionary has even given in and decided that the misuse is all right. Well, it isn't—at least for educated users of the language. Here is an example of the misuse—by a White House spokesman, of all people: "We can't believe the Governor of Texas would put himself in a position to deliberately *flaunt* the wage-price freeze." *Flaunt* means to display ostentatiously or impudently ("She *flaunted* her jewels"). *Flout,* believed to derive from the Dutch *fluiten,* to play the flute and hence to mock, means to display contempt for ("The student *flouted* the school's rules").

## FLOUNDER, FOUNDER
(Stumble and sink.) A radio report about a ship in distress used both the words *flounder* and *founder.* They are close relatives, but they can't do each other's work. When a ship *founders* that means it fills with water and sinks. *Flounder,* when it doesn't refer to a flatfish, means to stumble or thrash about awkwardly or to move or speak confusedly. *Founder* derives from the Latin *fundus,* meaning bottom, and *flounder* is believed to be a blend of *founder* and *blunder.*

## FLOUT
   *See* FLAUNT, FLOUT.

## FOOTNOTE TERMS
It might be helpful to list some of the more common footnote abbreviations along with the words in full and their meanings.

Hence:

*c.* or *ca.* (circa)—"about," used with a date or a century to indicate that the exact date is not known.

*cf.* (confer)—"compare," suggesting to the reader that he compare what has caused the footnote with another reference cited in the footnote.

*et al.* (et alii)—"and others."

*et seq.* (et sequens)—"and the following."

*f.* or *ff.*—"and the following page or pages."

*ibid.* (ibidem)—"in the same place," referring to a previous footnote and used to avoid having to repeat the name of the book, author, etc.

*op. cit.* (opere citato)—"in the work cited," referring to a work by the same author, which has been previously mentioned.

*passim*—"throughout," indicating that what is mentioned in the footnote turns up here and there in whatever source is being cited.

*q.v.* (quod vide)—"which see," directing the reader to a previously mentioned reference.

## FORBID, PROHIBIT

*Forbid* and *prohibit* mean just about the same thing, but they are not used in precisely the same way, and errors are most often made in the use of forbid. Frequently you will come across a sentence such as, "All city employes were *forbidden from* striking." Idiomatically the verb *forbid* is followed by a *to* infinitive, so that the sentence properly should read, "All city employes were *forbidden to* strike." A mnemonic device for remembering this is to think of two numbers, 4 and 2, and then associate them with *for*bid *to*, which should always be in combination. On the other hand, *prohibit* should be followed by an object noun ("The law *prohibits* the *possession* of unlicensed hand guns") or by a *from* phrase ("The law *prohibits* citizens *from* possessing unlicensed hand guns"). The advice to follow *prohibit* by *from* must have been taught to—but not quite understood by—an official on Long Island, N.Y., because along much of the Long Island Expressway there are signs that say, "Trucks, Buses and Trailers Prohibited From Left Lane." You cannot be *prohibited from* a place.

## FORCIBLE, FORCEFUL
(Forcible entry.) The purpose of this entry is to clarify the distinction between *forcible* and *forceful.* A news article contained this sentence: "It was unusual for the customarily reticent commissioner to speak out so *forcibly* in public." That is a misuse. The word *forcible* means having or using force. An important component of force is biceps, and you might think of the *b* in biceps as being related to the *b* in *forcible. Forceful,* a less literal word, means vigorous, strong or effective. Unfortunately, the distinction between the two words is so often ignored or unknown that there is danger it will disappear.

## FOREBODES (NO GOOD)
Not long after Gerald Ford assumed the Presidency, Indiana's Republican National Committeeman was quoted as having said: "Ford *forebodes* good things." That wording is almost self-contradictory. *Forebode* does mean to indicate beforehand or to portend, but it is almost always used in the sense of portending bad or evil things. In the sense of indicating good things *forebode* is just about verboten. Incidentally, people don't *forebode;* only facts or omens do.

## FORECAST, BROADCAST
(Cast system.) A financial ad contained this sentence: "He *forecasted* a major market decline—and was right." He may have been right, but I would have sworn that the ad writer was wrong in using the word *forecasted.* To my shocked surprise, four dictionaries gave *forecasted* as an alternative to *forecast* as the past tense and *broadcasted* as an alternative to *broadcast,* though none of them gave *casted* as an alternative to *cast.* Fowler's *Modern English Usage* offers a test, though it is almost impossible to apply, for deciding between *forecast* and *forecasted* as the past tense. The decision, says the book, depends on whether we regard the verb or the noun as the original form from which the other has been formed. If the verb is the original word (to guess beforehand), the past tense will be *-cast;* if the verb is derived (from to make a forecast) the past tense will be *-casted.* "The verb is in fact recorded 150 years earlier than the noun," the book concludes, "and we may therefore thankfully rid ourselves of the ugly *fore-*

*casted."* Yes, and that goes for *broadcasted,* too. (*See* VERB END-INGS.)

## FOREIGN WORDS
It is true that on occasion a foreign word or phrase expresses a thought better or more economically than it can be expressed in English. One of the first that comes to mind is *Schadenfreude,* which means enjoyment derived from the misfortunes of others. It is a German word that appears in some English dictionaries and it comes from *Schaden* (harm or damage) and *Freude* (joy). Then there is another German word, *gemütlich,* which can be defined only by using several words, such as cozy, cheerful, agreeable, congenial and conveying a sense of well-being. That word appears in some English dictionaries. From the French we borrow such phrases as *bête noir,* which means literally black beast and figuratively something or someone that is disliked, dreaded and avoided. And from the Yiddish we get *chutzpah,* meaning brazen, impudent, shamelessly brassy, full of unmitigated gall. There are, of course, dozens of other foreign terms that English welcomes with open arms because they fill a need, and the more popular of them find their way into our dictionaries.

## FORESEEABLE
A San Francisco columnist went on at some length about the phrase the *foreseeable future.* His point was that the future is not *foreseeable.* That is true if the word is interpreted narrowly. But a look at Webster's unabridged dictionary, third edition, discloses that the word need not be used and is not normally used in that narrow a sense. One definition is, "being such as may reasonably be anticipated," and a second one is, "lying within the range for which forecasts are possible." Thus, if we say that Jones will continue as bank president for the *foreseeable future,* the statement is within the range for which forecasts are possible and is not intended to take account of the possibility of Jones's being killed by a bolt of lightning.

## FORGO
Many words contain the prefix *fore-,* meaning ahead or front part, so the tendency to spell *forgo* as if it were *forego* is not really

mystifying. But it is wrong. The prefix *for* has the sense of apart or without. Thus *forgo* means to do without or give up and it should be spelled without an *e*. No *e* nohow.

## FORTE

(Two fortes.) Here are two different words that are spelled the same but pronounced in different ways. *Forte,* meaning one's strong point, is pronounced *fort* and *forte,* meaning loud in music, is pronounced *fortay.* Can both be pronounced *fortay?* Answer: no.

## FORTUITOUS, FORTUNATE

(More luck.) The discoveries by the Princes of Serendip (*see* SERENDIPITY) were both *fortuitous* and *fortunate,* but those two words are not interchangeable. *Fortuitous* means happening by chance; *fortunate* means marked by good luck. Probably because of the similarity of sound *fortuitous* is sometimes misused when *fortunate* is the desired word. Here is an example of the misuse: "He planned his investments so as to yield $5,000 a year and the result was *fortuitous*—he made just about that amount." The result did not come about through chance (unless you think all investments these days are chancy), but rather through planning. A proper use of *fortuitous* is illustrated in this sentence: "His meeting with his future wife was purely *fortuitous*—they found themselves side by side at a rock festival."

## FOUNDER

*See* FLOUNDER, FOUNDER.

## FOUR, FORTY

Why is the number 4 spelled *four* and the number 40 spelled *forty?* Of course those words that contain the *u* also include *fourth, fourteen* and *fourteenth,* and those that lack the *u* include *fortieth.* As far as we know and as near as we can get to an explanation, the difference in spelling reflects an ancient difference in the way the vowels were sounded, a difference that has largely but not entirely vanished. The words that include the *u* were pronounced in a rounder way with a deeper *oh* sound. Many people, possibly including you, still sound the vowels slightly differently. Try this little test: first say *four,* then say *forty.*

Notice any difference? No? Then try it again, this time paying close attention to what happens to the position of your tongue. In pronouncing *forty* don't you find that your tongue lifts to a tiny degree, making the vowel sound a little less rounded? If your tongue was not brought up, it might have something to do with where you were brought up. But don't worry about it.

## FREE LANCE

A *free lance* is a writer or actor who is not under any obligation or contract and who can and does work for whom he pleases. According to William and Mary Morris, in their *Dictionary of Word and Phrase Origins,* the term goes back to medieval times when it referred to Italian and French soldiers who felt free of any loyalty to a sovereign and fought for whoever paid the best fee.

## FRESH

Only a couple of decades ago *fresh* used as an adverb was considered colloquial, but it is proper these days to speak of fresh-baked bread or fresh-cut flowers. The adverbial use, though it appears mostly in commercial contexts, is acceptable except in the phrase "fresh out of" as in, "We are fresh out of eggs"; that is considered slang.

## FUDDY-DUDDY

Whence comes the word? As is true of most slang, the origin is not completely clear. The guessing is that the word derives from *dud,* meaning a weak, ineffectual person. One source says that the Scots used that word as far back as the early nineteenth century. In the United States it came into use in World War I to designate a shell or bomb that failed to explode and in the 1930's to designate that weak, ineffectual person or an ineffectual thing. The next step was apparently the process of reduplication, in which a new word is coined by repeating a sound of an older word. Thus we got *hanky-panky, itsy-bitsy, footsie-wootsie* and—building on that *ud* sound—*fuddy-duddy.* The meaning has changed, too, to designate not only an ineffectual person but also one who is elderly and old-fashioned. So there you have either etymology or a dud.

## -FUL, -FULS

(He had his hands full.) Trying out a recipe, a chap says, he filled his hand with dried fruit twice and added the contents thereof to the mixture. Did he add two *handfuls,* two *handsful* or two *hands full?* The plural of *handful* is *handfuls* no matter what the size of the hands or what you do with them. The same goes for *spoonful,* though it is customary to specify *teaspoonfuls* or *table-spoonfuls.* But *handfuls* are obviously a rougher kind of measurement.

## FULSOME

(Too full.) When the eighth vice president of the Grechko Manufacturing Co. retires, some newspaper or house organ is almost certain to print a sentence something like this: "Speaker after speaker heaped *fulsome* praise upon him." *Fulsome* is the wrong word there. It doesn't mean full; it means overfull, and more specifically offensive because overdone or insincere. So *fulsome* praise doesn't compliment the guest of honor; it downgrades him.

## FUNGO

(Baseball mystery.) No reference book gives the origin of the word *fungo,* meaning a fly ball hit to outfielders in pregame practice, so your host put Joseph Durso, knowledgeable sportswriter for *The New York Times,* to work on it.

First Joe called the late Casey Stengel, who had a 45-minute telephone monologue with him. Casey thought the word had something to do with Cuban wood, which was used in some bats early in this century. But others ruled that out because Cuban wood is rather heavy, whereas the *fungo* bat is always light and slender.

Next Joe tackled Oscar Kahn, managing editor of *The Sporting News* of St. Louis, who said his paper had once asked its readers to send in information about *fungo,* but had got no response. He added that Bill Bryson, a baseball researcher, said it came from a children's game: The kid with the bat would toss the ball up and chant, "One-go, two-go and (hitting it) fun-go." But there's no supporting evidence for that.

Finally, Joe tried Jack McGrath, retired vice president of the Hillerich & Bradsby Co., makers of the Louisville Slugger bats, who is the company's historian. He said he had tried to find the answer but had come up with nothing but a couple of suppositions.

There seems to be general agreement (except for Casey) that (a) the word *fungo* has nothing to do with the wood used in the bat, (b) that the word is somehow related to *fun* and (c) that the word dates back approximately a century. Beyond that man knoweth not; beyond that it's strike three.

**FURTHER**
*See* FARTHER.

**FUSED PARTICIPLE**
A clipping sent in from Columbus, Ohio, contained this sentence: "In a rehearsal room Miss Redgrave said, 'I play Mrs. Warren's daughter. My mother educates me from her brothel earnings without *me knowing* her profession.'" That combination of *me knowing* is what grammarians call a fused participle and in the view of some of those grammarians it is a serious offense. They contend that users of a phrase like that think of the *me* as being the object of the preposition *without,* whereas the participle *knowing* really is the object. Thus the *me* is left up in the air without any grammatical construction. Therefore they insist on changing *me* to *my.* In most instances that position is proper. From the days of Old English until the eighteenth century the use of a possessive ahead of the participle was almost invariable. But since then the rule has been eased. You wouldn't dream of writing, "I hate to see *this's* happening." In some constructions a possessive is just about impossible—for example: "He couldn't understand a *man* in his right mind *beating* his wife." The advice here is to use the possessive ahead of the participle, but not to feel compelled to use it when it is unidiomatic.

# G

## G-STRING

A *G-string,* as everyone knows, is a narrow loincloth worn by burlesque strippers and showgirls. Any dictionary will tell you that. But no dictionary will tell you why it is called a *G-string.* Sticking his neck out, this voyeur will hazard a guess. A violin has four strings: G, D, A and E. The E-string is the highest note; the *G-string* is the lowest. A burlesque show normally has a complement of musicians, all of whom would be familiar with the violin, and it's quite possible—nay, quite likely—that the expression *G-string* originated with them. The *G-string* occupies just about the lowest place possible on both femme and fiddle. Just a guess, you understand.

## GAG

(That is no choke.) In recent times there has been much discussion in and out of court of attempts at what the legal fraternity calls "prior restraint" on publication in the press of certain kinds of information. A New York state justice, J. Irwin Shapiro, spoke of the term "prior restraint" as "a fancy legal phrase for *gag,*" and much has appeared in the media about *gag* actions and *gag* laws. That use of *gag* is not a recent coinage, but it is definitely an Americanism; it was in use in Congress as far back as 1810.

## GALORE

The word *galore* is an unusual broth of a word in its current Irish usage. Authorities are divided on whether it is an adjective or adverb. We vote for adjective. Unlike most adjectives, however, it appears almost without exception after the noun it modifies. No one would say, "There are *galore* eggs in the refrigerator," but rather would use the word in what grammarians call a postpositive place: "There are eggs *galore* in the refrigerator." The word comes from the Gaelic *go leor,* meaning to sufficiency.

## GANTLET, GAUNTLET
(Run one, throw the other.) Here's a word on which the dictionaries are waffling: *gantlet.* A news article said, "The road to the Beirut airport, which lately has been a hazardous *gauntlet,* appeared to be secured." Strictly speaking, the word here should be *gantlet,* which literally means a form of military punishment in which the offender runs between rows of men who club him as he goes by. A *gauntlet,* on the other hand (and it's always on one hand or the other), is a protective glove worn by knights in armor. To *throw down the gauntlet* is to make a challenge. Probably because over the years the two words were confused the dictionaries now find *gauntlet* acceptable in both senses. But you don't have to do so.

## GAY
Homosexuals have recently been taking over the adjective *gay.* Two things about the adoption of that word are to be condemned: first, that its meaning of merry, lighthearted or joyous is not specifically descriptive of homosexuals and may be completely nondescriptive of some of them, and second and much more important, that if the word is applied in this way very much more, it is going to be lost to the language in its true meaning. Why homosexuals want to use it at all is not very understandable; it is an adjective and only an adjective, which leaves its users without a much-needed noun. How about inventing a word that would serve both sexes—but especially males—as both a noun and an adjective? For openers, how about *homex* (plural *homexes*)? There's no patent on that invention; help yourselves, folks.

## GET
(A versatile word.) A bank ad read, "If the travelers checks are lost or stolen, you can *get* them replaced." A friend questions

that use of *get*. He says he considers that phraseology in the same category as *getting married*. Shades of Ambrose Bierce, who contended more than 60 years ago that if it is correct to say *got married*, we should also say *got dead* for died! Trying to banish such *get* combinations is too extreme. There are occasions on which it is necessary, or at least preferable, to use the locution; for example: "He is married now, but I can't tell you when he *got married.*" The verb *get* in both speech and writing is a general utility word. Dictionaries list more than a score of meanings for the word, including the sense of *to cause*, in which sense the word is used in that bank ad above. Trying to get rid of some of those meanings will get you nowhere; they have gotten to be too well established in the language. Get it?

## GIVEN
*See* ABSENT.

## GLOSSOLALIA
The word *glossolalia*, derived from the Greek *glosso-*, meaning tongue, and *lalia*, speak, would appear to be a simple word meaning to speak with the tongue. Actually, it has the sense of a gift of tongues and has a religious connotation. The Holy Spirit is believed by some to manifest itself by causing *glossolalia* —Speaking in Tongues—in which the worshiper ecstatically utters unintelligible syllables that are regarded as a manifestation of a profound religious experience. To *gloss* a text, however, means to explain and interpret it.

## GOBBLEDYGOOK
The word *gobbledygook* was invented around 1940 by a United States Representative, Maury Maverick; about that there is no disagreement. But whereas most dictionaries connect the word with the sound made by a turkey, a professor has a different idea. The *gobble* part, he thinks, comes from an old French word for mouth and the *gook* is related to *goo* and *muck*. "In short," he says, *"gobbledygook* is sticky muck . . . issuing from the mouth." Somehow your host likes turkey better, especially white meat.

## GONNA

(A going concern.) Members of the Great Organization of Nescient Native Americans (GONNA) offer this prediction: The form using *will* and *shall* will become archaic; *gonna* will prevail. In common usage rarely does anyone encounter such sentences as, "I *will* study the theory of relativity tomorrow," but rather, "I'm *gonna,*" followed by the appropriate verb. Is the form *going* followed by the infinitive a grammatically acceptable replacement for *will* followed by the verb? Yes, it is; the construction has been in use since the 1400's. As to the broader question concerning the future of the future tense, it should be noted first of all that in American usage *shall* is becoming rarer century by century and *will* has replaced it in most situations. Next of all, although *going to* is making widespread gains, *will* is not likely to become archaic. In addition it appears in contractions such as *I'll* and *he'll* and is likely to survive in that form. Nevertheless, I would not be rash enough to rule out *gonna* (pronounced and perhaps spelled just that way) as the dominant form 100 years hence.

## GOOD

(No good.) "You never smiled so good," said a television advertisement and that evoked a protest to the advertiser. The protester wrote that a solecism of that sort works against the efforts of every English teacher . . . and every child who makes an effort to learn the English language. To which the advertiser replied, "We agree with you that it would be wonderful if everyone spoke perfect, grammatical English, but language is a changing thing, constantly adapting itself to new thoughts, new rules. A 'catchy' phrase sells products, and a company is in business to sell products. The success of the Winston commercial 'Tastes good like a cigarette should' was condemned and rightly so. But it sold cigarettes. . . ."

First, let it be noted that *good* may properly be used after a linking verb as an adjective modifying a preceding noun: "Her smile was *good.*" But it may not properly be used as an adverb modifying a verb: "She smiled good," which is the way it is used in the disputed ad. That usage is rejected by an overwhelming percentage of the usage panel of the American Heritage Dictionary.

Second, there is no evidence that language is "changing" toward acceptance of that use of *good.*

Third, in the Winston ad the use of *good* is in line with the acceptable use stated four sentences ago and there is some evidence that the present objection to the use of *like* as a conjunction may be softening a little. So the Winston ad offers little in the way of support for the "smiled so good" ad.

Fourth and finally, we don't need any help from advertisers to push the "changing" of language; we could use their help better in setting an example for school kids of educated English usage. (*See* ADJECTIVES AND ADVERBS.)

## GOT, GOTTEN

Doubts are often raised about the acceptability of *have got* and *gotten.* The words *have got,* as in "I *have got* a really good car," have long been put down by schoolmaster sticklers as an error, but most authorities agree that it is not. At worst they find it colloquial—that is, more common in everyday speech than in literary language. The words, of course, refer to mere possession and the *got* could be easily omitted. The words *have gotten* refer to the act of acquisition: "I *have gotten* enough bread to last a week." That is what Americans would say. The British, however, don't like the word *gotten;* they would feel compelled to substitute *bought* or *acquired* or *obtained* or some other word. As with *got,* the word *gotten* is acceptable in spoken language, but one of the more precise words would be preferred in written language.

## "GOT TO BE"

(Compulsive writing?) Exaggeration has always been a characteristic of slang and colloquial language, but today the tendency to go to extremes is more pronounced than ever. The chap who can tune the strings on his guitar is called *terrific* and the one who most of the time can sing in tune with his guitar is *fabulous.* But here is a reasonably conservative reviewer on a reasonably conservative paper writing about a dance program: " 'The Concert' has got to be one of the funniest ballets ever made." Not "may be" or "is," but *"has got to be."* Why does it got to be? In normal language "has to" (or "has got to") carries the implication of compulsion or imperativeness: "Pollution of the air has got to stop"; "You've got to eat your spinach." That ballet, however, is not under any compulsion to be funny.

But let's go a step further. What is usually understood with those normal "has to" phrases is, "There are no two ways about it." Viewed in conjunction with that corollary, the "has to" locution seems almost normal. What the reviewer was saying conceivably could be, "There are no two ways about it, 'The Concert' is one of the funniest ballets ever made." The question then arises, "Why didn't he say it that way?" Obviously because he was caught up in today's colloquial manners of expression and wanted to be down to earth—or, shall we say, "with it." All of which is, within limits, all right. But a penalty usually lurks behind those up-to-the-minute expressions. Today's tinselly crown of colloquialism may, without notice, become tomorrow's old hat.

## GOURMET, GOURMAND

The words *gourmet* and *gourmand* are both of French ancestry, but they mean different things. A *gourmet* is a person who is a connoisseur of food and drink, whereas a *gourmand* is also a good judge of food and drink, but in addition likes to stuff himself with them; he is a glutton.

## GOVERNMENTALESE

Two characteristics of bureaucratic jargon have come up recently. One is a tendency to use euphemisms—ways of getting around saying something unpleasant. When talk of gasoline rationing first arose, a bill to put it into effect did not use the word *rationing*. The framers of the bill dodged that word and called it instead *end-use allocation*. Another characteristic of governmentalese is the piling up of nouns used as adjectives. A recent public notice of the United States Environmental Protection Agency (that's a mouthful in itself) spoke of the *Ocean Disposal Permit Program*. What? The government is going to dispose of the oceans? What the program aims at, of course, is the disposal of waste and sewage in the oceans. Naturally, if that goes on long enough it may indeed dispose of the oceans, but that's another matter.

Here's another one. The title of a study made for the Department of Health, Education and Welfare is, "Evaluation and

Parameterization of Stability and Safety Performance Characteristic of Two and Three Wheeled Vehicular Toys for Riding."
That piece of gobbledygook was presented as a horrible example in an article by a Marine Corps professor of English, Argus
J. Tresidder, in the magazine *Military Review*. The professor
gave a simple translation of that far-out officialese as follows:
"Why children fall off bicycles." But the authors of that $23,000
study would not have felt as if they were earning their money if
they had written that simply. (*See* JARGON; REDUNDANCY.)

## GRADUATE (FROM)
A columnist who is a former teacher wrote, "Two fellows *graduated* high school, one went to college and one didn't." That use
of *graduate* is wrong. Three forms are correct: "He *graduated from*
high school," "He *was graduated from* high school" or "The high
school *graduated* him." Of course, you can also properly say, "He
*graduated* last year." But "He *graduated* high school" borders on
illiteracy. Certainly you wouldn't expect anyone who had *graduated from* high school to write it.

## GRANTED
*See* ABSENT.

## GRAY
(Black and white, mixed.) How do you spell that color? Is it *gray*
or *grey*? In the United States it is *gray,* but in England *grey* is more
common. A good way to remember it is *"a* is for America, *e* is
for England." Now that I've told you that, A and E are all I O
U. And don't ask Y. Just a bit of vowel play, that's all.

## GROUPIE, GROUPER
(Couple of newish words.) One recent entrant into the language
is *groupie.* When the word first came into use, it meant a teen-age
girl who was so enraptured by a rock *group* or any kind of celeb-
rity that she would follow her idols wherever they appeared.
Another perhaps more recent meaning of the word has to do
with young people who live together either on vacations or for
long spells. The similar word *grouper* applies to such people,
particularly if they engage in group sexual activities, and likewise to members of therapy encounter groups.

## GYNARCHY
If some of the extreme feminists have their way, we may one day
have a *gynarchy.* That word comes from the Greek *gyn-* or *gyno-,*
meaning woman, and the Greek *-archy,* meaning rule. *Gynarchy,*
pronounced JIN-ar-key, means government by women. Anyway,
it's better than anarchy.

# H

## HAD BETTER (IS BETTER)
A columnist wrote, "A new period is beginning and we better face up to it." The construction of the second clause in that sentence constitutes a grammatical error; it should read "we *had better* face up to it." Unfortunately the omission of the *had* is quite common in ordinary speech and is growing more and more common in writing. H. W. Fowler in *Modern English Usage* makes this point about the word: In such a context *had* is not a mere auxiliary of mood or tense, but a true verb meaning find and cannot be omitted. Thus, in his analysis of a clause such as "we had better face up to it" he declares it to be equivalent to "we would find to-face-up-to-it better." Other authorities have different explanations of the need for *had,* but careful writers had better pay attention to the point.

## HALFS AND HALF NOTS
A questioner wanted to know which is proper usage: *one and a half miles* or *one and a half mile.* His point was that one mile does not equal *miles* nor does a half mile equal *miles,* therefore why should one and a half of them equal *miles?* The way in which he put the question betrays that he knows which is proper usage, or at least common usage; he was questioning the customary. The easy explanation would be to set down the common usage as idiom, which is roughly what idiom is. But there is a logical answer, too. When you are speaking of one of those measures of distance the word to use obviously is *mile.* But as soon as you

exceed one of them you are speaking of more than one and more than one cannot be *mile*, it has to be *miles*. In the same way we speak of one and a half *dollars* or one and a half *times* (an amount) or one and a half *pounds*. Of course, if you can't swallow this explanation you are always at liberty to say *a mile and a half.*

## HAM ACTOR
How did the term originate? Two versions that appear in a book called *The Language of Show Biz* were quoted by a columnist in the St. Paul *Pioneer Press.* One traces the term back to about 1850 when Tony Pastor gave away hams to attract patrons to his opera house in New York. Another version, which has some support in Webster's New World Dictionary, is that ill-paid actors in the 1800's removed their make-up by using lard instead of the more expensive cold cream. Lard came from pigs, which also provided ham. In either version *ham* is supposed to be related to actors who were inept or overdid their acting. Still another version traces *ham* to the word *hamfatter,* which in turn came from a minstrel song, "The Hamfat Man." In addition, there may be a connection between *ham* and *am*(ateur). In short, no one really knows.

## HANDFULS
*See* -FULS.

## HANGED
*See* HUNG.

## HANG OUT
(Hangman's news.) In the press reports of the Watergate affair former President Nixon was quoted quite a few times as referring to taking the *hang-out road.* What he meant by the expression apparently was to disclose the complete truth. The phrase obviously derives from the Afro-American slang invention *let it all hang out,* meaning to speak out uninhibitedly, to tell it all. That expression has been with us some years and most probably had a vulgar derivation.

## HARD OF HEARING
A real puzzler is the expression *hard of hearing:* How did it de-

velop without similar ones developing for other infirmities such as *hard of seeing* or *hard of walking?* Actually in the days of Middle English similar constructions, though not always dealing with infirmities, were in use. For example, the Oxford English Dictionary contains this quotation dated 1400: "Yvil and hard of bileve" (which probably translates into "Evil and hard of belief"). Then, more to our point, there is this quotation dated 1564: "The testatrixe was hard of hearinge." Strangely enough, that *hard of* construction became obsolete in the language with just one exception: *hard of hearing.*

## HARDLY (CORRECT)

The word under discussion is *hardly.* It has a negative connotation and therefore should not be used in a sentence that already is negative in meaning. The following sentence is incorrect: "The Smiths do not own a television set or *hardly* any furniture." One way to correct the error is to introduce an affirmative verb in the second part of the sentence: "The Smiths do not own a television set and *have hardly* any furniture." Another error that is often made with *hardly* is to follow it with *than:* "*Hardly* had the Governor started to talk *than* the booing began." Change the *than* to *when.* The conjunction *than* indicates a comparison and properly follows a comparative adjective or adverb, as in, "No *sooner* did the Governor start to talk *than* the booing began." What has been said here about *hardly* applies equally to *scarcely.*

## HAS TO BE
*See* "GOT TO BE."

## HASSLE

(New irritation.) The word *hassle* (or *hassel*), meaning a quarrel, a dispute or a fight, has been with us a couple of decades, if not longer. Most etymologists think it is a combination of *haggle* and *tussle.* The Random House Dictionary, however, thinks it traces back to an obsolete word, *harsell,* meaning to irritate. Curiously enough, as used by the younger set these days, *hassle* has become a verb meaning to irritate, bother, annoy, as in "Don't hassle me, Pop." The curious part of it is that when the Random House traced *hassle* to that obsolete word meaning to irritate, the term hadn't acquired its current meaning. So the R.H. factor may be valid.

## HAVE
(The haves vs. the not-haves.) No one objects to a sentence like this: "I had my eyes examined last week." But some people object to a sentence like this: "I had my left leg broken last year." In the first sentence the verb to *have* is regarded as causative. In the second sentence those objectors still regard the *have* as causative and therefore regard the sentence as nonsense: A person wouldn't cause his leg to be broken, they argue. What the objectors are not aware of is that the auxiliary *have* is not always causative. Among its many meanings is one presented in the Merriam-Webster dictionary, second edition, as "to suffer or experience from an exterior source." That meaning is not a recent coinage; Shakespeare had Falstaff say, "The other night I fell asleep here behind the arras, and *had* my pocket picked. . . . " Those objectors have had their nit-picking spoiled.

## HERSELF, HIMSELF
See SELF WORDS; PRONOUNS.

## HIPPIES
In the youth-yak of olden days (that is, a dozen years or so ago) the young people who dressed in casual style (if that could be called style at all), who grew long hair and beards (if they were males) and who shot LSD (or any other dope that was available) were called *hippies*. Many of the characteristics remain the same, but the word *hippies* has disappeared (along with *flower children*). So today's question is: What do you call those weirdies? One youngster we know has heard the word *parkies*, an allusion to the fact that the youths often hang out in parks. But that does not seem to be a well-known word. Maybe we will have to wait for another generation to spring up.

## HISTORIC, HISTORICAL
Former President Nixon's original decision not to respond to subpoenas of the Senate committee was referred to in one news account as "a *historical* challenge." It was not that; it was a *historic* challenge (and not *an* historic challenge, by the way—See AN (A)

HISTORIC MATTER). *Historic* means figuring in history; *historical* means pertaining to history. A house that George Washington slept in would be a *historic* house, but a book about the house would be a *historical* work.

## HOCUS-POCUS
Just as there is phoniness in *hocus-pocus* there is phoniness attached to the word itself. It is believed to be based on a pseudo-Latin phrase coined in the sixteenth century and used by wandering scholars: *hax pax max Deus adimax.* The word, of course, refers to jugglery, trickery or sleight of hand.

## HOI POLLOI
From the Greek, *hoi polloi* means the masses; *hoi* means "the" and *polloi* means "many." For that reason it is improper to speak of *the hoi polloi;* the article *the* should be omitted. However, that makes for clumsy speaking and writing, so the best thing to do is avoid the expression altogether. Perhaps because *hoi* sounds to some people as if it were connected with "high," a man of our acquaintance said the other night, "He is a distinguished man, one of the *hoi polloi.*" That is wrong on every possible count.

## HOME
   *See* HOUSE.

## HOMONYM SLIP
A homonym is a word that has the same sound as another word but has a different meaning and usually a different spelling. Often homonyms provide the makings of gags: "As one dwarf said to another, *'We* are *wee.'* " Sometimes, however, they cause boo-boos. An ad for a book contained this sentence: "This book tosses out all pretense and gives sexual imagination full reign." Undoubtedly what was meant was "full (or free) *rein.*"

## HOMOSEXUAL, MALE
Most people think, as I thought, that there is no word meaning a male homosexual—that is, a word equivalent to lesbian, meaning a female homosexual. Well, by golly, there is one. The word is *urning.* It is a medical term that derives indirectly from *Ourania,* a Greek name applying to the love goddess Aphrodite. As a medical term and one that I could find only in Webster's unabridged dictionary, it is hardly a common word. But it

should be, to replace the undignified slang terms now in use. By the way, *urning* is pronounced oorning. Further by the way, there is a word for male homosexuality: *urningism*.

## HONKY
A black man's disparaging term for a white man in the United States is *honky* or *hunky,* but where the term comes from seems to be unknown. Far back *honky* was used by second-generation Americans to refer to new arrivals in this country—especially those of Slavic origin—and during World War II American troops referred to freed slave labor from all over Europe as *honkies.* A pure guess is that *honky* may have derived from *Hungarian,* just as *bohunk* is believed to be a blend of *Bohemian* and *Hungarian.* But how the word came to be taken over by blacks is a mystery.

## HONOR AMONG THIEVES
The idea underlying the phrase dates back as far as the first century B.C., when Cicero wrote, "Even thieves have a code of laws to observe and obey." Shakespeare wrote, "A plague upon it when thieves cannot be true one to another," and Cervantes put it this way: "Thieves are never rogues among themselves." In the eighteenth century Defoe produced this passage: "What thieves make a point of honor of; I mean that of being honest to one another." And finally in the nineteenth century Scott produced the familiar phrase when he wrote, "There is honor among thieves." There seems to be no touch of sarcasm in any of those passages and, indeed, even today we occasionally come across evidence that crooks have a code among themselves: the practices of the Mafia, for instance. Whether "honor" is the appropriate word for such rules is a debatable question.

## HOODLUM
What that word derives from is not known. What does seem to be known is that the word originated in San Francisco around 1870. One flimsy theory is that *hoodlum* approximates a reverse sounding of *Muldoon,* who was supposed to have been a dreaded thug. A sounder theory is that the word traces back to a German dialect term, *hodalump* or *hudilump* or *hodalum,* meaning a rowdy or miserable fellow, which approximates today's meaning.

Wherever *hoodlum* came from, it would be nice if he'd go back there.

## HOPEFULLY

(Word to be loosened.) Conflict continues over the word *hopefully*. The normal use of the term to which nobody objects is in the sense of full of hope, as in "We looked *hopefully* for a break in the stormy weather." The use to which many people object is in the sense of "it is hoped," as in, "The two sides began negotiations and *hopefully* an end to the strike is in sight." To be quite honest, a decade ago I was on the side of the objectors, but in recent years additional thought about the matter has changed my mind. In that secondary use the word makes sense; it is somewhat analogous to words such as *fortunately, luckily, regrettably* and *happily*. Unfortunately, no parallel word that means "it is hoped" exists. And happily, to use *hopefully* in that manner in no way distorts or corrupts the first meaning of the word. But strangely, the opposition continues to grow. Bruce Bohle, usage editor of the American Heritage Dictionary, tells me that approval of the secondary sense among the dictionary's usage panel was 44 per cent in 1968, 42 per cent in 1970 and 37 per cent in 1975. But he adds this personal opinion about the secondary meaning: "Realistically, I suppose it is *here.*" I think he is right. Those who continue to oppose that meaning are Canutists. That word *Canutists* was coined here just a moment ago. Can't you hear people saying, "I suppose it's related to King Canute. But what does Canute connote?" And then they will recall that Canute tried in vain to sweep back the waves of the ocean.

## HOUSE, HOME

(Making a house a home.) A dispatch about Angola said that *"homes* that cost the equivalent of $72,000 are being sold for as little as $17,000." As a matter of sentiment many users of English are agitated by the use of *home* in the sense of a structure designed for residential purposes. To them such a structure is a *house* until occupants fashion it into a *home*. That distinction between the words is correct, but more and more often it is being lost. Real estate operators frequently advertise not mere masonry but rather places of comfort, congeniality and family accommodation that make a *house* into a *home.* Sentiment usually enters the picture when purchase or sale is involved; a person most often speaks of buying a *home,* but selling his *house.* No one should discourage the sentimentalists from trying to keep the two words distinct, but success in that effort seems unlikely.

## HUMOR
A funny word. Originally it denoted any of the four principal fluids of the body: blood, phlegm, choler and melancholy. The proportions of these were believed to determine a person's disposition as well as health. In a roundabout way the emphasis of *humor* came to be laid upon the ability to perceive or create something amusing. Hence *humor* is funny.

## HUNG, HANGED
(Get the hang of it.) When the question of amnesty for former President Nixon was a live issue, Senator Hugh Scott was quoted as saying that "he has been *hung,* and it doesn't seem that in addition he should be drawn and quartered." The past and the past participle of *hang* are normally *hung,* but there is one exception: When the meaning is to put to death with a rope the preferred form is definitely *hanged.* This is not to say that Senator Scott committed an error, but rather to say that he was not in line with accepted educated usage.

## HYPHENS
(An anarchic field.) When and how to use hyphens is often headache-making because there are not many rules and such as there are sometimes become diluted by exceptions. A perplexing corner of the anarchic field is exemplified by the word *taxpayer,* which all dictionaries agree is one word. Suppose we wish to refer to a citizen who pays an income tax. Is he an *income taxpayer?* Likewise, *businessman* is one word, but how about a man who is engaged in a small business? Is he a *small businessman?* In each instance the normally solid word would have to be broken up: *income-tax payer* and *small-business man.* To complicate the matter further, examine a sentence such as this: "There are a large number of *ex-public schoolboys* in the Senate." (And let's not evade part of the issue by saying that the *ex-* could be changed to *former.* Maybe it's a headline and there isn't room for *former.*)

Since *school* is more closely related in this example to *public* than it is to *boys,* the preferred solution would be to make it *ex-public-school boys.* But there is no rule about it except to use common sense.

(With adverb preceding noun.) Compounds consisting of an adverb and an adjective preceding a noun are usually hyphened if there is even a remote chance that the adverb could be misread to be a modifier of the noun. A classic, if droll, example of a compound that could be misread is "a long felt want" (long and made of felt?); therefore it should be "a long-felt want." On the other hand, if a compound contains an adverb that ends in *-ly* and thus is readily identifiable as an adverb, the hyphen should be omitted.

(Fellow follower.) It is not uncommon to see in print terms such as *fellow-worker* or *fellow-Republican. Fellow* should be treated like any other adjective and the hyphen should be omitted, though it is necessary to make occasional exceptions—sometimes running the two parts together as a single word, as in *fellowship.* It is not feasible to lay down rules on the use of the hyphen, but it is possible to keep in mind what Winston Churchill said: "One must regard the hyphen as a blemish to be avoided wherever possible."

(With re- words.) In general a hyphen is not used after *re* except when its omission creates a homograph that might be mistaken to be a different word. (A homograph is a word spelled the same as another one but having a different meaning; for example, *lead* may mean to direct or be the name of a metal.) Several words beginning with *re* might be misunderstood—reform, react, re-cover, release, remarks, resign—but in most cases the context in which they were used would make clear what the word meant. However, if Mrs. Jones took her garments out of a closet and found them to be moth-eaten and then decided to place them in a different closet, the hyphen would be virtually mandatory in the sentence, "She decided to *re-store* her clothes."

Basically the function of a *hyphen* is to put two parts of a word under a single roof, and that is just about what the word denoted in its original meaning. It comes from the Greek *hypo-,* under, plus *hen,* one. *(See* PREFIXES.)

# I

## I.E., E.G.

Two common abbreviations are up for discussion: *i.e.* and *e.g.* The abbreviation *i.e.* (which is from the Latin *id est,* meaning that is) is normally followed by a kind of definition that clarifies what preceded it. Example: "Forests help provide us with newspapers, *i.e.,* paper is made of wood from trees." The abbreviation *e.g.* (from the Latin *exempli gratia,* meaning for example) introduces an illustration of whatever has just been said. Example: "One thing that will put on weight is a fatty food, *e.g.,* butter."

## "I" AND "ME" PHOBIAS

Some people are terrified at the thought of using *I* in certain constructions either because they think it is overrefined and therefore wrong or because their friends never use it. They are the ones who say, "Joe and *me* went to the ball game." Other people are sometimes fearful of using *me* because they think it sounds illiterate. They are the ones who say, "Between you and *I* it was a lousy ball game."

The grammatical subject of a sentence is the who or the what that the rest of the sentence is talking about. And the subject is always in the subjective (nominative) case. *I* is the subjective case; *me* is the objective case. Therefore, "*I* want to thank you," and "My wife and *I* want to thank you."

The object of the action or thought conveyed by the verb of a sentence is in the objective case: "He hit *me,* " "I like *her.* " Also in the objective case is the object of a preposition. (Prepositions are mere function words such as *among, between, of, for, into, to, within,* which usually relate the words they govern to some other part of the sentence, as, for example, "He fell *into* the pit.") Therefore, using the objective case for the word governed by a preposition, you get, "Her note aroused a feeling of warmth *within him*" or *"Between* you and *me,* it was a lousy ball game." (*See* OBJECTS; PRONOUNS; MYSELF.)

## IF
(Iffy question.) The little word *if* frequently introduces words in the subjunctive mood—that is, words expressing a hypothesis, a wish, a condition contrary to fact or something that is doubtful. Because of its frequent appearance in such expressions, some people leap to the conclusion that it must always be followed by a subjunctive. But whereas it is proper to say, "If I were you . . ." (not a fact), it is not proper to say, "He was asked if he were apprehensive over getting married." Sometimes *if* is the equivalent of *whether* and merely introduces an indirect question, as it does in the foregoing second example. The verb there should be *was,* indicative mood.

In other instances *if* introduces a clause suggesting doubt or uncertainty and then the subjunctive is normal: "If he *were* honest, his score for 18 holes would be 79, not 71." But when the emphatic point is not the *if,* but rather what follows it, the indicative is preferable: "If he *was* honest, his score for eighteen holes was 71." If you are in doubt (not "if you be in doubt"), use the indicative because the subjunctive, in most uses, is fading decade by decade. (*See* SUBJUNCTIVE.)

## IF NOT
(Spoken vs. written.) One of the things that make spoken language and written language occasionally quite different is a rise or fall in tonal register, something that written language cannot always indicate. The following sentence provides an example: "Senior government officials said that Mr. Yariv's remarks represented a new tone in Israeli statements on the Palestinians if not a substantive change in the official position." In print it is not possible to tell whether the phrase *if not* has the sense of *but not* or the sense of *and perhaps.* A speaker would leave no doubt about what was meant. If he dropped his tone a half note

beginning with *if not* he would indicate that "a substantive change" was not in contemplation. On the other hand, if he said "a SUBSTANTIVE CHANGE," lifting his voice and stressing *change,* he would be suggesting that such a thing was a real possibility. For the writer the solution to this ambiguity should be apparent: Don't use *if not* in this kind of context; if you mean *but not,* say so, and if you mean *and perhaps,* say so.

## IMPACT

(Overworked word.) No politician or social scientist who knows his business would ever use the word *effect, consequence, influence, result* or *significance* if he could possibly use *impact.* And that is too bad because *impact,* meaning violent contact, is a strong word that is being weakened by overuse. The *impact* on the word of overuse is distressing.

## IMPLY, INFER

These two words are frequently confused. *Imply* means to suggest or say indirectly; *infer* means to deduce or conclude from facts or indications. The mistake most often made by the confused users is to say *infer* when *imply* would be the proper word. Example: "I did not mean to *infer* that you were dishonest." Sir Alan Herbert has been quoted as illustrating the distinction between the two words in this way: "If you see a man staggering along the road you may *infer* that he is drunk, without saying a word; but if you say, 'Had one too many?' you do not *infer* but *imply* that he is drunk." In a general sort of way the implyer is the pitcher and the inferrer is the catcher.

## IMPRACTICABLE AND IMPRACTICAL

Perhaps the best way to tackle the difference between these two words is to examine first the distinction between *practicable* and *practical.* What is *practicable* is capable of being done; what is *practical* is capable of being done usefully or at not too great a cost. What is *impracticable* is not feasible; what is *impractical* is not useful or not valuable in practice or too costly. It may not be *impracticable* to set up a kindergarten on the moon, but it certainly would be *impractical*—at present, anyway. (*See* PRACTICABLE, PRACTICAL.)

## IMMINENT, EMINENT
A map caption in a newspaper said, "The courts have barred the state from exercising the right of *imminent* domain across the cemetery property." The use of *imminent* in this case is erroneous. *Imminent* means immediately impending. *Eminent* in this context means superior, and the phrase *eminent domain* refers to the superior right of a government to take over private property for public use.

## IMPORTANT, IMPORTANTLY
*See* MORE IMPORTANTLY.

## IN, INTO, IN TO
Three word forms—*in, into* and *in to*—are a source of trouble. The preposition *in* relates to position or condition: "She was *in* the classroom," "The team was *in* a joyous mood." No problem arises with that simple preposition. But *into* and *in to* sometimes puzzle people. *Into,* also a preposition, indicates motion from outside to inside or, figuratively, a modification of condition: "He stepped *into* the car," "She went *into* the doldrums." Sometimes the *in* is a "where" adverb used with the preposition *to:* "You may go *in to* see the patient," "He went *in to* his friends in the next room." When the *in* is used as an adverb, as in the preceding sentences, there is a rule: The *to* must not be joined to it.

## INCLUDE
*See* COMPRISE.

## INCOMPARABLES
(Free from error.) In a column I quoted a newspaper sentence that said, "The Viking test is considered at least *twice as accurate,* as the previous ones." Promptly that use of the word *accurate* was pounced on by three careful readers. All three made the same point: that something is *accurate* or it is not and that therefore one thing cannot be more *accurate* than something else.

I decided to let Bergen and Cornelia Evans answer that trio. In their *Dictionary of Contemporary American Usage* they say: "There are words, sometimes called *absolutes,* which . . . name characteristics that do not exist in degrees, such as *unique, complete, equal.* It is argued that words of this kind cannot be used in a comparison because, for a thing to possess the quality at all it must possess it completely, and therefore all things that possess the quality possess it equally. This argument disregards the facts of life. In this world we constantly do, and must, compare things in respect to qualities which, as seen from Olympus, they do not possess. We can and do say *this is squarer than that, make them more equal, this is more accurate, this is most singular."*

Let me add that Webster's unabridged, third edition, under the word *accurate* has this quotation from Lewis Mumford: "New inventions . . . had made it possible to chart and to hold a *more accurate* course at sea." And in the entry for the word *correct* it cites under synonyms a quotation from E.M. Forster that ends with the words "but the poet-writer must be *more accurate* than that."

It is not a good idea to try to add to the list of absolutes; they often create philosophical predicaments and literary straitjackets. A relatively few words such as *unique, fatal, final* and *unanimous* could appear in the list and such words should be unviolable. But let's not go looking for trouble.

## INCREDIBLE, INCREDULOUS

Two words that are virtually kissing cousins in sound and appearance are *incredible* and *incredulous,* but they mean quite different things and should be kept distinct. *Incredible* means unbelievable; *incredulous* means skeptical, unable to believe. *Incredulous* is the cousin that is subjected to the more maltreatment. It sometimes appears erroneously in a sentence such as this: "An *incredulous* edict was issued by the Premier." The edict wasn't *incredulous,* but those who read it probably were—they just couldn't believe it.

## IF EVER
*See* EVER.

## INFER
*See* IMPLY, INFER.

## INFINITIVES, PERFECT

One grammatical problem that is bothersome is how to use the perfect infinitive. Don't let the technical term floor you; the perfect infinitive is simply the one with a *have* in it and it is normally used to indicate a time level earlier than that of the main verb of the sentence. This item won't solve all the problems of the perfect infinitive, but the following three sentences may be of some help:

1. I would be happy (now) to have met her (last night or a year ago).
2. I would have been happy (last night or a year ago) to meet her (same level of time).
3. I would have been happy (last night or a year ago) to have met her (the night before last? two years ago?).

   Generally, sentences 1 and 2 take care of most situations. Sentence 3 is usually disapproved of by grammarians. Still there are rare occasions when it would be clear and sensible. Example: "Last summer when he applied for a job as tennis counselor he would have found it profitable to have won at least one tournament."

## INFINITIVES, SPLIT

Fasten your seat belts, folks, before you read the next sentence. The taboo against the split infinitive is on the way out. The split infinitive, of course, occurs when the "to" is parted from the verb, as in, "He proceeded *to* slowly *climb* the hill." When you come to examine sentences not containing infinitives you find that more often than not the natural position for an adverb is just ahead of the main part of the verb it modifies: "The plan was *universally approved*" or "The police will *quickly expel* any persons who make trouble." If we do not boggle at "He favors *really eliminating* discrimination," why should we boggle at "He wants *to really eliminate* discrimination"?

   The taboo against the split infinitive was clamped on writers by grammarians of the eighteenth and nineteenth centuries for some reason that is not entirely clear. But in the last few decades writers have more and more been ignoring it and the guess here is that within the next decade or so it will be for the most part ignored. Here are a few examples of splits by reputable news writers (some of them would be difficult to avoid): "He warned consortium members that they would have *to* more than *double* present production." "The Democratic nomination is thought *to* all but *insure* victory at the polls." "He said they were doing all they could *to* at least *maintain* what balance exists today." "The four women gave their names—believed *to* possibly *be* aliases—as . . ." Yep, the taboo seems to really be on the way out.

## INFLAMMABLE
*See* FLAMMABLE.

## INGENIOUS, INGENUOUS
One pair of words that are often confused are *ingenious* and *ingenuous.* The one that contains an I.O.U., *ingenious,* means clever, smartly adaptable, resourceful. Its original meaning was possessing genius, and that's a good word to keep in mind to remind you of the sense of *ingenious.* The other word of the pair, *ingenuous,* means innocent, without artifice, naïve.

## IN-LAWS
Is there a word in English that means the daughter-in-law's relationship to her husband's mother? Alas, in English there is none. There is one in Yiddish and it appears in Leo Rosten's *The Joys of Yiddish* as *machetayneste,* pronounced mokh-e-TANE-es-teh, with a harsh, guttural kh. Sometimes the TANE is pronounced TUN. Most commonly the word refers to the mother-in-law of a woman's son or daughter. The father-in-law of that offspring is referred to as *machuten.* Perhaps an English coinage for these characters could be distant-laws or even out-laws.

## INPUT
(Computer cant.) Jargon used by practitioners in a specialized field is one thing—it is usually precise and time-saving. But that same jargon taken over by nonspecialists striving to sound scientific or intellectual or simply out of the ordinary is something else again; it not only is not precise or useful, but rather is likely to be obscure and wordy. A simple example is the word *input.* In computer cant it denotes information fed into a computer. But laymen sometimes take it over to sound impressive

or perhaps to deliberately sound vague. Thus, a former high Administration official referred to himself as a possible source of "political *input,*" whatever that means. And the head of a doctors' association remarked, "Health of patients would deteriorate without adequate *input* by health care providers." Probably all he meant was "adequate health care," or maybe just "adequate care." The temptation to use technical words in nontechnical contexts is widespread, but it should be resisted lest our language degenerate into sound and fury signifying nothing. (*See* JARGON.)

## INSURE, ENSURE
There are those who try to find a distinction between these two words in the sense of make certain, but there is none. The only real distinction between them is when the meaning is to indemnify against loss. In that sense only *insure* will serve. In other senses the spelling that is preferred—on this side of the ocean, at any rate—is *insure.*

## IN ADDITION TO
*See* ADDITIONALLY.

## IN REGARD TO
(Best regards.) The phrase *in regards to* is wrong. In compound prepositions only the singular noun *regard* is proper. Therefore, use *in regard to* or *with regard to,* both of which mean in relation to or in reference to. *Regard* does appear with an *s* appended to it in the common phrase *as regards,* which means concerning. In the sense of good wishes the noun is always plural; that is why George M. Cohan sang, "Give my *regards* to Broadway," and why letters often close with the word *regards.*

## IN TERMS OF
(Show-off term.) Much writing these days shows a marked tendency by the scribes to try to appear technical or learned by using fancy phrases, and one of them is *in terms of.* Thus, we get a sentence that reads, "The Governor is thinking *in terms of* voter appeal," when all the writer means is that the Governor is thinking *about* or *of* voter appeal. Properly used, the phrase signifies a translation from one kind of language to another. For exam-

ple: "He is past seventy, but is young *in terms of* his thinking."
Even there, though the phrase is used appropriately, it could be
dropped in favor of "in his thinking." In most instances a simple
preposition *(about, of, concerning)* or a simple phrase *(with respect
to, in the matter of)* can be substituted for *in terms of* with no loss
except of pretension.

**INVOKE**
*See* EVOKE.

**IRREGARDLESS**
*See* REGARDLESS.

**IS WHEN, IS WHERE**
If you ask a little boy to tell you what boxing is, he is quite likely
to reply, "Boxing *is when* two guys slug it out in a ring," or,
"Boxing *is where* two guys slug it out in a ring." What has *when*
got to do with it? What has *where* got to do with it? No one
knows, especially the kid.

What authorities on English do know is that the construction
is faulty, though they do not find it easy to explain why. One
suggests it is not proper to use a word like *when* to join a clause
to a noun. But we do say, "Night is *when* the sun goes down,"
or, "The office is *where* I go every day," and no one finds such
sentences wrong.

The answer is that there is nothing grammatically wrong with
the kid's sentences; they are rather stylistically wrong because
the words *when* and *where* are being used in places where their
meanings are not relevant. Boxing is explained not by a when
or where idea but by a what idea. In the "night" sentence,
however, the when idea is relevant and in the "office" sentence
the where idea is relevant.

Next question: Why is the faulty construction a characteris-
tically juvenile mistake? You'll get no answer here; better see a
psychiatrist.

**ITS, IT'S**
(It's an error.) The heading of an ad in a newspaper read like
this: "CBS has *it's* eye on Perry tonight." *It's* (with an apostrophe) is a contraction of *it is* or *it has* and nothing else. The

possessive pronoun, which is what was wanted in the ad, is *its*. This was not always true. Beginning in the early seventeenth century the possessive pronoun was written *it's*, but since the early nineteenth century it has been written without the apostrophe. Maybe the writer of that ad is older than we think.

## IT'S (FOR IT HAS)

Webster's unabridged, second edition, does not give *it has* as a meaning for *it's*, but every newer dictionary does. *It's* taken some time for some dictionaries to catch up with modern usage, but they all have caught up now. Naturally you can't indiscriminately use *it's* in place of *it has;* for example, in speaking of a dog you can't say, *"It's* four legs." But in speaking of that dictionary you can say, "At last *it's* caught up."

# J

## JARGON

Ever notice how modern industry, principally in the mechanical field, tries to sound impressive by piling up words and phrases that might have meaning to its own personnel but are unintelligible gobbledygook to the lay public? That is jargon and we are immersed in it today. You read an auto ad and it speaks of "spring-strut suspension and responsive rack-and-pinion steering" and you are tempted to murmur, "You don't say!" Or you are introduced to a new color TV set with such words as "power sentry voltage regulating system maintains stable voltage to the chassis at or near the receiver design level" with the added information that the picture tube "features a unitized in-line gun system." You begin to wonder whether the writers of such words and the companies for which they speak are trying to tell you something or trying to keep something from you. If it's the latter, they are succeeding beautifully. If it's the former, it's about time they shifted from five-word obscure noun phrases to simple terms supplemented by simple explanations. The language does not need any further fogging. (*See* GOVERNMENTALESE; LEGAL LINGO; OUTDATED LINGO; PRETENTIOUSNESS.)

## JEALOUSY

*See* ENVY.

## JEW'S HARP

The derivation of the term *jew's harp* (sometimes the *J* is capitalized and sometimes *jew's* is pluralized into *jews'*) is a mystery.

One theory holds that the word *jew* in this context is a variant pronunciation of *jaw* and that the name comes from the fact that the lyre-shaped instrument is held between the teeth, or the jaws. Webster's Third New International Dictionary thinks the name might have come from the fact that the instruments were purveyed by Jewish peddlers. Webster's New World opines that the name is an alteration of the original Dutch term *jeugdtromp,* child's trumpet. And the Oxford Dictionary of English Etymology says that the ascription of the instrument to Jews "is unexplained." And there you are.

## JOCK

(Sporting word.) A news feature about the growing trend back to short hair for men quoted a graduate student as saying that he got tired of long hair and then adding, "Once the *jocks* grew their hair, you knew it's got to be wrong." In case you can't guess what a *jock* is, let it be said that the word means an athlete, particularly a college athlete. And in case you can't guess whence it derives, let it be said that it comes from the term *jockstrap,* an athletic supporter. *Jock* is a fairly recent piece of slang.

## JOHN DOE

Why the name *John Doe?* Why was that name chosen rather than the more common names *John Smith* or *John Jones?* Undoubtedly the idea was not to use a common name but rather to use an uncommon one so that the unknown party in a legal action who was dubbed *John Doe* would not accidentally have the same name as the man who lives next door. In other words, the idea was to employ a really uncommon name that would have only the sound of a real name. In the thick Manhattan phone book in New York City there are only five persons named *Doe* compared with well over 3,000 *Smiths.* And not one named *Doe* has the first name *John,* whereas there are something like 70 *John Smiths.* The use of *John Doe, Jane Doe* and *Richard Roe* began in England at least six centuries ago. Two additional names of unknown parties used sometimes in a legal action were *John Stiles* and *Richard Miles.*

## JOUNCE

The word *jounce* is known to most of us. It means to jolt or move in an up-and-down way. But its origin is apparently known to none of us. Three dictionaries flatly say just about that. The Oxford adds that similar words, such as *bounce, flounce* and *pounce,* all indicating abrupt movements, are likewise of unknown origin. An etymological dictionary suggests it is probably a blend of *jump* and *bounce.* Another dictionary guesses it is a combination of an obsolete word, *joll,* and *bounce.* Webster's unabridged, second edition, thinks it may come from an obsolete word *jaunce,* possibly influenced by *bounce,* and the third edition says right out that it derives from the Middle English *jouncen.* Not one of the books mentions the possibility of *jolt* plus *bounce,* which seems a not unlikely derivation. Anyway, there's plenty of bounce in there. (*See* BLEND WORDS.)

## JUST

(Mot juste.) A comic strip, noting that Franklin stoves and similar ones were making a comeback because of the energy situation, ended by saying, "The American family *might just move* back into the kitchen." Did the cartoonist mean to say *just might move?* The answer is yes, because the wording he chose is susceptible of a different interpretation from the one he intended. As it stands, it could be taken to mean that the American family might simply move back into the kitchen, that's all. What he apparently wished to say was not that the family would make a simple adjustment, but rather that there was a real possibility that such a thing would come about. Two things should be noted here. One is the importance of word order in English. In the instance at hand the change in meaning that results from the change in word order is a bit more subtle than it is in "Dog bites man" and "Man bites dog," yet is there and should not be ignored. The second point to be noted is that only one of the popular dictionaries—Webster's New Collegiate—gives the meaning of *just* as it is used in the corrected sentence above and as it is used by all of us day in and day out: the meaning of possibly or perhaps. (*See* ADVERB PLACEMENT.)

# K

## KARAT
*See* CARAT.

## KETCHUP
(With this word.) There are three versions of the word for that thick, spicy, tomato sauce: *ketchup, catchup* and *catsup.* But oddly enough, though dictionaries often bow to common usage, they are just about unanimous in listing *ketchup* as the proper word despite the fact that many people and most of the manufacturers of the stuff seem to go for *catsup.* The word derives from the Malayan *kechap,* meaning a fish sauce, and that in turn came from the Chinese *ketsiap.* Those facts answer the question of origin, but they don't answer the question of why so many people like *catsup* better than the two other words. A guess is that *ketchup* and *catchup* sounded to some as if they were slightly vulgar pronunciations of the prissier, more refined-sounding *catsup,* which therefore was judged to be the right word.

## KIND OF
(Kind of a solecism.) In speaking, you can get by with saying, "It's a *kind of a* muggy day," but in writing, which should be a more careful, more precise manner of expression, *kind of a* won't do. The articles *a* and *an* refer to a single thing, and a single thing does not by itself constitute a *kind* (or a *class* or a *sort* or a *type* or a *manner*). You probably wouldn't dream of saying, "What breed of *a* dog is that?" or "What class of *a* yacht is

that?" Likewise you should not dream of saying, "What kind of *a* day was it?" Drop the *a*.

Another *kind of* error arises when plurals are involved. Frequently you will hear *"those kind* of cars," but the frequency of the occurrence of that locution does not make it right. *Kind* is a singular noun and you can't properly affix a plural adjective —*those*—in front of it. One solution is to make it *"that kind* of cars." If that seems slightly stilted, you can make it "cars of *that kind."* But *those kind,* never.

## KITH AND KIN
*Kin,* of course, means relatives. But *kith and kin,* contrary to a prevalent impression, is not confined to relatives; it also includes friends and acquaintances. That is because *kith* derives from an Old English word meaning knowledge; hence, someone who is known, but not necessarily related. *Kithin'* cousins are something quite different. They are not even spelled that way.

## KOWTOW
To *kowtow* to someone is to show subservience, to be obsequious, to behave in a servile manner. Originally it demanded even more of the kowtower; he had to hit his forehead on the ground. That explains the word *kowtow,* which is a Chinese term meaning to knock the head.

# L

## LACKADAISICAL
It began as *alackaday,* an interjection expressing regret over a bad day; then it was extended into *lackadaisy,* and finally Laurence Sterne, the eighteenth-century English novelist, made out of it the word *lackadaisical,* meaning listless, languid, exhibiting no spirit or interest. Sterne's coinage is today's word. The loss of that first *a* from *alackaday* results from a process known as *aphesis.* It is a gradual development that causes the dropping of an unaccented vowel at the beginning of a word. It was aphesis that produced *lone* out of *alone.*

## LAGNIAPPE
A *lagniappe* (pronounced lan-YAP) is something extra, a bonus. The word comes from the Spanish *la* (the) and the Quechuan Indian *yapa* (something additional, a gift). Here is how it might be used: "The restaurant serves a four-course meal and throws in a flask of wine as *lagniappe.*" If someone asks you how you can remember such a word, just say, "It's a gift."

## LAST, PAST
For years and years nit-pickers have been trying to force on the rest of us a distinction between "the *last* year" and "the *past* year." Their point seems to be that *last* means final and that since time is still marching on we have not seen the final year. A rejoinder that has been made to that argument is that *past* cannot be right either since all years except the current one are *past.* The argument is meaningless and is not going to get us

anywhere because since the days of Middle English *last* and *past* have been used interchangeably to mean gone by immediately before the present. It is not likely that after centuries of such usage the nit-pickers are going to effect a change. The same may be said about those who try to force a distinction between *last* and *latest,* which also have been used interchangeably for centuries.

## LATTER
Three things should be noted about the word *latter.* First, it means the second of two, not the last of three, five or whatever. Therefore, it is not proper to write, "The candidates are Smith, Jones and Doe and the *latter* is favored to win." Make it the *last-named.* Second, if you are speaking of three persons, you should not refer to the *latter two.* The phrase *latter two* would be appropriate only if you had already mentioned a first two: "The bridge players will be John and Jane Smith and Henry and Mary Jones and the *latter two* are favored to win." Third, use of *latter* often compels the reader to look back to see who or what is meant, and that can be annoying unless the sentence is a short, simple one. The reader won't object to repetition of a name or of a thing, but he may be irritated if he has to retrace his steps.

## LAUNDERING
(Coming clean.) A word that has been coming up from time to time in the area of politics is *laundering.* It refers to the disguising of the source of a contribution to a candidate for office. The donor sends his gift to a committee backing a number of candidates with instructions that it go to Candidate A. Then the committee deposits the check, sends a check of its own to Candidate A and he lists it as a contribution from the committee. Thus the name of the donor doesn't appear, which is what he had in mind. The practice was supposed to have been outlawed by the campaign act of April 7, 1972, but *laundering* did not completely stop then. The laundry suds continued to bubble here and there.

## LAUNDRESS
*See* SYNCOPE.

## LAY, LIE

Many people seem to have more trouble with these two verbs than with any others. Therefore, although the subject has been taken up many times, we shall try another explanation. Perhaps this one will be more graphic.

| *lay,* transitive (as in lay an egg) | *lie,* intransitive (as in lie down) |
|---|---|
| Present tense —lay | Present tense —lie |
| Past tense —laid | Past tense —lay |
| Past participle —laid | Past participle —lain |

Notice that the transitive verb, *lay,* is always followed by an object: "I always *lay* the newspaper on my desk" (present tense); "I *laid* the newspaper on my desk yesterday morning" (past tense); "I *had laid* the newspaper on my desk before the boss came in" (past participle). The intransitive verb, *lie,* never is followed by an object. It goes like this: "I always *lie* down after dinner" (present tense); "I *lay* down after dinner yesterday" (past tense); "I had *lain* down before our friends arrived" (past participle). For each verb the present participle is formed by adding *-ing;* for *lay* we get *laying* and for *lie* we get *lying.* All clear?

## LEAVE AND LET

Words are not always used as precisely as they should be. *Leave* and *let,* followed by *alone,* are examples of such words. *Leave alone* should exclusively mean to cause to be in solitude. *Let alone* should exclusively mean to allow to be undisturbed. Common usage, however, has given *leave alone* both meanings and the ambiguity raises questions. For instance, a newspaper editorial, discussing the right of a dying person to prevent his body from being invaded by life-saving measures and equipment, said, "The right to privacy is the right to be *let alone.*" A letter writer asked whether that is proper usage. It is, and it is not a bad illustration of the distinction between the two words. *Let alone,* as used there, means to be undisturbed, not interfered with. If *left alone* were substituted it would mean that no one would be in the room with the patient, and that surely is not the intended meaning. What we have been speaking of is strict usage, which is not always followed even by skillful writers. One thing they would agree upon, however, is that *leave* should not be substituted for *let* when the sense is to allow or permit. Don't, for instance, say, *"Leave* me buy you a drink."

## LEAVE IN A HUFF

The meaning and origin of the phrase *leave in a huff* have stirred curiosity. The meaning is certain enough: a *huff* is a heightened condition of anger or arrogance and to *leave in a huff* is to walk away in that condition. The derivation of *huff* is unsure, but the conjecture is that the word is echoic—that is, imitative of the huffing and puffing of an irate person.

## LEFT/RIGHT

*See* RIGHT/LEFT.

## LEGAL LINGO

(Whence it comes.) A lawyer friend tells us that sometimes redundancy in legal phrases is a vestigial remnant of the Norman Conquest. Of course, to the lowly worker in the fields a particular animal was *sheep* in his Anglo-Saxon tongue, whereas to the conquering lord presiding at the table the flesh of that animal was *mutton* in his Norman-French speech. To insure understanding on all sides, some legal phrases included both languages. An example is *will and testament,* in which the Anglo-Saxon and the Norman-French words are coupled to describe the same document. All right, but 900 years later should we still have to *indemnify and hold harmless* (there's one for you) the perpetrators today of these annoying tautologies? (*See* JARGON.)

(Stilted phrases.) The abundance of lawyers who asked questions and answered them at the United States Senate Watergate hearings introduced the public to a variety of stilted phrases that the legal profession delights in. The motto seems to be, "Never say anything in one or two words if it can be said in six." Here are some samples, followed by rough translations:

At a certain period of time . . . *(once* or *ever).*
At that particular time . . . *(then).*

Did there come a time when you . . . (did you *once* or *ever*).
In that time frame . . . *(then)*.
To the best of my recollection . . . *(I think)*.
During the course of that meeting . . . *(during* or *at* that meeting).
Subject matter . . . *(subject)*.
I have no knowledge of . . . (I *don't know* about).

Part of the trouble comes from the desire to sniff out and plug all possible loopholes that other lawyers might discover and part comes from the fear of deviating from language that has become traditional and what lawyers consider safe. A simple example is the *if, as and when* fixation. A contract may provide that a real estate broker will get his commission *if, as and when* title closes. The *if* doesn't set any time limit, the *as* suggests he will get his money while the title is closing and the *when* definitely fixes the time of payment. But the *when* covers all the contingencies. Why, then, the *if* and the *as?* The full, traditional phrase is scarcely ever necessary. But it will disappear only *if, as and when* lawyers become aware that it is excess baggage.

## LEND, LOAN
(Distance loans enchantment.) An ad for air conditioners carries the line, "If we can't fix your new air conditioner on the spot, we'll *loan* you one." In Britain that use of *loan* would be disapproved, and in the United States, although it is quite common, it is not acceptable to careful writers and speakers. In careful usage the verb is *lend,* while *loan,* if it is used as a verb at all, is restricted to business dealings: "The bank loaned him $5,000." Even there, of course, *lent* not only is acceptable but is preferred by educated people. As for nonbusiness uses, how would you like, "Friends, Romans, countrymen, *loan* me your ears," or the words that top this item?

## LESS, FEWER
In careful usage *less* applies to quantity (*less* food, *less* courage) and *fewer* applies to countable things (*fewer* potatoes, *fewer* noble deeds). *Fewer* is never misused, but there is a tendency to misuse *less.* People will often say, "There were *less* mosquitoes around this year," when strictly speaking the word should be *fewer. Less* is sometimes used with plurals when they really refer to quantity rather than number. For instance, it would be proper to say, "He

makes *less* than $100 a week"; the $100 is not thought of as individual dollars but rather as a sum of money. Likewise it would be proper to say, "It is *less* than ten miles to town"; again ten miles is not thought of as individual miles but rather as a distance figure. Let's all try to make *fewer* mistakes and have *less* loose usage.

## LETHOLOGICA
(Don't forget this word.) The term that is applicable when you can't recall a word is *lethologica* (pronounced lee-tho-LOJ-i-ka) and it means the temporary inability to remember the proper word or a name. It appears in only one general dictionary, Webster's New International, second edition, where it is so buried that it is almost unfindable. Webster's third edition has tossed it out altogether and other dictionaries apparently never let it in. I understand that many people, especially those over 65, suffer from temporary attacks of *lethologica,* so by golly the word merits a revival. Let's start a campaign to revive . . . what's that word again?

## LET
   *See* LEAVE AND LET.

## LIABLE, LIKELY
*Liable* denotes legal or other liability and should not be used in place of *likely,* says Miss Thistlebottom. Up to a point *liable* does denote legal responsibility, but it doesn't stop there. Just about every dictionary gives another meaning of the word denoting subject to the possibility of something, or likely to have or to undergo something, undesirable or unpleasant. And there is no label "loose" or "colloquial" or "informal" attached to that meaning. It would be inappropriate to say, "We are *liable* to go to the ball game tomorrow," but it is quite proper to say that something "is *liable* to cause resentment."

## LIFE STYLE
(Word that has caught on.) Four of the newest editions of dictionaries include *life style* as a standard, accepted term, which it has become within relatively few recent years. The most appropriate definition appears in the 1973 edition of the American Heritage

Dictionary: "An internally consistent way of life or style of living that reflects the attitudes and values of an individual or a culture."

## LIGHT VERSE
(Strange change.) Something in our civilization has been lost in the last decade or so, something that your host sadly misses. So here goes a feeble start to an attempt to regain it:

TRIOLET
Containing Plaintive Questions

What has become of light verse?
  Where are the humor, the rhymes?
Why can't we revel, rejerce?
What has become of light verse?
On blankety-blank verse a curse!
  And so I repeat countless times:
"What has become of light verse?
  Where are the humor, the rhymes?"

## LIGHTED, LIT
Now for light prose: A couple have had a difference of opinion for years. "I say the lamp is *lighted,*" he says, "and she says the lamp is *lit.*" Take it easy; no cause for divorce. Usually either word is acceptable. However, when the past participle of the verb *light* is used as an adjective, *lighted* is more common; thus, "a *lighted* lamp." On the other hand, when the verb is used in the simple past tense *lit* seems more natural: "He *lit* the lamp" gets the vote over "He *lighted* the lamp."

## LIKE
(A likable like.) Do you say, "He looks like *me,*" or "He looks like *I*"? The *me* sentence is correct. Some authorities say that *like* used in that way is a preposition and the following word, which it governs, should therefore be in the objective case—*me.* Other authorities say that the *me* is correct but for a different reason: In that construction *like* is an adjective, they say, and the following word is the object of the preposition *unto,* which is understood. In any event, like me, like my dog. (See COMPARISONS.)

## LIKE, AS

(No like.) The subject before the house is the use of *like* as a conjunction as in, "Winthrops taste good *like* a pizza pie should." There are no logical or historical reasons why *like* should not be used that way to introduce a clause containing a verb. Still for generations grammarians have outlawed that use and the taboo is a force in the language—a force that a careful writer defies at the peril of being classed as illiterate or semiliterate. The taboo applies not only to *like* instead of *as* (as in the sentence quoted above), but also to *like* in place of *as if,* as in, "He works his head off *like* there was no tomorrow." It does not apply, however, when *like* precedes a noun that is not followed by a verb—that is, when the *like* does not introduce a complete clause. Thus it is proper to say, "He runs *like* a deer," or, "Nothing develops muscles *like* swimming." There can be no doubt that what is considered the improper use of *like* is slowly but steadily gaining ground—in spoken language at least—and the guess here is that in another couple of generations the taboo will collapse.

(A look at as.) Let us now examine the use of *as* where the word should be *like*. The trouble is that after all the fuss that has been made—quite properly—about the misuse of *like,* many people have become gun-shy about using the word at all. For instance: "Controllers can make mistakes *as* anyone else." Another for instance: "While Mr. Jones is listed as an associate editor of the magazine, he merely submits articles *as* any other columnists." In each instance the word should be *like*. With *as* those sentences sound as hell. Ugh.

## LIKELY

From a news article: "A number of countries are cautioning that such a move *likely* would prompt the United States to cut off funds." The use of *likely* in that way is not an outright error, but it is unidiomatic and therefore comes close to being an error. When *likely* is employed as an adverb, idiom calls for preceding it with *very, quite* or *most.*

## LIKELY vs. APT

"A person who is appalled is *apt* to blanch or turn pale." Right or wrong? The quickest way to dispose of the case is to quote a usage note in the American Heritage Dictionary: *"Apt* and *likely,* when followed by an infinitive, are often interchangeable. *Likely* is always appropriate when mere probability is involved: *It is likely to snow.* . . . When probability based on a natural or known tendency is implied, *apt* is the choice: *He is apt to stammer when he is excited."* In the original sentence either *likely* or *apt* would be all right, but on the basis of that dictionary note *apt* is the better of the two. But the word *liable* is not proper. (*See* LIABLE.)

## LIKE SO

Often we hear sentences such as, "You do it like so." Is that just idiomatic or is it incorrect? It's a borderline case, which is best set down as idiomatic or colloquial. If someone said, "You do it like this," no question at all would arise. But the words *like so* mean like or as in a certain manner. The two words have virtually the same sense and, indeed, the *like* could be dropped without altering the meaning or the correctness of the construction. On the other hand, in the sentence, "You do it like this," the *like* could not be omitted. Let's say simply that the careful writer or speaker would not use the *like so* version.

## LIMOUSINE

Some top officials ride around these days in *limousines* and perhaps you have wondered where that word came from. In a former province of central France called Limousin the natives wore cloaks with hoods that enclosed their heads. The word *limousine* then was used to designate such a cloak and it is still a word in the French language. When enclosed vehicles came into use the word was attached to them and today it denotes a large sedan, especially one driven by a chauffeur. As you see, the meaning of the word was changed; you might almost call *limousine* a convertible.

## LIPOGRAMS

(Writing without ease.) Imagine a 50,000-word novel written without the use of a single letter *e!* Willard R. Espy's fun book, *An Almanac of Words at Play,* identifies the work as Gadsby, by Ernest Vincent Wright, published by Wetzel, Los Angeles, in

1939. A composition of that kind, in which a letter is omitted throughout, is a *lipogram*. James Thurber wrote a story about a country in which no one was allowed to use the letter *o*. And back in ancient times there appeared the *Odyssey of Tryphiodorus,* which, according to the Merriam-Webster unabridged dictionary, contained no *alpha* in the first book, no *beta* in the second and so on. (That rare word *lipogram* is composed of a Greek prefix *lipo-*, meaning to be wanting, and a Greek combining form *-gram*, meaning something written or a letter of the alphabet. In other words, it means a letter is missing. But let's not bother the post office about a missing letter.)

## LIT
*See* LIGHTED.

## LITERALLY VS. FIGURATIVELY
A reporter, writing about a governor, said, "I don't think I've ever heard him say, 'No comment.' Instead he will literally bury you with words. . . ." You could bury, swamp, flood, inundate someone with words, but not do so *literally* any more than you could *literally* beat someone over the head with words or *literally* trip someone up with words. When a writer uses the word in such senses he is intending to employ it as an intensive to strengthen what he is saying, but actually he is committing an error. *Literally* has the meaning of really, in fact, true to the exact definition of the words. But in the instances cited what the writer meant was *figuratively*, that is, not in the words' exact or usual sense but rather in an analogous or metaphorical sense.

## LITOTES
(Not too good.) When we say that something is "not bad" we mean it is good. That form of understatement is called *litotes,* which is a commonly used figure of speech. *Litotes* involves taking the thing you wish to say—"good"; finding the reverse of it —"bad," and then negating it—"not bad." It's often a useful and effective manner of expression. But leave it to some lawyers to carry it to incomprehensible extremes. Here is a sentence by an Assistant United States Attorney General: "After consideration of the proposed plan to reapportion the Legislature, I must inform you that the Attorney General is unable to conclude that

the reapportionment plan does not have the purpose and will not have the effect of abridging the right of Negro citizens of Louisiana to vote on account of race or color." *Litotes* aside, what he was trying to say was that the reapportionment plan would abridge the rights of blacks. On the other hand, a politician can sound reserved, even modest, if he says, "I am not unmindful of the support you have given me." For some purposes, as you can see, *litotes* is not bad. That word *litotes* comes from the Greek *litos* meaning simple or plain. Someone ought to tell the Assistant Attorney General about that.

## LITTLE, A LITTLE

By itself, *little* has a negative connotation, meaning not very much, as in, "The boys in the back of the room gave the teacher *little* difficulty." When *a* is inserted ahead of it, however, the word takes on a positive connotation, meaning some or a small quantity, as in, "The boys in the back of the room gave the teacher *a little* difficulty." And if a negative element is introduced, *little* becomes much: "The boys give the teacher *not a little* difficulty." (*See* FEW, A FEW.)

## LIVE (IN)

Let's look at just one utterance by one of our public servants. Not that they utter any worse than most of their masters. It's rather that the things they say come to public notice more. This is former President Ford writing to a ten-year-old boy: "With your help and that of all Americans, I am confident we can overcome the problems we face and make our country a better place to live." Do you live a place—even a better place? No. It must be changed to "a better place to live *in*" or "a better place *in which* to live."

## LIVID

If a news story reads, "The defendant's attorney turned *livid,* banged his fist on the table and shouted at opposing counsel," many readers visualize the learned lawyer as becoming red-faced, and, alas, the reporter probably visualized that, too. Perhaps it's because of the sound association with the word *vivid.* But it's an unsound association. *Livid* means black and blue or lead-colored or ashen, not red-faced or flushed.

## LOAN
*See* LEND.

## LOATH VS. LOATHE
A reputable newspaper contained this sentence: "But, curiously, in an institution *loathe* to make decisions, they are ready to judge a President." That is a gaffe that is not uncommon. *Loathe* is a verb that means to hate, despise or detest. *Loath,* a much milder word, is an adjective meaning reluctant or unwilling. That is clearly the word that should have appeared in the quoted sentence. What a world of difference that final *e* makes!

# M

## MACHO
The word *machismo* has not been in the English language very long, but an even more recent entrant, derived from the same Spanish root, is *macho*. As a noun it means a virile man and as an adjective it means strongly masculine.

## MAKE A MOTION
*See* MOVE.

## MALAPROPISM
The word *malapropism* is built on the word *malapropos*, which was minted in the seventeenth century by Dryden. *Malapropos* is a combination of *mal-*, poor or unsuitable, and *apropos*, to the purpose or object, and the combination means not suited to the purpose or inappropriate. A century later Sheridan wrote a play called *The Rivals*, in which there was a character called Mrs. Malaprop. The inappropriate things she said were dubbed *malapropisms*. Sample: "The Soviet stance mitigates against any real disarmament."

## MANY A
(A singular plural.) One would think that *many* would always be followed by a plural verb. But not so. Look at this sentence: *"Many* a citizen *is* studying the national candidates these days." The fact is that *many a*, which is always followed by a singular noun, invariably takes a verb in the singular. The reason for this is what grammarians call "attraction": the proximity of the verb

to the singular noun causes the verb to be singular. A similar situation arises with the phrase *more than one:* "It appears that *more than one* candidate *is* going to face financial difficulties." (*See* AGREEMENT.)

## MASTECTOMY

Because of the mastectomies performed on wives of prominent men, the subject of surgical breast removals has become a topic of open discussion. What has been overlooked is that the notion of removing a breast, though not for health reasons, figures in Greek mythology. The Amazons, that mythical nation of warring women, supposedly removed the right breast of every female at puberty so that it would not interfere with use of the bowstring in battle. According to folk etymology, the word *Amazon* was derived from the Greek *a-* meaning without, and *mazos,* breast.

## MASTERFUL, MASTERLY

Two words that should be kept distinct but often are not are *masterful* and *masterly*. *Masterly* is rarely misused, but *masterful* frequently is. *Masterly* means in the manner of a master. *Masterful* means imperious or domineering. Thus, a critic who writes of a painter that "he paints in a *masterful* manner" is not saying what he means. One reason for the misuse of *masterful* may lie in the fact that it lends itself more readily to an adverbial form than does *masterly*. To say "He paints *masterly*" sounds a little odd despite the fact that *masterly* is either an adverb or an adjective, but "He paints *masterfully*" sounds proper even if strictly speaking it isn't.

## MATINEE

Here's a mystery that dictionaries don't explain: Since *matinee* is French for *morning* why is it used to mean an afternoon performance? The big Oxford dictionary pretends to explain it this way: "A 'morning' (i.e., afternoon) theatrical or musical performance." That's a big help, eh? Bergen Evans in his book *Comfortable Words* gives a more helpful explanation, to wit: "The simplest answer is that part of the period which we call *afternoon* used to be morning. The mystery lies, really, in the much stranger word *noon,* which comes from the Latin *nona,* meaning nine. The day used to be computed from sunup (not as we compute it from midnight—what owls we have become!) and the ninth hour, noon, was three hours after midday. Anything before that was morning."

## MAVEN
(Expert, shmexpert.) In current slang a *maven* is an expert, usually a self-proclaimed expert. Although the word has been in use for twenty years or more, it does not appear in any conventional unabridged dictionary. Wentworth and Flexner's *Dictionary of American Slang* does list it (as *mayvin*). It originated in the Hebrew word phonetically spelled *mayveen,* meaning to understand. From there it was taken over by Yiddish as *maven* with the meaning of a buff or self-styled expert. From the Yiddish it has crept into slang in this country. That's all you can get out of this *word maven.*

## MAVERICK
In general use a *maverick* is a nonconformist, one who goes his own way, a politician who bolts from his party. In more specialized use a *maverick* is an unbranded animal on a Western range. The word derives from the name of a Texas rancher, Samuel A. Maverick, who died in 1870. Unlike other ranchers, he did not brand his animals.

## MAY, MIGHT
These two words are in most instances just about equivalent. The shade of difference between them is that *might* expresses a slightly greater degree of uncertainty than *may.* If you say, "I *may* go to the city tomorrow," you are holding out the possibility of making the trip. If you say, "I might go to the city tomorrow," you are holding out that same possibility, but also seeming to suggest that in the back of your mind there are contingencies that could interfere with your plan. *May* in some situations changes to *might* to satisfy proper sequence of tenses. For instance, if the woman says, "I *may* get my hair cut tomorrow," in indirect discourse it becomes, "She *said* she *might* get her hair cut tomorrow," with both verbs in the past tense. But that by no means implies that all *may's* should be converted to *might's.*

## MC, MAC

(Hi, Mac.) Sometimes the three-letter prefix *Mac-* in Irish and Scottish names is contracted to the two-letter abbreviation *Mc-*. As to why the contraction occurred no answer seems to be available. It may be noted, however, that in British usage the prefix is often abbreviated further to *M'*, so you might have *MacDonald, McDonald* or *M'Donald*. There seems to be no difference in connotation in the three versions; they all signify "son of." The prefix *O'*, as in *O'Reilly* is broader; it means "descendant of."

## ME

*See* "I" AND "ME" PHOBIAS.

## MEANTIME

According to the American Heritage Dictionary, *"meantime* serves principally as a noun: 'In the *meantime,* we waited.' In expressing the same sense by a single adverb, *meanwhile* is more common than *meantime: 'Meanwhile,* we waited.' " As an observation of fact that note is quite true. But if it was intended as a caution against using *meantime* as an adverb, it may safely be disregarded. Such use of the word dates back at least to Shakespeare's day. Bartlett's *Concordance of Shakespeare* lists sixteen such uses of *meantime* by the Bard against only four such uses of *meanwhile*.

## MERE

There are those who declare that the only adjective in the English language that has a positive degree and a superlative degree but no comparative degree is *mere*. We speak of *"mere* details" or "the *merest* detail," but did you ever hear anyone say that one detail was *merer* than another? Webster's New International Dictionary, second edition, has a peculiar comment on the word, as follows: "The comparative is rarely or never used." One might say that if it's "rarely" it's not "never," and that if it's "never" it's not "rarely." Maybe what the dictionary should have said is "rarely if ever."

## METAPHORS

(Mixaphors.) In the sentence, "Thus the word *enthuse* was coined," *coined* constitutes a metaphor, a figure of speech that implies an identity or comparison. In this instance the comparison was to the minting of a new piece of money. (A simile differs from a metaphor in stating a likeness explicitly by the use of *like* or *as:* "The word *enthuse* was created *as* a coin is.") Getting back to metaphors, we may say that they are a concise and colorful way of expressing ideas and sometimes they border on poetry. But one caution is in order: Beware of the mixed metaphor or, to use the centaur word your host has minted, the *mixaphor.* Example: "His boss backs him to the hilt whenever the chips are down." There you have an absurd mixture of swordsmanship and poker. Another example: "Almost drowned in a torrent of abuse, the Senator was a pillar of strength." A drowning pillar? We almost had a third example when, in the opening sentence above, the writer was tempted to say, "The word *enthuse* was coined out of the whole cloth." (*See* CLICHES.)

## METER
*See* POETIC METER.

## MIDNIGHT
*See* A.M., P.M.

## MIGHT
*See* MAY.

## MILITATE
*See* MITIGATE.

## MINUSCULE

(It's a small matter.) How can we get people to spell the word that means tiny in the proper way: *minuscule,* instead of *miniscule,* as so many spell it? The only way to set them on the right course is to give them a minus every time they misspell the word; then they will have the minus handy the next time they have to spell *minuscule.*

## MISANDRY

Most of us are reasonably familiar with the word *misogynist,* meaning a woman hater, but is there one word to describe a female who detests males? The word that comes to mind immediately is *misanthrope* because there's a man at the bottom of it, but that word won't do because it means someone who hates mankind, men and women alike. A bit of searching at last turned up a word, which strangely appears only in Webster's unabridged, third edition. It is *misandry,* from the Greek *mis-,* hatred, and *andros,* man. Just the word you've been looking for, girls.

## MITIGATE, MILITATE

A Federally sponsored study concluded that school children of today are ahead of those of the 1950's and earlier in their reading ability. The head of the research project, an Indiana University reading authority, was quoted as saying, "Everything *mitigated* against showing greater reading achievement, yet that is what happened." If the head of the project could be guilty of that kind of flagrant misuse of a word, it makes one wonder about the value of the study and the validity of his conclusions. Among ordinary folk the confusion of *mitigate* and *militate* is common, but among academics it is inexcusable. *Mitigate* means to soften, moderate, make less severe. Having those meanings, it obviously cannot be followed by *against. Militate,* on the other hand, means to have an opposing effect and most of the time is followed by *against.* A look at the derivations of those two words, *militate* and *mitigate,* may help to drive home the distinction between them. *Militate* comes from the Latin *militare,* meaning to serve as a soldier. *Mitigate* derives from the Latin *mitis,* meaning soft, gentle, mild. The two words look something alike and sound something alike, but in meaning they are about as different as two words can be.

## MNEMONIC

There are fewer than a dozen words in English beginning with *mn* and almost all of them are related to that word *mnemonic.* The underlying root of such words is the Greek *mneme,* memory. *Mnemonic* pertains to assistance to memory. A related word is *amnesia,* loss of memory. And another related word is *amnesty,* which is a deliberate forgetting of an offense. Mnot so hard to remember all this, is it?

## MODIFIERS

(Poor positioning.) Improper placement of words or phrases can on occasion make a sentence anything from ludicrous to obscure. Here is one illustration: "Israel has developed a bullet-proof helmet for soldiers made of plastic." Soldiers made of plastic? Writing "a bulletproof plastic helmet" would have solved that one. Another illustration: "Neither woman was able to lift a 25-pound bar bell with one hand over her head as required in the Civil Service examination for the job." Get the picture—one hand over her head? Nothing of the kind. The phrase "over her head" belongs after "bar bell." Still another illustration: "She asked for time off to testify at a hearing into charges of sexual, ethnic and racial discrimination against the American Telephone and Telegraph Company and its subsidiaries." Discrimination against the company? No. The "against the company" phrase should be placed after "charges." In putting together a sentence be sure everything is in its proper place.

(Say what you mean.) Sometimes the misplacement of a word or phrase will cause a statement to say not quite what the author is trying to get across. Take the slogan of the United Negro College Fund: "A mind is a terrible thing to waste." Quite obviously, the coiner of the slogan did not mean in any sense that a mind is a terrible thing; if he had meant that, he would not have advocated educating it. What he did mean is the sentence: "It is a terrible thing to waste a mind." Of course, ad men often indulge in deliberate distortions of good English to slam a point home to what they conceive of as the common people. But bad usage is a terrible thing.

(Adverb ambiguity.) A term that doesn't sound at all pedagogical is used by grammarians to denote the sloppy usage in this kind of sentence: "The bars he patronized frequently are mere dives." The grammarians' term for that word "frequently" as it is placed in the sentence is *squinting modifier* or *squinting construction.* The idea is that the word seems to look in two directions: Does it tell you about the bars he patronizes frequently or about the frequency of their being mere dives? If the first alternative is meant, the sentence should say, "The bars he frequently patronizes. . . ." If the second alternative is meant, it should say, ". . . are frequently mere dives." Squinting has no place in precise language.

(Danglers.) Here's a recipe for you: "When dipped in melted butter or Hollandaise sauce, one truly discovers the food of the gods." The trouble with the sentence, of course, is that the participial phrase, "when dipped, etc.," is out of contact with the noun it modifies, "food," and is in close contact with a word it does not modify, "one"; it suggests one is dipped in butter. That type of error is known as a *dangler* or *dangling participle*. It is not so much the bad grammar that makes a *dangler* intolerable as the ludicrousness of what the sentence inadvertently says.

Some participle phrases appear to be danglers, but actually are not, yet there are fussbudgets who point to them as if they were. An example is this: "Considering the handicaps, Jones made a good race for alderman." No one thinks there is any individual doing the "considering." The test of whether a participle is a dangler or a nondangler is the presence or absence of an agent that is performing the action or is related to it. Like "considering," there are a score or more of participles that are used without any suggestion of an agent, and they are called absolute participles. A few of the more common ones are *assuming, barring, concerning, depending, following, given, granted, judging, provided.*


## MOMENTARILY, MOMENTLY

(Of no great moment.) If the plane pilot says, "We will be taking off *momentarily,*" is that a correct use of the word? Time was when some authorities on usage objected to employing *momentarily* in the sense of what may happen or is expected to happen at any moment. To convey that sense they demanded *momently.* However, that time has just about passed. *Momently* is not used very often these days and when it is used it denotes the idea of from moment to moment ("The noise of the rioters grew *momently* louder"). It is quite proper to expect the plane to take off *momentarily.*

## MOOT
The origin of *moot,* meaning debatable or hypothetical, lies in the Old English *mot* and *gemot,* meaning a meeting or discussion. Originally a noun denoting an early English assembly, the word developed into an adjective as well and it is often used that way these days, as, for example, in *moot point.*

## MORE IMPORTANT(LY)
(Here's an argument.) One of the easiest ways to start an argument among people interested in grammar is to use the phrase *more importantly.* There is no wish to start an argument here, but rather a desire to set forth the case on both sides and hint at a leaning.

The case against the phrase is established, albeit perhaps established on a superstition. Take a typical sentence that is approved by the standpatters: "The treaty calls for peace, but *more important* sets up a border commission." The standpatters say that *more importantly* would be wrong. The far-out radicals retort that they should take some equivalent adjective and try to substitute it for *important*—for example, *specific, substantive, fundamental, concrete, realistic, pointed, practical.* It is evident, the radicals say, that in virtually every instance it would be necessary to use the adverbial form: *specifically, substantively, fundamentally,* etc. The standpatters return to the fray by arguing that the reason for using *important* is that it is part of an ellipsis for "what is more *important.*" Which prompts us radicals to ask, "If that is so, why shouldn't the same reasoning apply to all the other words cited?" But it doesn't; the adjective form simply would not do. The American Heritage Dictionary reports that its usage panel divided 50–50 on this momentous question concerning a usage —i.e., *importantly*—that "is not defensible grammatically." Well, if a grammatical defense is necessary, call *importantly* what is known as a "sentence adverb" and maybe that would take care of it. The intention of all this is not to argue that *important* is wrong, but rather to suggest that *importantly* is not necessarily wrong either.

## MORE THAN, OVER
(A superstition.) An ad for a magazine spoke of *"over* 114,000 readers." Should the *over* be changed to *more than*? Alas, here's

a superstition that grips many writers. Apparently it originated with Ambrose Bierce, who objected to that use of *over* without stating any reason for his objection. However, the meaning "in excess of" has been attached to *over* in reputable use since the days of late Middle English. Oddly enough, the foes of *over* do not fire any shots at *above* or *under*. They do not hesitate to say, "The company's profits were 10 percent *above* last year's," or, "His income is *under* $20,000." It's time for the war on *over* to be over.

## MORNINGS
*See* ADVERB.

## MOST
*See* ADVERB PLACEMENT.

## MOVE, MAKE A MOTION
(Motion sickness.) If you attend a parents' association meeting, the chances are that at some point someone will use this kind of construction: "Mr. Chairman, I would like to *make a motion* that every pupil be able to spell 'cat' before he gets a diploma." There is nothing in any rule book about it, but good parliamentary language would call upon the parent to *move* rather than *make a motion.* The proposal he has put before the meeting is a motion to be sure, but in preferred usage he *moves* rather than *makes a motion.*

## MUCKRAKING
In 1906 President Theodore Roosevelt became aroused by writers who unearthed real or alleged corruption and he compared them to a character in *Pilgrim's Progress* who was so intent on raking muck that he was always looking downward. Lincoln Steffens and such writers seized delightedly on the coined words *muckraker* and *muckraking* and soon the terms were in widespread use. Despite the derogatory sound of the words they were not deemed disparaging. Nevertheless, in keeping with the modern trend toward euphemisms and fancy phrases *muckraking* today is called *investigative reporting.*

## MUGGING

Friend Dear Abby asked where the word *mugging* came from. Just about the only place a clue to the origin of the verb *mug* appears is Webster's New Collegiate Dictionary, which is based on Webster's Third New International. The Collegiate says that *mug* is a back formation from the noun *mugger,* which in turn "probably" comes from the obsolete English verb *mug,* meaning to punch in the face. If that is true, there has been a kind of back formation in the assault itself. Instead of a punch in the face today's *mugging* usually is a robber's attack from behind.

## MUTUAL, COMMON

The word *mutual,* properly used, indicates interaction or reciprocity between two or more. Thus, Jack and Jane can have *mutual* admiration, and if John and Jill feel the same way toward them and toward each other and Jack and Jane feel that way, too, the four of them can have a *mutual* admiration society. But if Jack and Jane merely both admire John, what they have for him is a *common* admiration, not a *mutual* admiration. Likewise it is improper to say, "China will not obstruct aid by the Soviet Union to their *mutual* ally, North Vietnam." In that sentence no adjective at all is needed, but if one is used it should be *common.* *Reciprocal* is often equivalent to *mutual,* but not always. For one thing, *mutuality* designates a relationship that is simultaneous, whereas *reciprocity* can designate something that occurs later than what is being reciprocated. For another thing, *mutual* is not used to refer to concrete things; people can indulge in *mutual* criticism, but they cannot exchange *mutual* punches. As a postscript, it may be said that strictly speaking *mutual friend* is improper, but the Dickens novel *Our Mutual Friend* has brought it into acceptance and, in addition, to use the phrase *common friend* might sound like a derogatory term. That, however, is an exception to the rule concerning the misuse of *mutual.*

## MYSELF AND I

It is not unusual to hear such utterances as these: "Fran and *myself* went to the movies" or "Fran invited Bill and *myself* to a party." The misuses of *myself* have persisted for years, and they are caused by a fear of the words *I* and *me.* In the first of those quoted sentences it should be "Fran and *I*" and in the second it should be "Bill and *me.*" But the same people who stumble into "between you and *I*" use *myself* because they can't discriminate between a nominative case and an objective case. In the first of those sentences it should be a nominative *(I)* because it is the subject of the verb *went;* in the second sentence it should be objective *(me)* because it is the object of the verb *invited.* The *-self* words are used for only two purposes: for emphasis ("I repaired the car *myself"*) or for reflexive purposes, that is, to turn the action back on the grammatical subject ("She dressed *herself* quickly"). (*See* "I" AND "ME" PHOBIAS.)

# N

## NAUSEOUS, NAUSEATED

*Nauseous* and *nauseated* are used by many people as if they were interchangeable, but they are not. They are, of course, related; both are based on the Greek *naus* (ship). A ship produces seasickness and *nausea* is not far removed from that. A thing is *nauseous* if it makes one sick to the stomach; the victim of that sickness is not *nauseous*, he is *nauseated*. A person who feels sick is not *nauseous* any more that a person who has been poisoned is poisonous.

## NEITHER, NOR

(Wrong number.) The *neither-nor* combination often induces grammatical errors. For instance: "Neither Jack nor George were properly equipped for their careers." If the *neither-nor* combination links two singular nouns, the verb and the following pronoun and noun should be singular, thus: "Neither Jack nor George *was* properly equipped for *his career.*" If the conjunctions link a singular and a plural, the number of the verb is normally determined by the nearer noun, thus: "Neither Jack nor the other *students were* properly equipped for their careers." (*See* CORRELATIVES.)

## NICKNAME

*Nickname* raises the question, What has Nick got to do with it? The answer is, nothing. It's not Nick, but *eke,* and *eke* has to do with augmentation or supplementing. Originally, an additional or supplemental name was an *ekename*, then, just as children say "a napple" when what they are talking about is "an apple," so an *ekename* came to be a *nekename* and then a *nickname*. Adding something to the beginning of a word in that way is a process called prothesis or prosthesis.

## NINCOMPOOP

Nobody knows the origin of the word *nincompoop,* meaning a foolish or simple-minded person. A guess that has become popular is that it came from *non compos mentis,* meaning not of sound mind. But the Oxford English Dictionary discards that idea on the ground that the spelling of the earliest versions of the term, such as *nicompoop* (1676) and *nickumpoop,* do not suggest such a derivation. (Warning: the following sentence is rated PG.) Such versions come up in Captain Francis Grose's 1785 *Classical Dictionary of the Vulgar Tongue,* which has this entry: "Nickumpoop, or Nincompoop. A foolish fellow; also one who never saw his wife's ****." (That is the entry edited in the twentieth century by Eric Partridge.) A quite plausible theory of the word's origin is advanced by the Oxford Dictionary of English Etymology. It says that those earliest forms of the word suggest derivation from a proper name, such as Nicholas or Nicodemus—it mentions the French word *nicodeme,* simpleton—plus the obsolete *poop,* befool. That last syllable could also be related to the Dutch *poep,* a fool. Anyway, you and I have now done a lot of work on that word, but it's more fun to work on a nincompoop than on a nincometax, isn't it?

## NOISOME, NOISY

Two words that are often confused are *noisome* and *noisy,* but they bear no relation to each other. *Noisome* has nothing to do with noise, but rather means foul smelling, disgusting, harmful, filthy. The confusion between the two words is not tolerated by authorities on usage. In a new edition of the American Heritage Dictionary 99 percent of the usage panel decided that the "sound" meaning of *noisome* was unsound.

## NONCE

The word *nonce* resulted from a kind of reverse confusion. In Middle English there was a phrase *for then ones* (in which *then* was a definite article), but the *n* got detached from the *then* and the result was the word *nonce,* meaning the present occasion. (The process of attaching a syllable or letter to the beginning of a word is called *prosthesis,* as was noted on the preceding page.)

## NONE
Whether the pronoun *none* should be followed by a singular verb or a plural seems to be continually bothering people. Miss Thistlebottom (or a close relative) taught us that none should be followed by a singular verb. Miss Thistlebottom's point was that *none* derives from *not one.* That is true enough, but the word does not always mean not one; it often means not any. Take a look at this sentence: *"None* of the stockholders, officers or directors *are* receiving remuneration for services." In that sentence the *none* leans more toward the *not any* side than the *not one* side. Dictionaries and authorities on English generally agree that often the plural verb is to be preferred. When the singular idea predominates the verb should indeed be singular: "All three schools have excellent health records, though *none* has a full-time physician." Likewise when *none* is followed by a singular noun it is usually treated as a singular: *"None* of the food *was* fresh." Although a flat rule is not advisable, it can be said that in most instances the singular sounds pedantic and the plural is to be preferred. (*See* AGREEMENT.)

## NOON
*See* A.M., P.M.

## NOR
*See* OR.

## NORMALITY, NORMALCY
(Not so abnormal.) One myth that has persisted in the face of sound evidence against it is the one asserting that President Warren G. Harding coined the word *normalcy.* Even Ernest Klein's respectable two-volume *Comprehensive Etymological Dictionary of the English Language* speaks of the word as "a hybrid coined" by the President, noting that "the correct form is *normality."* It may well be that President Harding had never heard of the word *normalcy,* but merely had an impression there was such a word and let it drop from his lips without giving a thought

to it. In that sense he may have "coined" it. But the word had, as H. L. Mencken points out, a respectable ancestry and was in use more than 60 years before Harding appeared on the scene. The *Oxford English Dictionary* quotes from an 1857 book on mathematics that employed the term. Myths die hard, but it's high time this one expired.

## NOT ONLY . . . BUT ALSO
*See* CORRELATIVES.

## NOTORIETY
*See* PUBLICITY.

## NOUNS
*See* COLLECTIVES; COMPOUNDS; CONVERSIONS; POSSESSIVES; SINGULAR CONCEPTS.

## NOUS
(A woman with it.) Some women, addressing a United Nations forum, voiced annoyance over what they considered to be a patronizing approach by men speakers. "After all," said one woman representative, "we have some *nous.*" A rare word, *nous* means intelligence or common sense. Pronounced either noose or nowce, it denotes mind, intellect or reason in the highest sense.

# O

---

## O AND OH-OH

A paperback book bears the title on its cover and on its title page, *If I Forget Thee, O Jerusalem*. But Pyramid Publications, in its publicity material about the book, four times gave the title as, *If I Forget Thee, Oh Jerusalem*. Notice the difference in the o-zone. Which is right, *o* or *oh?* The answer is *o*. As a word of address to a being or thing, the word is *O*, always capitalized and never followed by any punctuation. Therefore, the title as it appears on the book itself is correct: *If I Forget Thee, O Jerusalem*. When used as an utterance followed by a pause, the word is spelled *oh*, it is not capitalized except at the start of a sentence and it is set off by one or two commas, thus: "Jerusalem is, *oh*, about 35 miles from Tel Aviv." As an exclamation it is also spelled *oh* and is usually followed by an exclamation point: "*Oh!* How could you kiss me in front of all those people?"

## OH!

If your zip code is 71860, the chances are that people will pronounce that final numeral "oh." Some say there are three "correct" words to use: *zero, ought* or *nought.* (The second and third could be spelled *aught* and *naught.*) Those three words are correct all right, but so is *O;* every dictionary says so. Undoubtedly most people prefer *O* because it takes slightly less effort. In handwriting and typewriting the letter *O* and the figure *0* look alike, though in printing the numeral looks as if it has been watching its calories whereas the letter is slightly overweight. If the typesetter is willing, you can compare them right here: 0—

O (the first is the numeral, the second is the letter). If incorrectness attaches to any of the three words mentioned, *ought* is the one. It has a shady background because it came about through faulty division of *a nought* into *an ought.* Some naughty scribes probably did that.

## O.K.

It is doubtful whether any expression has had more guesses made as to its etymology than has *O.K.* They range all the way from *aux quais,* supposed to have been used in the American War of Independence by French sailors dating American girls, to *okeh,* a Choctaw word meaning it is so. The best evidence, collected from many sources, appears in Mencken's *The American Language.* The use of initials was a vogue in Boston in 1838 and it spread to New York within the succeeding year. In Boston the initials O.W., standing for "all right," as if it were spelled "oll wright," appeared in 1838 and the following year *O.K.* ("oll korrect") appeared in both Boston and New York. However, *O.K.* did not become a national by-word until the political campaign of 1840 when it was part of the Democratic O.K. Club, which was supporting Martin Van Buren for a second Presidential term. The *O.K.* was an abbreviation for Old Kinderhook, Van Buren's Hudson River birthplace, and when the club held its first meeting in New York the initials caught on and spread rapidly. That's the story about *O.K.* to the best of O.K. (our knowledge).

## OKAY?

A typical recounting of a trivial incident might go this way these days: "I was walking down the street minding my own business. *Okay?* So I was approached by this guy—y'know, beard, beads, tangled hair, boots—hippy type. *Okay?* He says to me, 'Excuse me, have you got any spare change?' So I looked at him and I said, 'That's funny, I was just about to ask you the same question.' *Okay?*" *Okay* runs third as today's most prevalent speech-filler ("y'know" and "like" are the leaders). For at least a half century such meaningless things have been with us. At one time the popular one was "see?" Then there was "get it?" Then "right?" Then, more recently, "you dig?" All are, or were, mannerisms used by speakers who do not understand, as actors do, the value of a pause. And to many listeners they are irritating. So next time you find your tongue forming *okay?* why not clear your throat, blow your nose or light up a joint?

## OBBLIGATO

The musical term *obbligato* is an Italian word conveying the sense of being obliged. It originally referred to a part of a musical composition, often performed by a solo voice or instrument, that was required, that the performers were obligated to include. But now the meaning has been almost reversed. Today it often refers to a section of a composition that is optional, a section that may be skipped. It almost looks as if music took the lead in the spread of permissiveness.

## OBJECTS, DIRECT AND INDIRECT

(She teaches school.) When the Teacher of the Year received her award she was quoted as saying, "I don't teach subjects, I teach children." That prompted a professor of education at the Johns Hopkins University to write a letter to a newspaper observing that the words *children, pupils* or *students* are never the direct object of a sentence that answers the question, What do you teach? Rather, he said, those words are indirect objects; for example, "I teach *children* art." However, they are used as direct objects in stating whom one teaches. What the Teacher of the Year was saying, therefore, the professor concludes, was, "I teach children, but I don't teach them anything." We disagree. The teacher was not denigrating the importance of subject matter. Rather she was emphasizing the importance of getting through to the pupils, teaching them how to learn as well as teaching them history, arithmetic or whatever. In a way she was making a play on words to emphasize the idea of well-rounded instruction.

## OFF OF

(Something to lay off of.) The use of the preposition *of* after off is at least superfluous and at most close to vulgar. That is because the "of" idea is built into *off*. A locution such as, "Signs directed motorists *off of* the damaged road" is considered poor usage. Still worse, of course, is "I got a loan *off of* my brother-in-law," but there the fault lies in the misuse of *off* for *from*.

## OMISSION
*See* ELLIPSIS.

## ON (OFF) THE WAGON
When someone goes *on the wagon* or *off the wagon* he is, as everyone knows, either abstaining from alcoholic liquors or returning to them. These phrases came into use in the early 1900's and alluded to the water wagon, which was a truck used to transport water. If someone was *on the wagon,* he was confining himself to water or other gentle beverages; if he was *off* (or *fell off*) *the wagon,* he had returned to spirituous beverages.

## ON ACCOUNT OF
(Calling to account.) It is acceptable to say, "She will not attend the party *on account of* illness," but it is not acceptable to say, "She will not attend the party *on account of* she is ill." That is downright illiterate. *On account of* is synonymous with *because of* and just as you would not say, *"because of* she is ill," so you should not say, *"on account of* she is ill."

## ON RELIEF
A Washington magazine editor saw in a story about baseball a mention of a pitcher who was called a *reliefer.* He said he thought the word should be *reliever* and asked which was correct. The answer is both or either. They mean the same thing, but *reliefer* is a relatively recent word to designate the hurler who takes over late in the game to keep the opposing batters in check. It appears in the newer dictionaries and has a secondary meaning denoting a person who is on relief.

## ON THE OTHER HAND
Does one have to introduce one hand before speaking of *on the other hand?* A few purists insist one does, but it isn't so. Can you conceive of a reader who would encounter the phrase *on the other hand* and then ask himself or anyone else, "What other hand?" The fact is that *the other hand* phrase is an old but useful cliché. The normal reader does not think of clichés in terms of their literal meanings; he instantly grasps their abstract sense and moves on. If he reads that someone has *pulled the chestnuts out of the fire* he doesn't stop to visualize a fire or some chestnuts; he

knows at once what the meaning is. It is not always necessary to be literal.

## ONE ANOTHER
*See* EACH OTHER.

## ONE . . . HE/SHE
(More than one "one.") In a column I wrote, "In that example *one* is assuming as fact the very thing *he* is professing to prove." A reader asked whether the *he* should not have been *one.* The authorities on usage are divided on whether such a use of *one* is a must. There are those who find the *one . . . one* construction too prissy. And then there are sentences in which the repeated *one* would produce a slightly absurd result. One example: "In the art exhibit *one* finds little to interest *one.*" Second example: *"One* who hopes for a passing grade had better read *one's* assignments and think carefully about *one's* answers when *one* takes *one's* final examination." This question of using *he* rather than *one* is discussed in the *Harper Dictionary of Contemporary Usage* by William and Mary Morris and one question that was put to the book's usage panel of 136 leaders in the field of usage was whether they favored repetition of *one* rather than using *he* to avoid the implications of male chauvinism. Ninety-one percent voted no.

## ONE-TO-ONE
(One thing and another.) A phrase that has been coming into wide use with a slightly different meaning from the one it had originally is *one-to-one.* Its early meaning was the correlating of two elements exactly and uniquely. Today's users employ it to mean person-to-person or face-to-face. Example from a news article: "One casualty of the new sophistication in medicine is the old, straightforward *one-to-one* relationship between doctor and patient." In that instance, as in many others, the phrase is not needed at all.

## ONE FELL SWOOP
(Terrible descent.) Mr. So-and-so (that's not his name) wrote to ask about the meaning and origin of *one fell swoop.* A *swoop* is a sudden pouncing or descent and *fell* means fierce and meant—

archaically—deadly. So *one fell swoop* is a terrible dive or blow. Whether Shakespeare originated the phrase or not, he did use it in *Macbeth* this way: "What! all my pretty chickens and their dam at *one fell swoop?*" When Shakespeare gave a "dam" he was using a word of his day for "mother."

## ONE OF THOSE (MISTAKES)

In a common construction in English the word *one* is so dominant that it leads writers and speakers into error. Look at this sentence from a newspaper article: "Are you *one* of those people who *is* perpetually misplacing spectacles?" The writer's mind focused on *one* to such an extent that *is* seemed the proper verb. But it is not. This becomes evident if you turn the sentence around to get at its real meaning: "Of those people who *are* perpetually misplacing spectacles are you one?" The error is one of those things that betray (not betrays) the thoughtless writer.

## ONE WORD, TWO WORDS

Is it *everyone* or *every one,* is it *anyone* or *any one,* is it *someone* or *some one?* Take a look at the following sentence and the answer will begin to become clear: "There were a dozen apples in the basket and *everyone* was rotten." A partial answer is that if you can substitute *everybody* (or *anybody* or *somebody*), then the single word is correct. That is clearly not the case in the apples sentence; therefore it should in that sentence be *every one.* Another test is whether the combination involves two stresses (or accents) or one. If there is a single stress, as there would be if *everyone* meant *everybody,* the term is a single word. In the apple sentence there are two stresses—EVERY ONE—and therefore two words are proper. The only exception to that rule is *no one,* which is always two words lest people pronounce it noon.

## ONLY

The proper placement of the word *only* is a problem that seems to bother many writers. Take this headline: "They Only Kill Their Masters." Does *only* limit "they" or "masters" or "kill"? To begin with, let's eliminate "they" as the modified word because to convey that sense either the *only* would have to precede "they" or it would have to be changed to "alone." Probably we

can also eliminate "kill" as the modified word because to suggest that "they" don't do anything worse would border on the
humorous. That leaves only one possibility: that they kill *only*
their masters. If that is the intended meaning, as we assume it
to be, the technically correct place for the *only* is right ahead of
"their masters." But that doesn't mean that we must rule out
every other position, no matter how clear and idiomatic it is. It
is perfectly acceptable to say, "John *only* got a job two days ago,"
though in the strictest sense the wording would be, "John got
a job *only* two days ago." We are not encouraging loose usage;
we *only* wish to be helpful. (*See* ADVERB PLACEMENT.)

## OR

(How to handle your or.) What verb should be used in the
following sentence: "That book was written before you or I
*(was? were?)* born."? Some conservative authorities say that the
verb should be made to agree in person and number with the
nearest subject. The nearest subject in this instance is *I*. Thus,
just as you would say, "before I *was* born," those authorities
would make the sentence read, "before you or I *was* born."
Other authorities favor the plural verb *were* in this instance on
the ground that the idea here is addition of subjects rather than
separation of them. It must be conceded that they have a case
and that *were* sounds more natural than *was*. All of which proves,
perhaps, that we have here a deficiency of the language and a
situation in which there is no flat right and no flat wrong. (*See*
AGREEMENT.)

## OR, NOR

(A couple of more negatives.) Often a *no* phrase may be followed by either a *nor* phrase or an *or* phrase, and the choice of
which to use may be subtle though not unimportant. If the two
elements that are to be linked are merely synonyms, *or* would
be appropriate. For example: "The Senator has *no* power *or*
influence to win passage of the bill." The words "power" and
"influence" mean about the same thing and *or* is a natural link
between them. However, if two words of that sort mean different
things, *nor* would be the appropriate way of stressing the difference. For example: "The Senator has *no* power *nor* desire to
obtain passage of the bill."

(No negative carryover.) Here is a sentence that exposes a fairly usual error: "No hunting is allowed in the demilitarized zone, or can unauthorized persons enter it." The *or* should be changed to *nor.* The reason is that the negative idea in the first part of the sentence is complete in that part and cut off from the second part, which therefore needs a negative of its own. On the other hand, the sentence could be rephrased so that the negative idea applied to both parts, thus: "Persons are not allowed to hunt in the demilitarized zone *or* to enter it without authorization." In that construction the *or* is perfectly proper.

## ORAL VS. VERBAL
(Spoken vs. written.) The word *oral* presents no problem; it refers to spoken words. *Verbal,* however, is subject to ambiguity. What it means and should mean is in the form of words whether spoken or written, but it has become fuzzy because of a widespread tendency to use it as if it meant only pertaining to spoken words. Thus, if someone speaks of a *verbal* agreement, there may be uncertainty concerning whether it is an agreement reached in conversation or is one set down on paper. It would be well if *verbal* could be confined to communication by means of words as distinguished from communication by gestures, sign language, extrasensory perception or whatnot. Then the word *written* could be used in referring to words committed to paper. Precision is helpful to the cause of clarity in language.

## ORIENT, ORIENTATE
These words mean the same thing: to get into a proper position with respect to circumstances or surroundings ("The course is designed to *orient* students to the program of the college"; "He spent his first day in New York trying to *orient* himself to his new environment"). However, the desire to sound impressive that is inherent in officialese and pedagoguese causes an undue preference to be given to *orientate,* the longer, more important-sounding word. If you wish to sound important, use *orientate,* but if you favor simple, precise expression, use *orient.*

## OTHER
(Be "other"-wise.) Strictly speaking, *other* refers to something distinct from a like thing already mentioned; for instance, "one

book and the *other* book" or "five players and the *other* five." Sometimes, however, we encounter a locution that could not be called incorrect but that is not precise. Here is an example: "Former Prime Minister Tanaka and his secretary were the 14th and 15th persons arrested in the case. The *other* 13 persons were all businessmen." Since a first set of 13 persons was not mentioned, it is not prissy pure to speak of "the other 13 persons"; it would be preferable to say "the 13 *other* persons." Here is another example: "Ten people were involved; three confessed their wrongs, but the *other* seven did not." Since the sentence does not mention a first seven, it would be better not to say "the other seven" but rather to say "the seven others."

### -OUGH
(Pronounced failure.) Under the title "Hough's That Again," a friend tells this droll story: "A Frenchman learning English was having trouble mastering the many ways in which common English letter combinations are pronounced. *Through, though, tough, bough*—there you have four different pronunciations of the combination *ough*. Disheartened, he was passing a theater one night when he happened to glance up at the dancing lights on the marquee: 'The Brothers Karamazov—Pronounced Success.' The Frenchman went back to his hotel and killed himself."

### OUGHT (TO)
(What ought to be said.) Some purists insist that the auxiliary verb *ought* must be followed by an infinitive including the word *to*. In most instances they are right. The *to* certainly should be inserted in this sentence: "Car owners *ought* drive carefully." But omission of the *to* is permissible and idiomatic in a sentence like this: "Car owners *ought* never exceed the speed limit." Two experts on usage explain this by saying that omitting the *to* is proper in a negative statement. That is true, but we can go further and say that the *to* may (not must) be omitted if any qualifier, negative or not, intervenes between the *ought* and the main verb. For instance: "The police *ought* always be on the lookout for muggers" or "Your newspaper *ought*, no matter what the weather, be delivered to your door."

## OUTDATED LINGO

An editorial in *The Chapel Hill Newspaper,* a North Carolina daily, observed that inflation and new life styles have played hob with some old standbys of American colloquialism. As one example it mentioned *chicken feed,* meaning a trifling sum, and suggested running down to your neighborhood grain store and buying some chicken feed. As another example it spoke of *selling like hotcakes.* It quoted a restaurateur, who at first seemed puzzled by the term hotcakes, and then said, "They get a play now and then. But the big thing is black coffee and dry toast. Everybody's on a diet." Obviously, some colloquialisms with the passage of years become old hat. And there's one for you. Who knows what a hat is these days?

## OUTSIDES?

Yes, there is a word *outsides.* One of the players in a word game used it and won 80 points with it. But its role in that game is almost the only use anyone would ever have for it. According to Webster's unabridged, third edition, *outsides* refers to the top and bottom quires of a ream of writing or drawing paper. *Insides,* as everyone knows, are something else again.

## OVER
*See* MORE THAN.

## OVERSIGHT

(Word with opposite meanings.) A newspaper clipping said that "a distorted Attorney General's opinion . . . would make Congressional *oversight* meaningless." To many people that use of the word would be puzzling, yet it is quite proper. One meaning of *oversight* and by far the commoner one is a careless error or omission. But another meaning, which is not unusual in legislative circles and is the one used in the quotation above, is supervision, management or careful watchfulness. So the same word can denote something careless and something careful.

## OWING TO
*See* DUE TO.

# OXYMORON

An *oxymoron* is a figure of speech in which contradictory terms are joined, sometimes in a sharply silly way—the Greek roots of the word mean sharply silly. Examples of *oxymorons:* the height of the Depression, conspicuous by its absence, a deafening silence.

# P

## P'S AND Q'S
(Watch those tails.) As almost everyone knows, the expression "Mind your p's and q's" means to be careful, to watch your step, to be circumspect in your behavior. But what no one knows is where the expression comes from.

Brewer's *Dictionary of Phrase and Fable* passes on three explanations that have been suggested. One is that in the old-time bars the beer accounts used *p* for pints and *q* for quarts and when the customer got around to settling up he found it was a good idea to mind his *p's and q's* or he might overpay. A second possible explanation traces it to France in the time of Louis XIV. Huge wigs were worn and deep bows were made with great formality, so that two things were necessary: a "step" with the feet and a low bend. When the bow was made the wig was liable to get disarranged and even fall off. The caution of the tutor to pupils, therefore, was, according to Brewer, "Mind your *p's* (i.e., *pieds*, feet) and *q's* (i.e., *queues*, wigs)." The third explanation is that the expression was an admonition to children learning the alphabet and even more so to printers' apprentices sorting type, because in both handwriting and print the side that the tail is on determines whether the letter is a *p* or a *q*. The vote here goes to the third explanation, which seems by far the most likely. But the whole business is quite p-q-liar.

## PAIR, PAIRS
(A singular question.) An ad will sometimes speak of "three *pair* of stockings." Using *pair* as a plural is not wrong, but. . . . Here

is what the Oxford English Dictionary has to say on the subject: "After a numeral *pair* was formerly used in the singular form; 'three pair (of) shoes' = German *drei paar Schuhe;* this is still retained colloquially, and in certain connections; but the tendency now is to say 'three pairs.' " In short, after a numeral *pair* is not wrong, but *pairs* is far preferable.

## PALINDROMES

(Backward in reading.) A *palindrome* is a word, a phrase or a sentence that reads the same backward as forward. A classic example is Adam's supposed introduction of himself to Eve: "Madam, I'm Adam."

Only a very short time ago a long-forgotten *palindrome* was found among the graffiti on the walls of a tavern of the Roman imperial age. In Latin it read: "Roma summus amor." Translated that means, "Rome supreme love."

One of the longer ones was the fancied utterance of Napoleon after his banishment to exile: "Able was I ere I saw Elba."

But there are even longer ones. The earliest recorded *palindrome* in English was by the seventeenth-century poet John Taylor and it was longer: "Lewd I did live, & evil I did dwel."

That ampersand (&) for *and* is a bit of cheating. But *dwel* was the spelling of his time.

Willard R. Espy in his book *The Game of Words* includes a few more long ones:

"Sums are not set as a test on Erasmus."

"I, man, am regal; a German am I."

"Egad, a base tone denotes a bad age."

"Dog, a devil deified, deified lived a god."

"Live dirt, up a side-track carted, is a putrid evil."

Perhaps the all-time best was inspired by Goethals's building of the Panama Canal:

"A man, a plan, a canal—Panama!"

Then there are short ones, of course:

"Step on no pets."

"Never odd or even."

"Name no one man."

"Dennis and Edna sinned."

A still shorter one, if you will tolerate an original contribution, concerns present-day fabrics and is the exact opposite of the truth:

"Knits stink."

## PARA-(GRAPH)

The prefix *para-* is not something new, but its use has widened in recent years. It has the meaning of alongside or auxiliary, or related to but not the same, or supplementary to. Thus we have *paramedics,* who are doctors' assistants; *parajournalists,* who work for the underground press; *paramilitarists,* who are civilians prepared for action on a military basis and *paraprofessionals,* who are assistants in professional fields. The first thing you know, the prefix will be attached to any jobholder who has a para hands and a para feet.

## PARALLELISM

(Linguistic linguini.) A silly Italian proverb makes for grammatical confusion. It goes like this: "You're not a man until you've had sex in a tree, underwater and with a jealous husband knocking at the door." The trouble is that there are three elements involved—a phrase, an adverb and another phrase—and it is not clear at first how they are to be separated. One way to do it in this instance is to repeat the verb for each element. Therefore: "You're not a man until you've had sex in a tree, had it underwater and had it with a jealous husband knocking at the door." Another way is to make all three elements phrases by changing the second to "under the water."

(Series out of control.) Here is an example of careless writing: "He said most married actors he knew either worked a second job, appeared in commercials or their wives worked." The first two items in the series are quite all right: the actors "worked"; the actors "appeared" but take a look at the third item: the actors "their wives worked"? It makes no sense and is grammatically impossible. To straighten it out you would have to say something like "had wives who worked."

## PARAMETERS

(Fad word.) Lend an ear to the Chief Justice of the United States: "While I would not undertake to make a definitive statement as to the *parameters* of the court's ruling . . ." A good guess is that what the Chief Justice had in mind was the *limits,* perhaps the *perimeter,* of the court's ruling. Had he gone to a dictionary he would have found that *parameter* is a mathematical term meaning a constant, the value of which can vary according to how it is applied. And for Pete's sake don't ask what that means. Clearly the Chief Justice did not go to a dictionary, but rather tossed in a word that sounded as if it should mean something like *perimeter* and that many people are using—correction: misusing—to sound technical and impressive.

## PARENTHETICAL INTERPOLATIONS
(How to stage a break-in.) Commas, parentheses or dashes may be used to set off matter interpolated in a sentence, and the closeness of such matter to the main thought usually determines which punctuation to use. With a close relationship, commas are used: "The pupils, who are all about the same age, are in the fifth grade." If the relationship is more remote, either parentheses or dashes may be used. Usually dashes are preferred to indicate a sharp break or shift in the sentence: "The host of the party—he made a fortune in Wall Street as well as in the theater—was widely complimented on the gourmet dinner he served." Parentheses are versatile; they can take care of most interpolations. And they have an additional advantage: Since they are used in pairs, the first parenthesis alerts the reader to the fact that he is going to come to a second one and thus that he is reading interpolated matter. That is not true of dashes, which may be used singly as well as in pairs. (*See* COMMAS.)

## PARTICIPLES
(Open and shut case.) A problem that puzzles some language buffs concerns the words *closed* and *open,* as in the sentence "The store is *closed* over the long weekend, but is *open* on Tuesday." The former word is a past participle, but the latter is not. Offhand it does seem to be a puzzle, but really it is not. *Closed* can be a past participle ("He had *closed* the safe before leaving the office"), but when used as in the cited sentence it is an adjective, just as *open* is. To be sure, *closed* as an adjective derives from a verb—*close*—but it has been an adjective for more than seven centuries. Nor is the use of past participles as adjectives uncom-

mon: "He discovered his pencil was *gone,*" "*Barking* dogs kept the whole neighborhood awake," "He used *guarded* words in speaking of the candidate." *Participles* are two-faced creatures; they can serve in the role of both verbs and adjectives. The word *participle* derives from the Latin *particeps,* meaning sharing or partaking.

## PARTING SHOT
You will look in vain in almost all dictionaries for the quite common phrase *parting shot.* What you will find in a few of them is *Parthian shot,* which apparently was "corrupted" into *parting shot.* It seems that Parthian horsemen in ancient times had a tactic of firing arrows from their bows when they were retreating or pretending to be retreating. That was their final tactic before either victory or defeat. Hence, the phrase *Parthian shot* or, as everyone except the dictionaries says, *parting shot.*

## PAST
*See* LAST AND PAST.

## PED-
A few words begin with *ped-:* for instance, there are *pedagogue* and *pedantic* and *pedal* and *pedestrian.* There is no connection to the word "child," as in *pediatrician;* the words derive from two different roots. The word *pedagogue* derives from the Greek *pais* (child) combined with *agein* (to lead); a *pedagogue* is one who leads children, a teacher. *Pedantic* and *pediatrician* have the same childish basis. *Pedal,* on the other foot, derives from the Latin *pedis* (foot) and so do *pedestrian* and *pedestal.* The word *peddler* has nothing to do with either of the foregoing categories. It seems to come from a word meaning basket. A *peddler* is also a *hawker,* which was originally a peddler of hawks. It's getting to sound *pedantic,* isn't it?

## PEEPING TOM
With skin flicks being shown everywhere and porno mags flourishing, maybe there aren't quite as many *peeping Toms* around as there once were. Still you may be interested to know where the term came from. Legend has it that the Lord of Coventry in 1040 imposed on his tenants certain taxes that his wife, Lady Godiva,

begged him to cancel. He said he would do it if she would ride naked through the town. She did so and he kept his promise. Years later an addition to the legend reported that everyone stayed indoors that day and one man, a tailor, peeped through his window as the lady went by and was instantly struck blind. He became known as the *Peeping Tom of Coventry.* Today a *peeping Tom* is a lasciviously prying person or a voyeur. (This paragraph is rated PG.)

## PEOPLE VS. PERSONS
Were you taught that *people* was the plural for *person* and that *persons* was incorrect? If Miss Thistlebottom taught you that, she led you astray. The plural of *person* is *persons,* though *people* may be used in the same sense. A general guide is to use *people* for large uncounted groups and *persons* for an exact or small number. Thus, it would be well to say, "Thirty-two *persons* signed the petition," and, "One hundred people attended the meeting," but preferably not to say, "The meeting was attended by 431 *people.*"

## PERQUISITES, PREREQUISITES
(Two look-alike words.) A news agency dispatch, speaking of President Nixon's resignation, said that it "would preserve his retirement pension and the *prerequisites* to which a former President is entitled." The word intended there was *perquisites.* Confusion of those two words is not an uncommon error. *Prerequisites* refer to things that are required in advance; for example, a *prerequisite* for voting is registration. *Perquisites* refers to benefits or rights to which a person or institution is entitled because of the status or position that is held; thus, a pension is a *perquisite* of the office of President. The thing to keep in mind is the prefix *pre-* in *prerequisites,* which means beforehand.

## PERSONS
   *See* PEOPLE VS. PERSONS.

## PERSUADE
   *See* CONVINCE.

## PERTINENT, PERTAINING

There is a shade of difference between *pertinent* and *pertaining* despite the fact that they come from the same Latin root. *Pertaining* is the more general word, suggesting relationship or applicability. *Pertinent* is more specific, conveying the idea of relevance or connection with the particular point or matter at hand.

## PLAYWRIGHT

(Wright? Wrong.) This sentence exhibits an error that crops up occasionally: "For 25 years he has been happily engaged in *playwrighting.*" The chap who writes plays is a *playwright,* but he *writes* plays, he doesn't *wright* them; therefore he is engaged in *playwriting,* not *playwrighting.* A *wright*—the word is used chiefly in combination, as in *wheelwright* or *shipwright*—is one who fashions or constructs something. The word has no connection with *write.* That should right a common wrong.

## PLEAD, PLED

Some of us don't especially care for *pled* as the past tense of *plead,* as in, "He *pled* guilty," and one or two dictionaries go along with us, terming *pled* colloquial or dialectal. But other dictionaries find it acceptable. Thus, there is no flat rule. Wilson Follett's *Modern American Usage* says that "in American usage *pleaded* is educated, *pled* is not." In Scottish law *pled* is approved, but elsewhere in Britain it is frowned upon. This judge's opinion is that *pled* may be all right for ordinary folk, but that *pleaded* has a more literate sound.

## PLEONASM

*Pleonasm* means the use of expressive words. It comes from the Latin word *pleonasmus,* which in turn comes from the Greek *pleonazein,* meaning to be more than enough. Have you had it? (*See* REDUNDANCY; TAUTOLOGY.)

## PLUMP FOR

The expression *plump for* means to come out strongly in favor of something or someone. The verb *plump* denotes falling heavily or with strong impact. When the word is switched over to figurative use it means to throw one's weight on the side of or to cast strong support for a candidate or a cause.

## PLURALS

(Rule for compounds.) Which should it be: *breakthroughs* or
*breaksthrough?* The rule, subject to exceptions, is to form the
plurals of compounds that are written as single words by adding
the "s" at the end. Thus the proper form would be *breakthroughs.*
Compounds that are written with a hyphen take the "s" at the
end of the noun that is dominant in the compound; for example,
*mothers-in-law.*

(Foreign words.) One word that needs watching is *graffiti* because so many people are tempted to say, "*Graffiti* is spreading
like wildfire," or "*Graffiti* is something that must be stopped."
The thing to be noticed is that *graffiti* is a plural noun; the
singular is *graffito.* Other foreign words that need watching are
*strata,* which is also plural (so that you can't say "every strata
of government"), and *media,* likewise plural. The singular
is *medium.* Three yes-and-no cases are *agenda, trivia,* and *data.*
Strictly speaking they are plural nouns, but their use as singu-
lars is of such long standing that it is now pretty generally
accepted.

(-ics words.) A question that arises from time to time is whether
a word like *politics* is always singular. It is singular most of the
time, but not always. When an *-ics* word refers to a subject, a
science, a profession or a system it is construed as a singular:
"World *politics was* his life study." But when such a word refers
to practical activities or qualities it is sometimes construed as a
plural: "*Politics keep* the Senator busy from morning till night."
Two more examples: "*Statistics* is a principal course at the business school"; "*Statistics prove* nothing in this instance."

(Names.) The headline read, "Stars and Friends Help the Con-
nors' Celebrate Their Silver Anniversary," and that prompts us
to discuss the plurals of names ending in *s.* As a general rule the
plurals of such names are formed by adding *s* or *es* to the singular. Following that rule, the headline writer should have made
it the *Connorses.* That form may sound awkward to some people,
but they wouldn't blink an eyelash at the *Joneses* or the *Charleses*
or the *Davises.* If adding an *es* does produce an awkward pronunciation—the Euripideses of drama, for example—or produces
ambiguity—the *Louises* (two girls named Louise?), for example

—the use of an apostrophe is acceptable. Normally, however, it is not acceptable; one should not write the *Smith*'s.

("A" or "the" decides it.) How about this sentence: "An average of 3,000 letters a month arrives at the magazine's office." Should the verb be *arrives* or *arrive?* The rule that generally applies to the word *average,* as well as to *number* and *total,* is to use a plural if the subject is *an average* (*a number, a total*) and a singular if the subject is *the average* (*the number*, the *total*). Thus you would write, *"An average* of 3,000 letters a month *arrive . . ."* but *"The average* of letters received each month *is* 3,000." Likewise: *"A large number* of people *were* at the rally," but, *"The number* of people at the rally *was* large."

## PLUS
(A minus for plus.) A common colloquialism these days goes something like this: "She is beautiful *plus* she has a fine mind." It is decidedly improper. *Plus* may be a preposition meaning increased by ("His pension *plus* Social Security will be ample"), or it may be an adjective indicating additional ("His Social Security is a *plus* quantity") or it may be a noun meaning something added ("His Social Security is a definite *plus"*). But the sentence cited at the beginning of this item uses the word as a conjunction, as if it were equivalent to *and.* That, to be colloquial about it, is no go.

## POETIC METER
(Remember your feet.) In verse a foot is a combination of syllables, and there are five common combinations, with their accents differently placed. They are as follows: the *iambus* (as in proDUCE), the *trochee* (as in JOYful), the *dactyl* (as in HELPfulness), the *anapest* (as in disreGARD) and the *spondee* (as in AMEN). Note that each of these feet has two syllables except the *dactyl* and the *anapest,* which have three. Now the question arises as to how to remember what the five sound like. Don't despair. Some time back your host composed a stanza that is easy to memorize and illustrates how each of the feet is accented. It goes like this:

> *Iambus,* King of all the North,
> Sucking *trochees,* ventured forth.

> Galloping *dactyls* emerged from their nest,
> But he struggled and conquered this *anapest.*
> *Spondee!*

## PORTMANTEAU WORDS
*See* BLEND WORDS.


## POSSESSIVES
(No hissing, please.) The possessive case of most nouns is formed, of course, by adding an apostrophe and an *s:* father's, Pennsylvania's, etc. However, exceptions occur when the noun ends in *s* or the sound of *s* and is followed by a word that begins with an *s* sound. Take a look at this passage from a review by Robert Brustein of Yale of a book by John Simon: ". . . the critical John Simon is composed of divided personae . . . which, for convenience sake, we'll call the good, the bad and the ugly." Normally, *convenience* in the possessive case would be *convenience's,* but when it is followed by *sake* the succession of three *s* sounds would be difficult to pronounce. In such situations, therefore, the *s* is omitted, but the apostrophe is retained to indicate the possessive case. It should be "for *convenience'* sake."

(Apostrophe or no apostrophe.) Is it *Womens Day program* or *Women's Day program*— should one use the possessive apostrophe? The answer is yes, use the apostrophe. The apostrophe is dropped these days in some instances in which the plural is indicated by a final *s*—for example, Teachers College, Citizens Union, Doctors Hospital. But when the plural is indicated without any final *s*—as it is in *women* or *men*—the apostrophe plus the *s* is necessary.

(Plurals that take possession.) One news article said, "Commander Brant, a lawyer with *11 years service* in the Navy, declined to comment." Another said, "He had had *three hours sleep* and innumerable telephone calls during the night at his home in Jamaica, Queens." Those phrases—*11 years service* and *three hours sleep*— should be in the possessive case or more aptly, since there is no real possession involved, the genitive case. Therefore they should be rendered with apostrophes: *11 years' service* and *three hours' sleep.* (*See* APOSTROPHE; DOUBLE GENITIVE.)

## PRACTICABLE, PRACTICAL

There is a distinction between those two words. *Practicable* refers to something that can be done; *practical* refers to something that can be done usefully or valuably. On another occasion I gave an illustration of the distinction between the words by presenting a pet idea of mine, which has gotten nowhere: It may be *practicable* to get double use out of the nation's railways by retaining the freight trains but also converting the tracks into airways for electronically guided, low-flying, safe, all-weather jet passenger planes that would not require vast tracts of real estate for airports. But the plan may not be *practical.* Incidentally, has anyone ever investigated to see whether the plan is *practical?*

## PRACTICALLY, VIRTUALLY

As strictly defined, *practically* means in practice or for practical purposes and *virtually* means in effect or as good as or almost. In common usage, however, *practically* has practically come to mean virtually the same thing as *virtually.* Some strict purists do not approve this overlapping, but they are indulging in Canutism (remember King Canute trying to make the ocean waves recede?). Trying to make the distinction between the words normally would require too close a study of the context. What should be avoided is the use of *practically* in the sense of almost. A baseball slugger whose drive went foul by two feet did not *practically* hit a homer.

## PRECIPITATE, PRECIPITOUS

Two words that speakers and writers seem to have trouble telling apart are *precipitate* and *precipitous.* Recently 15 Senators signed a letter asking that telephone service on Metroliners not be *"precipitously* terminated." The proper word there would have been *precipitately. Precipitous* is usually, but not always, applied to physical things and means steep; *precipitate* is applied to actions and means hasty or abrupt. A good way to remember the distinction is to think of the *a* in *precipitate* as standing for "abrupt" and the *s* in *precipitous* as standing for "steep."

## PREDOMINATE, PREDOMINANT

(Ate the improper word.) The word *predominant,* meaning superior or authoritative, is definitely an adjective. It has a niece, *predominate,* which should be nothing but a verb, meaning to be superior. But under the influence of the *-ant* the niece has been altered into a similar, if not entirely proper, adjective. It appears in a couple of dictionaries as an adjective, but it is not fully established and the advice here is to forget it.

## PREFER

(Try to avoid "Rather than.") A letter to the editor in a New York paper contained a sentence that said, "It is for these reasons that we *prefer* Richard H. Kuh *rather than* Robert M. Morgenthau." There are circumstances in which *prefer* may be followed by *rather than,* but that is not one of them. Normally it is followed by *to:* "We *prefer* Kuh *to* Morgenthau." However, a difficulty arises when an infinitive follows *prefer.* You cannot say, "I *prefer* to watch baseball *to* to watch movies." Here is an occasion on which *rather than* may be used despite the fact it makes for redundancy since *rather* conveys the sense of preference. It is idiomatic to say, "I *prefer* to watch baseball *rather than* to watch movies." If you don't like the redundancy, you can say, "I *prefer* watching baseball to watching movies," and all will be well.

## PREFIXES

(Be-.) How does one explain the word *behead,* which ought logically to mean put a head on just as the prefix in besmirch, beget, etc., means to add rather than take away? The answer is that the prefix *be-* has half a dozen meanings. Here are some: around, as in *beclothe;* completely, as in *becrowd;* off, as in *behead;* about, as in *bemoan;* make, as in *beknight,* and furnish with, as in *befriend.* All of which proves—if it proves anything—that we must not think of the English language in too narrow terms. It is rich and versatile.

(Bi-.) The prefix *bi-* causes more confusion in the language than you would expect from so tiny a thing. It has several meanings, all of which have something to do with two, but the one that causes confusion is the one that means "every two" or "twice a." Here's a list of common ones with the definitions parenthesized: *biannual* (twice a year), *bimonthly* (every two months in standard usage), *biweekly* (every two weeks in standard usage), *bidaily* (every two days, if there were such a word) and bilingual (operating in or proficient in two languages). It might be useful at this point to quote the usage note under the word *bimonthly* in the American Heritage Dictionary: *"Bimonthly* is rigidly restricted to the sense of once in two months, and *biweekly* to that of once in two weeks, according to 84 percent of the usage panel." The sense of "twice a" is more properly conveyed by *semi-*. Maybe it would be most helpful if in this sense we could say *bi-bi-* to that two-letter prefix.

(Re-.) Scrabble players and others are bothered about when the prefix *re-* may be hitched to a word. There seem to be no rules governing the use of the prefix and the nearest approach to a rule is the observation that the prefix is of Latin origin and therefore is most commonly attached to words of Latin derivation or to words from the Romance languages, which derive from Latin. But just to complicate matters, the prefix is sometimes hooked on to loan words that are not of Latin origin, for example, *restrengthen.* Perhaps the best rule that can be laid down is to look up the word in the nearest unabridged dictionary.

(Un-.) A news article said that "politicians expressed *unease* at the situation." There is nothing wrong with the word *unease,* but there almost is. Most other nouns are converted in the negative forms by the use of the prefix *dis-,* but obviously this one cannot be *disease,* which means something else. Actually very few nouns convert by taking the prefix *un-* unless the adjective form already has the *un-* (untidy, untidiness, for example).

## PREPOSITION AT END
Miss Thistlebottom may have told you that a preposition was a bad word to end a sentence *with.* Up to a point she may have known what she was talking *about.* But there are more exceptions to the rule than she dreamed *of.* The rule traces back to Latin, a language that most modern writers are strangers *to.* And it is a rule that can well be done away *with.* As H. W. Fowler says, "The fact is that the remarkable freedom enjoyed by English in putting its prepositions late . . . is an important element in the flexibility of the language." The people who insist on the rule do not always know *about* what they are talking. They do not know *for* what rules are. And it makes one wonder *to* what they are up.

Sometimes, it is true, placing the preposition at the end makes for a weak sentence. Example: "German is not the best language to write poetry *in.*" There the sentence ends in weakness. But in an idiomatic sentence such as, "They don't know what they are talking *about,*" the words at the end are sufficient to sustain the stress that normally falls toward the end. To paraphrase Winston Churchill, the rule about ending sentences with a preposition is nonsense *up* with which we shouldn't put.

Occasionally we run into a sentence in which the same preposition is used in two adjoining positions: "The welterweight fought hard but he was forced to give *in in* five rounds," or "He was operated *on on* April 2." Are these constructions incorrect? The answer is, no; they are simply stylistically poor. They can be improved either by the substitution of a word (*"within* five rounds") or by slight reconstructions ("On April 2 he was operated on."). In other words, that that is is often correctable.

# PREREQUISITES
*See* PERQUISITES.

# PRESENTLY
(Now or soon.) Time was when *presently* meant at the present time or now. But, according to the Oxford English Dictionary, that meaning became obsolete in literary English in the seventeenth century. The meaning from then on was soon, shortly. In the last decade or so, however, there has been a reversion to the obsolete meaning, fostered chiefly by those people who seem to think that the longer word is more impressive than the shorter one. When they could easily say *now* they prefer to say *presently.* The result has been that *presently* has become a blurred word. If the receptionist says, "The doctor is ready to see you *presently,*" who knows whether she means "Come on in" or "It will be only another hour or so"? How much better it would be if the word could be restricted to a single meaning, preferably the one that has predominated for the last few centuries. How much better it would be to avoid any possibility of ambiguity. Why not say *now* or *immediately* if that's what you mean and reserve *presently* for the sense of in a short time or before long or soon?

## PRESTIGIOUS

Much used these days, the word *prestigious* means possession of or imparting of high standing. It developed from the word *prestige*. But its original meaning was quite different. The Shorter Oxford English Dictionary defines it as meaning "practicing juggling or legerdemain; cheating; deceptive, illusory." The reason for that is that the word came from the Latin *praestigium*, meaning delusion and hence sleight of hand. But the present-day sense derives from *prestige*, which also derives from a similar Latin word that meant to bind and therefore to impress. Complicated, eh? It's current cant anyway.

## PRETENTIOUSNESS

(Thought turns into mud.) A speaker suggested more emphasis on vocational guidance and placement and on what he called "attitudinal reconditioning, particularly in terms of value structures relating to nonprofessional job opportunities." If one might essay a translation into plain English, what he seemed to be saying was, "Get them not to look down on blue-collar jobs." But note the pomposity of the quotation. Look at "attitudinal reconditioning." Look at "in terms of." Look at "value structures." Then consider how the speaker, in seeking to sound impressive, has muddied his thought. Everyone's trying to be a social scientist these days—or to sound like one. A little more windyfoggery like that and human beings won't be able to communicate with one another.

(More language pomposified.) An industrial psychologist connected with Muzak, the music distributing outfit, said in a recent speech that "among the interrelated matters of a time and place, Muzak is a thing that fits in. The things that go together, including the Muzak, are *synomorphs.*" And he added that "Muzak is *synomorphic.*" But he wasn't finished yet; he went on to say that "Muzak promotes the sharing of meaning because it *massifies* symbolism in which not few, but all, can participate." *Synomorphs,* from the Greek *syn-,* together, and *-morph,* a formed thing, obviously is designed to mean things that go together, as he said. And *massify* presumably means to spread to the masses, or something. Thus do the pretentionists wordify in the hope that they will be recognizified as scientologists, or something.

(Polysyllabification.) Take the words *preventive* and *preventative,* now interchangeable, according to most dictionaries. But the preference is definitely given to the shorter version; the longer one is usually tossed in with an "also" in front of it. A failing among not a few writers is to consider polysyllabic words always to be scholarly words and to think that length of words has some connection with breadth of intellect. So we get *experimentalize* for *experiment, administrate* for *administer, usage* for *use, service* for *serve* and *preventative* for *preventive.*

## PRETTY
How did the word *pretty* come to mean fairly or moderately? Only a partial answer is possible. *Pretty* came from the Old English *praettig,* meaning sly or tricky, but that sense was softened to mean a term of admiration, especially when applied to children. Other words, such as *cunning,* went through the same process. When *pretty* was applied to appearance it was again softened to refer to something less than beautiful. And when it was used as an adverb, as in *pretty* good, it underwent a similar softening process and came to mean something less than *very.* The word *fair* received similar treatment, so that *fairly* good does not mean *very* good. Such changes in word meanings may not be numerous, but neither are they exceptional.

## PRINCIPAL, PRINCIPLE
Many people have trouble differentiating *principal* from *principle,* and a rescue operation is about to begin. Let's start out by noting that the two words come from the same Latin root: *princeps,* meaning the first or chief. As a noun *principal* denotes a leader or a top man (or woman). As an adjective it denotes foremost or chief or highest ranking. The general idea in both noun and adjective is topmost, first-rate, A1. Hold in mind that A1 designation because that's how you're going to remember the proper spelling. The word *principal* ends in *al* and in print or typewriting *al* looks like A1. Got it? The other word, *principle,* tracing back to that Latin root meaning first, refers to the first or foundation expression of something, a fundamental truth, an elementary guide. Even if you have trouble remembering *principle,* how could you ever forget that the *principal* is not only a *pal* but also an A1 fellow?

## PRIORITY

A common phrase these days is *first priority* or sometimes *top priority*. Isn't that redundancy? Yes and no. *Priority* refers to precedence in rank or time and therefore to first or topmost position. On the other hand, it is possible to have a second *priority*, which would mean that the second in rank would become first once the topmost was disposed of. That's why the answer is yes and no.

## PROHIBIT
*See* FORBID.

## PROMISE

(Peculiar promise.) Occasionally you will hear this kind of sentence: "I *promise* you it never happened." *Promise* pertains to the future, not the past. Properly used, the word does have a future connotation. The meaning in the quoted sentence above is to assert emphatically or to give assurance and Webster's New World Dictionary correctly labels it colloquial. Why not make it, "I assure you it never happened"?

## PRONE

The adjective *prone* has at least three meanings: 1. liable or tending to; 2. inclined or willing to, and 3. lying flat, face down. The word derives from the Latin *pronus,* which means inclined, or leaning forward. Thus, the root is almost a pun; it involves the literal meaning of *inclined*—bent forward—and the derived meaning of the word: having a tendency or disposition to, leaning toward. Another postscript: *prone* used in its literal, physical sense does not mean merely lying flat; it means lying flat on one's belly. The word for lying on one's back is *supine.* And the word for just plain lying is *prevarication,* but that's something else —forget it.

## PRONOUNS

(He, she, it.) A news story about a wandering black bear cub said, "Apparently *it* had not escaped from a zoo and the police speculated *he* may have wandered into town from the hilly countryside." Two things should be noted about that sentence: first, the pronouns should be made consistent; second, as a general guide it is best not to use a personal pronoun in referring to an animal unless its sex has been established or it has a name. In this instance the bear was an *it.*

(He should watch hisself.) A TV commentator was talking about a guest of honor at a dinner and said, "He deserves a banquet because he has given a lot of *hisself.*" *Hisself* does appear in two dictionaries, but both label it substandard. The proper form is, of course, *himself.* The other form conceivably could be used as two words, as in, "He put *his self* above his party." Quite irrelevantly, the *self* words have a mysterious peculiarity in that four of them have the prefix in the objective case *(himself, herself, itself* and *themselves),* while three of them have it in the possessive case *(myself, yourself* and *ourselves).* And don't ask why.

(It's me.) When a columnist apologized for having written, "That picture is *me,*" a professor of English wrote a letter indicating that maybe *me* wasn't wrong after all. He wrote: "With *I* and *me* two separate aspects of personality seem to be involved: one, the *I* of individuality (you as a person) and two, the *me* (you as an object distinct from your personality)." The distinction he was making is a subtle one—indeed, too subtle for a speaker to decide on the spur of the moment. According to strict grammatical rules, the pronoun following a copulative, or linking, verb such as *is* should be in the nominative case: "That picture is *I.*" But, as Fowler says in *Modern English Usage,* "The use of *me* in colloquialisms such as 'It's *me*' and 'It wasn't *me*' is perhaps the only successful attack made by *me* on *I.*" The Evanses in *A Dictionary of Contemporary American Usage* go even further and say, "In natural, well-bred English, *me* and not *I* is the form of the pronoun used after any verb, even the verb *to be.*" That statement may go too far, but there can be no doubt that in widespread usage "It's *me*" is common even among educated people. "It's *I*" is beginning to sound prissy and affected these days. (*See* "I" AND "ME" PHOBIAS.)

(Confusing references.) The following paragraph from a news article is an example of how to confuse a reader by using pronouns without clear antecedents: "Bertran said *she* has accompanied Mills to the restaurant on several occasions in the three months that *he* has been manager of the night club. She was with *him* on Sunday night, *he* said." Since no *she* had been mentioned later than the third paragraph ahead of the one quoted, some readers might think that the *she* referred to Bertran, which it doesn't. Next, the *he* could be taken to refer to Mills, which would be wrong. Then the *him* and the *he* toward the end refer to two different persons. A frequently offered guide is that a pronoun has an affinity for the nearest noun, but that is not invariably true. The best guide is to reread what has been written and be sure that no ambiguity is possible.

(Sexless word needed.) There is a tendency to support the use of the plural pronoun *they* or *their* after a singular antecedent; e.g., *"Everyone* rose to *their* feet." At least it is one way to handle the problem of the lack in English of a sexless pronoun. The Oxford English Dictionary lists half a dozen well-known English writers who used *they* or *their* in similar locutions. Without doubt the use of those pronouns is the popular and conversational solution to the problem, but also without doubt that solution, as Fowler says in *Modern English Usage,* is one that "sets the literary man's teeth on edge." Fowler goes on to ask, "Have the patrons of *they,* etc., made up their minds yet between 'Everyone *was* blowing their noses (or nose)' and 'Everyone *were* blowing their noses'?" The advice here is either to reconstruct the sentence to duck the problem or to use *him* or *his,* ignoring the masculinity of such pronouns, which is only nominal anyway. In any event, everyone should write whatever she thinks is best.

Pronouns, by the way, tend to change over the centuries so perhaps the word *they* someday will become a legitimate singular. The pronoun *you* originally was only a plural word, the objective form of *ye,* which was exclusively plural. Maybe that word will eventually become a precedent. (*See* SEX AND LANGUAGE.)

## PROOF
If your gin is labeled 86 *proof* in the United States that means it contains 43 percent alcohol by volume; the number that indicates alcoholic strength is double the percentage of alcohol. The term *proof* relates to the arbitrary standard of an alcoholic liquor called *proof spirit,* which contains 50 percent alcohol by volume.

## PROPER NAMES (MADE PROPER)

A sign outside the home of John Doe reads, *The Does,* but we have seen signs recently that read, *The Doe's.* The second is not proper. Two uses *are* proper: one, *The Does* to indicate that the people who live in that house or trailer are the Does, and two, *The Does'* denoting that the home belongs to the Does, that is, an apostrophe is included after the plural to indicate possession. And the Does should be glad they *are not the Aristophaneses.* (*See* APOSTROPHES.)

## PROSTHESIS

*See* NICKNAME and NONCE.

## PROVED, PROVEN

The verb *prove* has two participial forms—*proved* and *proven*—but in most situations *proved* is used, as in, "He has proved his value to the company." The form *proven* is used as an attributive adjective (ahead of a noun) and particularly in certain technical locutions, such as "a *proven* oil field."

## PROVIDE

It is on record that Shakespeare used *provide to* once in *Two Gentlemen of Verona,* in which Thurio says, "You must *provide to* bottom it on me." It is doubtful whether William S. or any other writer has used that combination in that way since, so let's forget it. Three other uses are all common and simply depend on meaning. *Provide for* (or against) means to prepare for (or against) some contingency: "Social Security *provides for* one's old age." *Provide with* means to furnish with or equip with: "He *provided* his children *with* all the clothing they needed." You could make that one read, "He *provided* clothing *to* his children." Finally, *provide* can be used by itself in the sense of stipulate: "The will *provides* that the widow is to get the entire estate." It is also possible to use *provide* unattached in a sentence such as, "The Lord will provide," but that is simply an ellipsis; a noun or a phrase has been omitted after *provide* and is understood.

## PROVIDED, PROVIDING

If, like many of us, you had Miss Thistlebottom as your grammar teacher, she probably told you never to use *providing* as a conjunction, but always to use *provided*. Miss Thistlebottom's reasoning probably was that *provided* is an elliptical form of "it being *provided,*" whereas you can't say that about *providing*. But you can't say it about *supposing* either, yet no one ever objects to that word. *Provided* and *providing* may be used interchangeably.

The only caution to be sounded about either *provided* or *providing* is that it cannot always be used as a synonym for *if;* both words imply a stipulation of some kind. For instance you could properly say, "He will not get into trouble *provided* he takes the normal precautions," but you should not say, "He would not have got into trouble *provided* he had taken the normal precautions."

## PUBLICITY, NOTORIETY
(Public notice.) Although *publicity* and *notoriety* have something in common, they are by no means synonymous. What they have in common is the condition of being known to the public. But whereas *publicity* is often sought for and desirable, *notoriety* is seldom desired. *Notoriety* is a condition of widely known but unfavorable publicity, and who wants that?

## PUNCTUATION
Punctuation marks guide us in reading. They tell us when to slow down and when to stop and sometimes indicate the nature of the road ahead. When were such signs invented and were they in existence in ancient times? In the earliest forms of writing the letters simply ran on and on without even spaces between words. Gradually words were separated by spaces. Later punctuation points were introduced and Aldus Manutius (1450–1515), an Italian printer who devised the italic form of type, got up a code of punctuation. (*See* APOSTROPHES; COLONS; COMMAS; HYPHENS; QUESTION MARKS; QUOTATIONS; SEMICOLONS.)

## PURPORT
A strange word this. Nominally an active verb, *purport* has the sense of a passive verb—the sense of "is supposed, or is represented, to be." Therefore it may not properly be used in the passive voice. The following newspaper sentence is improper: "The documents were *purported* by the C.I.A. agent to have been

stolen." To make matters more complicated, the subject of *purport* may not be a person: If that sentence were turned into the active voice—"The C.I.A. agent *purported* the documents to have been stolen"—the subject would be a person and the sentence would be improper on that ground. Two remedies are possible. One is to make the sentence read, "Papers *purporting* to be stolen were shown by the C.I.A. agent." The other is to change the verb altogether: "The documents were alleged by the C.I.A. agent to have been stolen."

## PUTTING ON THE DOG

Whence comes this expression? Dictionaries are no help, as is frequently the case when one tries to find the origin of slang phrases. Dictionaries can tell you the derivation of a normal word that came into use three centuries ago but not of a slang word that appeared three years ago. In this instance Bergen Evans, in his book *Comfortable Words,* comes to the rescue. The expression "putting on the dog," he says, originated about 1870 as college slang and probably referred to men's high stiff collars, women's diamond chokers and military officers' heavily braided collars, all of which were referred to as "dog collars." And since all were used on formal occasions, "putting on the dog" would mean preparing for such an occasion and dressing with pretentious splendor.

# Q

## QUA

It was in a Scrabble game that we first used the word *qua*. It means as, or in the capacity of or in the character of. Example of its use: "The physician *qua* friend advised the hard-working broker to take it easy." That means that the physician was speaking in the capacity of a friend rather than as a doctor. The word is an adverb and is a rare, show-off word.

## QUALITY

The sentence read, *"Quality* merchandise is offered by our shop on Main Street," and it prompts two questions. One concerns the meaning of the word *quality.* It can be assumed that high *quality* is meant in the sentence. The primary meaning of the word *quality* concerns the characteristics that make something what it is, but a secondary meaning concerns the attributes of excellence of a thing. The second question is whether it is proper to use the noun *quality* as an adjective in the phrase *"quality merchandise."* The answer to that one is yes. From time immemorial nouns have been pressed into service as adjectives, giving us such now familiar terms as *railroad, law school, mountain top* and *paperback.* The thing to watch out for is an awkward noun pile-up, such as *submarine missile test ban agreement,* which may be necessary in newspaper headlines but is clumsy in ordinary writing.

## QUESTION MARKS

In a sentence such as, "How is your sore throat?" there is no doubt that a question mark belongs at its end. But how about such sentences as, "May we have the pleasure of hearing from you soon," or "Would you please send us a duplicate copy of that invoice." Maxwell Nurnberg supplies the replies succinctly in his paperback book, *Punctuation Pointers,* where he says, "We do not use the question mark when we are merely making a request or when we expect no answer." In the first of the above sentences no answer is expected and in the second the writer is merely making a request. Therefore, use no interrogation mark in either instance.

## QUOTATION MARKS

(They're everywhere.) The growing misuse of quotation marks is amazing. There can be no doubt that letters and sign painters tend to go wild in their use of those inverted commas. They are not content to let the sign in the shop window say, SALE—BARGAINS; they make it say, SALE—"BARGAINS." All that those quotation marks do is to cause a literate person to think that maybe they are not bargains after all. Then you will see one that says, *Special "Mother's Day" Dinner,* or even one that says, *"No Trespassing."* What's the point of the quotes in those signs? The proper uses of quotation marks are few: to enclose the exact words of another that are being cited; to set off titles of books, plays and the like; to mark a word that is being used in an unusual way or is being downgraded, and sometimes to indicate a piece of jargon that has not come into widespread use.

(How to use them.) American practice is to use double quotation marks before and after quoted words, phrases or sentences and single quotation marks for quotations within quotations. For example: The Senator said, "I think the President used 'expletive deleted' too often." (It may be noted that the British often reverse the American practice in the use of double and single quotes.) A question that usually arises with quotation marks is whether you put other punctuation marks inside them or outside. There is no rule, but most style authorities prescribe that the period and the comma should be placed inside the quotes and the colon and semicolon outside. The placement of question marks and exclamation points depends on the meaning. Examples: *The audience cried, "Bravo!" Don't you dare tell me again "all is lost"! "Why do you call some educators 'elitists'?" he asked. Have you read "The Perils of Smoking"?* Yes, the use of quotes is a bit complicated.

(Stops and quotes.) In a sentence that ends with a quotation where should the period go—outside the quotation marks or inside? It depends on where you are. If you are in Britain, you should follow the British practice and write your sentence as follows: *He said, "I am going to have a drink".* However, if you are in the United States, you should follow the American practice and write: *He said, "I am going to have a drink."* The British practice is more logical since the period in such an instance marks the end of the sentence rather than the end of the quote. Thus the American practice does not make perfect. But it is so close to a rule on this side of the Atlantic that you had better follow it.

# R

## R.S.V.P.

The only odd thing about *R.S.V.P.* is that there was once a university professor who did not know what it meant. For his benefit let it be known that the initials are an abbreviation of the French phrase *répondez s'il vous plaît,* meaning reply, please.

## RACK

*See* WRACK.

## RAILROAD TALK

The terms *highballing, balling the jack* and *gandy dancing* are all railroad terms. A *highball* was an early railroad signal calling for high speed. It consisted of a metal globe raised to the crossarm of a pole. From that piece of railroad lingo came the phrase *balling the jack,* meaning to work or operate rapidly. (*Jack* at one time meant a locomotive or train.) *Gandy dancing* was a little harder to track down and is related to the Gandy Manufacturing Co. of Chicago, which made tools for railroad section hands. It refers to the workers who lay tracks, dig ditches and do similar work and it derived from the dancelike movements of such workers. So there you have three track terms that have been tracked down. (*See* BASEBALL TALK; LEGAL LINGO.)

## RAP

At the height of the House Judiciary Committee's debate a few years back on the articles of impeachment some Republican Congressmen decided to hold what they called *rap sessions* on the

187

subject. The phrase *rap session* has been with us for several years and it means simply a discussion by a group. It derives from *rap*, a slang word for talk or converse. But the origin of *rap*, like the origins of most slang terms, is a mystery. One reference book suggests it may derive from *rapport* and another thinks it may come from *repartee*. If the two reference works don't mind the comment, both theories sound unlikely, chiefly because at the low level at which *rap* apparently originated both those words are probably unknown. A better guess—but only a guess—is that the slang word derives from one of the standard meanings of *rap*, to make a sharp utterance, as in, "The captain rapped out a command."

## RATHER
Sometimes *rather* presents a minor problem. Example: "The group is more interested in experimenting with recipes rather than in pursuing rare specimens." Technically *rather* is an adverb in the comparative degree and since the comparative *more* has already been introduced into the sentence the *rather* becomes redundant and should be removed. Right? Rather!

## RATHER THAN
*See* PREFER.

## RAUNCHY
As I have noted before, it has always seemed odd to me that etymologists can trace back the derivation of an ordinary word three centuries and lots more, but often cannot trace back the origin of a slang word even three decades and sometimes not even three years. A common slang word today is *raunchy*, meaning earthy or openly sexual. In the sense of sloppy or careless one slang dictionary dates it to 1939 and in the sense of dirty or ugly to 1950, but the book offers no clue to the origin of the word. Nor does any other dictionary at this writing.

## REASON . . . IS BECAUSE
What about the use of those two terms together in a sentence? Miss Thistlebottom was prickly about that and she was right in this instance. Here is an example of the disapproved construction: "The *reason* many voters stayed at home was *because* a heavy

cold rain fell all day long." When you are alerted to the fact that the meaning of *because* is *for the reason that* it becomes obvious that the same thing is being said twice; the construction involves a redundancy. There are two ways out: Either strike out *the reason* and the *was* ahead of *because* or substitute *that* for *because*. (*See* REDUNDANCY.)

## RECIPE, RECEIPT
*Recipe* and *receipt* derive from the same Latin root: *recipere,* with the general meaning of receive. And, strangely enough, they at one time denoted about the same thing, but today neither of them usually denotes that thing. A *recipe* used to be what is now a medical prescription and a *receipt* meant the same thing and in addition what we now refer to as a *recipe*—a formula in cooking. In modern times they have gone their separate ways, the word *receipt* picking up additional meanings as it went along.

## REDUNDANCY
(Too many words.) There are differences among the words *pleonasm, tautology, redundancy* and *verbosity,* but let's first examine the sameness of the words: In general, they all mean you talk too much. *Pleonasm* refers to the use of a word or words that could be omitted without altering the meaning ("true facts"). *Tautology* means repetition in different words ("Actually and in fact it has been a record rainfall"). *Redundancy* calls attention to the use of more words than are needed ("I don't need it, I have no use for it"). *Verbosity* designates wordiness ("He talks too much, he never stops, he goes on and on, he speaks endlessly"). As is evident, the differences among those words are not great. And ironically, of the words in English that denote a lot of words there are a lot of words. In addition to the four just mentioned there are *prolixity, diffuseness, verbiage, circumlocution* and *periphrasis.* To say nothing of *shut up.*

(Examples.) The phrase *each and every one* makes us wince. Its originator could have been a lawyer since the legal profession tends to say things twice or thrice either for emphasis or to be pompous or to be sure no loophole has been left open. Think, for example, of *null and void* or *without let or hindrance* or *aid and abet* or *ways and means.* But laymen, too, have been responsible for such redundant clichés. Here are a dozen that everybody has heard—and heard far too many times: *one and only, bits and pieces, you and you alone, part and parcel, betwixt and between, upright and honest, kith and kin, jot or tittle, lo and behold, fair and square, leaps and bounds, rack and ruin.* And there are lots more. Really and truly. (*See* LEGAL LINGO.)

(Repetition record.) Familiar-sounding phrases sometimes lead people into uttering meaningless verbiage and outright repetition. Here is a remark by a public official that must set an all-time record for tautology in a single sentence: "I have not in fact done anything wrong in terms of actual wrongdoing of any sort by my conduct." What does "by my conduct" add to the single word "done"? What does "actual wrongdoing" add to "wrong"? What does "of any sort" add to "anything"? What do the phrases "in fact" and "in terms of" contribute to the sentence? What the official was saying, in short, was, "I have not done anything wrong," and in short was the better way to say it. (*See* TAUTOLOGY; PLEONASM.)

## REDUPLICATION
*See* FIB; FUDDY-DUDDY.

## REGARDLESS, IRREGARDLESS
(Without regard to lexicology.) How about the word *irregardless?* So many people use it that some wonder whether it has become proper. Flatly, no. It is a redundant word—that is, repetitious— since the negative suffix *-less* is duplicated by the negative prefix *ir-*. Every dictionary characterizes it as erroneous or nonstandard, though it is sometimes used humorously. The Random House Dictionary says that the word does "creep into the speech of good English speakers, perhaps as a result of attempting greater emphasis." Strike out the words "good English" and substitute "illiterate."

## RELUCTANT
*See* RETICENT.

## REPLICA
*See* COPY.

**REPLY**
*See* ANSWER.

**REPRESENTATIVE**
Even a dignified word like *representative* is sometimes used loosely. Sportswriters and athletic directors speak of sending the "most *representative*" team in the league to the Rose Bowl game. Undoubtedly what they mean is the best team capable of representing the league. But *representative* has the meaning of typical or being an example of a kind of thing. Thus the users of that word were unintentionally advocating the sending of the most nearly average team in the league, rather than the best team. Not the most heinous offense to the language perhaps, but if we all used words with precision maybe we'd know what we were talking about.

**RESPECTIVE(LY)**
Sometimes one of these words is useful. For example: "Simon and Pinter write comedies and serious plays *respectively.*" Without *respectively* the reader would be justified in assuming either that they collaborated or that each wrote both kinds. On the other hand, more often one of the words is excess baggage, as in, "Manhattan Island borders on three rivers—the Hudson, the East and the Harlem *respectively.*" There the word *respectively* tells us nothing and should be dropped. Even when the word is used properly the user should re-examine what he has written to see if the sentence could not be reworded to eliminate it. The reason is that it compels the reader to go back and do a little job of matching, and anything that avoids making the reader retrace his steps is an aid to swifter and easier comprehension. Take that first example. Wouldn't it be simpler to write, "Simon writes comedies and Pinter writes serious plays"? Surely that discloses their *respective* fields of drama clearly, doesn't it?

**RESTIVE, RESTLESS**
(Stubborn misuse.) If *restive* meant the same thing as *restless,* who would need it? Despite widespread misuse, it doesn't mean the same thing. *Restless* describes a condition of impatient activity, of inability to relax, of fidgetiness. *Restive,* which comes from the Old French, means unruly, resistive, stubborn, balky. Thus:

"The crowd became *restless* when the show was delayed because a *restive* horse shied away from the hurdles."

## RETICENT, RELUCTANT

Here is a misuse of *reticent:* "Every time I go to church or to a meeting of any kind I wonder why so many of us are *reticent* to go up front." That appeared in a newspaper column, the writer of which should have known better. *Reticent* means disinclined to speak. The word the columnist undoubtedly had in mind was *reluctant,* which means averse or unwilling.

## RETORT

*See* ANSWER.

## RIGHT/LEFT

One thing that has long fascinated your host is how he would define *right* (or *left*) if he were writing a dictionary. A couple of dictionaries tell you that it relates to the hand that is the stronger or the side of the more-used hand (but how about the lefties?); another says it pertains to the side of the body on which the liver is situated (that's a big help). A very recent dictionary says *right* designates the side of the body that is toward the *south* when one faces the sunrise. Fine. So let's look up *south* in that same dictionary. Here's what it says: "The general direction to the *right* of sunrise." In short, the dope who doesn't know anything and who is looking up *right* finds that *right* means *south* and that *south* means *right.* That brings us to an important point worth noting: No dictionary or any other basic, elementary book should define two words in terms of each other. The phrase that designates that type of circling back (a phrase that seems to be findable in only one word book, Webster's unabridged, third edition) is *circulus in definiendo,* meaning a vicious circle in definition.

So you want to know how your host would define *right* if he were getting out a dictionary? All right: it is the side opposite the heart side or opposite the side to which the heart's apex points. Right?

# S

## SAME AS; JUST LIKE
(Similar but not identical.) A question fired at this editor is whether *the same as* and *just like* are interchangeable. The answer is no. The phrase *the same as* conveys the sense of identicalness, whereas *just like* conveys the sense of closely similar. You might say that frozen grapefruit juice is *just like* freshly squeezed grapefruit juice, but you wouldn't say it is *the same as* the freshly squeezed juice; it's not identical with the fresh drink.

## SANCTION
The noun *sanction* is, in a way, two-faced. On the one face it means permission or approval to do something ("She had the *sanction* of her parents for living outside the dormitory"). On the other face it means, especially in the language of diplomacy and the United Nations, a penalty or coercive action to prevent the doing of something ("The Security Council approved *sanctions* against South Africa"). At latest reports, however, nobody has complained of being confused about the word.

## SCAN
*Scan* is another *two-faced word.* In its primary meaning it is synonymous with *scrutinize:* to examine closely and carefully. In its prevalent modern use it means almost the opposite: to view hastily and superficially, as to *scan* the headlines. Why the change? No one seems to know. It may be that *scan* is a quick-sounding word—particularly as contrasted with the ponderous-

sounding *scrutinize*—so that people came to believe it had something to do with speed.

## SCAPEGOAT

*Scapegoat* was coined by William Tyndale, a Bible translator, in the sixteenth century and apparently involved some confusion of two Hebrew words, one of which had something to do with a goat. It was a goat over which the high priest confessed the people's sins on the Day of Atonement and which he then allowed to escape into the wilderness. From that *scapegoat* comes today's sense of someone or something that gets the blame for someone else's mistakes. The *scapegoat* was made the *goat* of the sinners, and that shortened form is also in use today.

## SCARCELY

*See* HARDLY.

## SCHOOL

The teacher shouldn't let the kids in on this, but underlying the word *school* is the idea of leisure—in fact, the word comes from the Greek word *schole,* meaning leisure. The leisure referred to was employed in discussion, teaching and learning, and that's what it should be used for today.

## SCOTCH

(The Scottish drink Scotch.) The term *Scottish* has replaced *Scotch* and *Scots* in Scotland's usage and is the preferred term also in American and British formal literary usage. Likewise *Scotsman* or *Scot* is preferred in the homeland to *Scotchman.* However, *Scotch* is retained in some combinations such as *Scotch* tweed and, of course, *Scotch* whisky.

## -SELF WORDS

*Himself, herself* and like words are properly used for two purposes: for emphasis ("She repaired the roof *herself*") and for turning the action back on the grammatical subject ("She dressed *herself* quickly"). In the latter sense such a word is called a reflexive pronoun. In other situations the use of the *-self* words in place of the simple pronoun *he* or *she* is considered improper.

Thus, in the sentence, "He said his wife and *himself* would attend the dinner," the pronoun should be changed to *he*. An Irish dialectal usage in which, for example, the wife says, *"Himself* has gone to the soccer game," is perhaps amusing but off the proper beaten track.

Lately one notices that the word *myself* is being used as a substitute for *me,* and gradually it is being used as a substitute for *I*. It is not quite correct to say, "Joe gave a book to my brother and *myself,"* or, worse, "My brother and *myself* went to the football game." These misuses are quite common. They seem to be caused by an uncertainty bordering on fear concerning the words *me* and *I*. In the "book" sentence above the pronoun is the object of the preposition *to* and therefore should be *me*. In the "football game" sentence the pronoun is the subject of the verb *went* and therefore should be *I*. (*See* "I" AND "ME" PHOBIAS.)

## SELF-DESTRUCT

(New and needless.) An editorial about New York City in *The New York Times* bore the title of *"Self-Destructing* City." Why *self-destructing;* why not *self-destroying?* The word *destruct* originated with the missile men as a back-formation from *destruction* (that is, a made-up word that a real word is supposed to derive from) and it may have had a limited legitimate use in the missile field to denote deliberate destruction rather than destruction by accident or by an enemy. But it's hard to see what purpose it serves outside that limited field.

## SELF(-ISH)

A self-propelled vehicle is one that propels itself and a self-pollinated flower is one that has been pollinated by itself. Is a self-addressed envelope one that has been addressed by itself? Without taking the question too seriously, we should point out that *self-* does not mean only by itself or of itself; it can also mean to itself or to oneself. Consequently that envelope need not take pen in hand. However, that question borders on one that is more meaningful: There are several words containing *self-* that would be better off without the prefix, such as *self-opinionated, self-conceited, self-composed.* And then there is one that is a favorite

of newspapermen and is a glaring redundancy: *self-confessed.*
Only the person who is confessing can confess, so why the *self-?*
Forget it.

## SEMICOLON
There seems to be reluctance to use the semicolon, though it is
a useful piece of punctuation. One place where it is definitely
needful is in what is termed a run-on sentence: "The teacher is
responsible for classroom discipline, if there is to be learning
there must be order." The comma there does not produce
enough separation of the different grammatical structures or a
long enough stop, and a period might cause too long a stop.
Abraham Lincoln was aware of the value of the semicolon. We
are indebted to Richard Hanser of Mamaroneck, New York, for
passing along a quotation from a letter Lincoln wrote to Noah
Brooks in 1864: "With educated people, I suppose, punctuation
is a matter of rule; with me it is a matter of feeling. But I must
say I have a great respect for the semicolon; it's a useful little
chap."

## SENSUAL, SENSUOUS
(Coming to our senses.) The words *sensual* and *sensuous* both
have something to do with the pleasures of sensation, but they
have quite different meanings. *Sensual,* the coarser of the two,
applies to preoccupation with the bodily senses and has over-
tones of lewdness. *Sensuous* applies to enjoyment produced by
appeal to the senses. Thus, a *sensuous* piece of art might provide
*sensual* desires.

## SENTENCES
(Fragments thereof.) Miss Thistlebottom laid down a rule that
"a sentence is a group of words containing a verb and its subject
and expressing a complete thought." When we and our school-
mates wrote compositions they often were returned with the
marking "Inc" in the margin, meaning that a sentence was incomplete. Other teachers write in the margin "frag," meaning
sentence fragment, for the same purpose. The reproof usually
comes when a pupil writes something like this: "My parents
scolded me for having dirty hands. And my brother, too." By
schoolroom standards those final four words are not a sentence;

they are a sentence fragment. For most pupils—indeed, for most people—those standards are good to follow.

But modern usage permits sentence fragments for emphasis, for dramatic effect or for expressing a comment—in general, for putting life into the written word by making it akin to the spoken word. Here is an example from an ad: "Tell your travel agent where in the world you want to go. How much you can spend. And how long you can get away." Two words of caution are necessary, however. First, a writer should know what he is about and second, he should not overdo the sentence fragment; it should be used sparingly. If he obeys those two cautions, he may substitute for Miss Thistlebottom's definition of a sentence the one that appears in the Oxford English Dictionary: "In popular use often such a portion of a composition or utterance as extends from one full stop to another."

(Run-on types.) Sentences that contain two or more independent clauses, which are in effect sentences in themselves, should contain, according to some textbooks, adequate punctuation between the clauses. An example of such a sentence without punctuation would be, "Darkness fell bitter cold came on I was hungry." Even if one *and* were inserted after *fell* and another after *on,* those textbooks would prescribe a comma before each *and* in what they call a run-on sentence. My view is that commas are not necessary if *and* is inserted twice in that simple a sentence, but they might be advisable in a longer, more complicated one. Likewise a comma is often advisable before a *but* because that word tends to change the direction of the sentence. If two independent clauses in the same sentence are not joined by a conjunction, a comma is not sufficient and a semicolon is indicated. Example: "He gave the beggar a $5 bill; that's the kind of man he was." Run-on sentences present a situation in which it is best not to lay down rules. Rather the writer should decide how independent the clauses are, how long the pauses should be.

## SERENDIPITY
(Pure luck.) Some people seem to have the happy faculty of slipping into a puddle of mud and finding a bag of gold at the bottom of it. Such an aptitude is called *serendipity.* The word was

coined by Horace Walpole in the eighteenth century in allusion to a Persian fairy tale, "The Three Princes of Serendip," about princes who had an aptitude for stumbling on those bags of gold or other treasures. Their discoveries were *serendipitous.*

## SET, SIT

A Southern judge believes it is correct to say that a house *sets* upon certain acreage. The judge's case is denied without appeal. *Set* is almost exclusively a transitive verb—that is, conveying action from the subject to the predicate. You *set* the stage, you *set* a pencil on the desk, you *set* your hair. There are a few exceptions: the sun *sets,* the concrete *sets* and the hen *sets.* But that house doesn't *set* on the acreage, it *sits* there. Sorry to have to reverse you, judge.

## SEX AND LANGUAGE

(Another kind of man.) A recent news article began this way: "The rape of a *freshman woman* . . ." That phrase is mighty clumsy. Of course, the word *rape* would permit, in this instance, omission of *woman.* But suppose the story were about a mugging or a robbery and the sex of the victim had to be indicated, what could be done? *Freshwoman? Freshperson woman? Frosh woman?* All are pretty ridiculous. The only solution seems to be the lengthy phrase *first-year woman student.* Maybe all women should skip the first year of college.

(Dear—what?) Some women are concerned about what salutation to use on a business letter. *Dear Sir,* they think, is inappropriate, *To Whom It May Concern* is too verbose and *Greetings* suggests induction. Of course, there is always *Dear Friend* if you don't mind having your letter tossed into the wastebasket unread. Then there is *Dear Corporation,* unless the recipient has a bay window. But how about *Dear Addressee,* which is about as insipid and noncommittal as anything anyone could dream up? All right, now let's worry about the *Dear;* isn't that a little too sexy?

(Feminine Ms-take.) All hail, women's movement! Women want equality and they should have it. But when some keep trying to popularize the coined honorific *Ms.* to apply to all classes of women—single, married, divorced, widowed—they are Ms-guided. They wish to be on a par with men, for whom the title *Mr.* covers all categories, but their approach is wrong. They should get on a par by doing something to the masculine title, not to their own.

From a linguistic point of view, the deplorable tendency in popular language these days is toward ambiguity and fuzziness, and adoption of the *Ms.* would be another step in that direction. What the women should agitate for is greater specificity in the masculine titles to match theirs. After all, a woman has a right to know whether the chap who is making a pass at her is married or single or what. Therefore let's have more titles for men. The titles shouldn't be hard to come by. For instance: for a married man *Mr.*, for a bachelor *Bar* (which would be all right provided his first name wasn't Mitzvah) and for a widower *Wow.* In short, the women's slogan should be, "Make the honorific/More, not less, specific."

(Wowom, wow.) In a "news release," the reason for which is neither disclosed nor apparent, Temple University said that Professor James F. Adams, chairman of the university's department of counselor education and counseling psychology, believed that the English language was far behind the times of the women's liberation movement. "Take a look at Webster's dictionary," said the professor, "and you'll be amazed at the mass of words that discriminate against the female." He suggested a basic reformation by indicating the gender of the word through substituting *wom* for *man* and he listed some thirty examples of what he had in mind. Four or five ought to give you the idea without boring you too much: Dr. Adams suggested changing *manic* into *womic, manicure* into *womicure, manifest* into *womifest, manure* into *womure* and *manuscript* into *womuscript.* One point the professor overlooked was mentioned earlier by your host. Every *woman* embraces a *man* in the very composition of the word and therefore a start might be made by getting rid of the word *woman.* The thought that was thrown out here was to call one of those lovely creatures a *woperson.* Dr. Adams obviously is throwing out the idea that she should be called a *wowom.* Both ideas are all right just so long as they are thrown out.

## SHALL, WILL

(A use for shall.) Miss Thistlebottom taught you that to express simple futurity *shall* should be used in the first person and *will* in the second and third persons, whereas to express determination or emphasis that order should be reversed. However, that rule has largely vanished and *will* has just about taken over in declarative sentences. There are some exceptions and legal language provides a few. For example, a New York law states: "Whenever in his judgment the public interest requires it, the Attorney General may, with the approval of the Governor, and when directed by the Governor, *shall* inquire into matters concerning public peace, public safety and public justice." As the Attorney General remarked when that law came to public notice recently, *"Shall* is a very strong word." It is especially strong in the quoted law because of its contrast with the word *may.*

## SHAMBLES

Sentence from a news article: "At the school, faculty meetings are disorganized and record-keeping is in a *shambles."* Basically and originally *shambles* meant a bench where meat is sold, but it was broadened to mean a slaughterhouse, then a scene of slaughter or carnage and then a scene of great destruction or wreckage. More recently writers searching out the lurid word have applied *shambles* to mere confusion or turmoil. Thus the word has lost much of its power. It would be well to tighten up on its use and keep it strong, though that may be a lost cause. Incidentally, the use of the preposition *in* ahead of it is not usual or idiomatic.

## SHOP (AT)

Is it wrong to use *shop* as a transitive verb, as in *"shop* Jones's Knickknacks Store" if you need a knickknack? That use of *shop* is, to be sure, a modern innovation, although the use of the word as a transitive verb is not; it was used long, long ago in British informal speech to mean to arrest or to inform on or betray. More recently it has come into good colloquial usage in the sense of visiting a store to examine what it has to offer. The more common use of the word in the phrase *shop at* probably made some people's hair curl when it was first introduced, but it became standard. There is no reason to believe that the more economical *"shop* Jones's" will not become standard, too, ere long.

## SHORT SHRIFT

To *make short shrift* means to dispose of something quickly, and the phrase dates back to medieval times. A condemned person was granted a brief time to confess his sins and receive absolution before he was dropped with the rope around his neck. *Shrift,* which comes from Old English, refers to the confession and absolution ceremony.

## SHOT DEAD

A newspaper editor asked us about the phrase *shot dead.* He observed that we often read that "a store owner was *shot dead* by a hold-up man," though we never read that anyone was *beaten dead* or *stabbed dead,* but rather that he was *beaten to death* or *stabbed to death.* The phrase *shot dead* is quite proper. There is a subtle difference between *beaten to death* or *stabbed to death* and *shot dead.* The difference is one of time. In a beating or a stabbing it normally takes a bit of effort and a bit of time before death occurs, but in a shooting, unless the gunman is a bad marksman, one or two quick shots do the trick. In other words, *to death,* which means *until death,* suggests a somewhat more prolonged process. Of course, this distinction does not rule out the phrase *shot to death,* though one old-time editor used to insist that it not be written unless the death resulted from repeated firings. If the distinction does not suit you, you can always say that the store owner was fatally beaten, fatally stabbed or fatally shot, poor fellow.

## SHOWED VS. SHOWN

The past tense of *show* is *showed,* and no one disputes that. The past participle, however, raises a question of usage. A news article contained this sentence: "The marshal was asked in the interview whether the Secretary had *showed* him a copy of the agreement." People in the know would class that use of *showed* as a rarity and would favor making it *shown.* In the passive voice *shown* is mandatory: "The marshal was *shown* (not *showed*) a copy of the agreement."

## SIC

That little word *sic* is a Latin word meaning thus or just so. It is normally enclosed in brackets and inserted into quoted matter to indicate that the preceding word or words, mistaken though they may be, were just that way in the original. Thus the word *sic* gets the quoter off the hook and leaves the quote on it.

## SIMILES: TRITE AND BRIGHT

We all use similes frequently in both speech and writing. A simile, as you know, is a comparison beginning with *as* or *like;* for example, *as American as apple pie.* That is an example of a trite one and there are dozens and dozens of them ranging from *as bald as a billiard ball* to *as white as a sheet.* They are everyday tools of conversation and it would be futile and perhaps undesirable to try to get rid of them. Similes, even trite ones, often add a touch of color to everyday speech. But the eloquent speaker who can come up with original ones as easily as rolling over in bed or the imaginative writer who can coin them as quickly as your landlord sends his rent bill can often brighten a dull subject. In general be bright, not trite.

## SIMPATICO

(Loan word that's not alone.) From the Italian, the English language has taken over *simpatico,* and a versatile term it is. Some fifty meanings have attached themselves to *simpatico.* Space does not permit listing them all, but they range from *amiable* and *amicable* through *benignant* and *brotherly, compatible* and *companionable, delightful* and *devoted, enchanting* and *engaging* and lots more, to *understanding, winning* and *winsome.* Of course, not all of them are precise definitions of the word, but they do convey its flavor. With a complement like that, no wonder the word is complimentary.

## SINCE

This is a word that occasionally produces a grammatical error, as in the following sentence: "Since the Sinai war in 1956, Egypt took the position that guerrilla raids were counterproductive." *Since* means from then until now, and that calls for what is termed the present perfect tense ("has taken"). The present perfect represents an action at an indefinite time up to, and perhaps including, the present.

## SINGULAR CONCEPTS
Do spectators at a thrilling auto race hold their *breaths* or their *breath?* Do Japanese students live in this country to complete their *educations* or their *education?* Logically, since the spectators and the students have individual noses, shirts and friends, you'd expect them to hold their *breaths* or complete their *educations.* That's the logic of it, but it's not the idiom of it. Idiomatically the noun applying to more than one person remains in the singular when (a) it represents a quality or thing possessed in common ("The audience's *curiosity* was aroused"); or (b) it is an abstraction ("The judges applied their *reason* to the problem"), or (c) it is a figurative word ("All ten children had *a sweet tooth*"). Occasionally there is a choice of a singular or a plural noun: "The men were held *prisoner*" (abstract) or "as prisoners" (concrete). But that kind of choice is an exception to the general—quite general—rule. (*See* AGREEMENT.)

## SLANG
Some prissy, pedantic persons seem to have almost an innate aversion to slang. But, as John Moore points out in *You English Words,* those who deplore some current piece of slang are wasting their breath. "It is odds on any given word being forgotten in a season," he says. "But should a slang word by chance escape the common fate, then woe betide the pedant, for it will live to mock his memory. So do the words *bamboozle, banter, sham, mob* and *bully* take their long revenge upon Dean Swift, who was so unwise as to describe them in 1710 as 'Certain words invented by some Pretty Fellows . . . now struggling for vogue,' and to attribute to such words the 'Continual Corruption of the English tongue.' " Some slang terms—but by no means all or even most —contribute to the vitality of the language and win places in the aristocracy of words.

## SLEIGHT OF HAND
(Slight slip.) In a recent book review the reviewer twice wrote (or maybe the printer printed) references to clever *slight of hand.*

It should, of course, have been *sleight of hand.* The two words are pronounced the same, but come from different roots. *Slight* derives from a Middle English word meaning smooth, soft or slim, whereas *sleight* derives from an Old Norse root meaning crafty or clever and that derivation led on to the phrase *sleight of hand,* which denotes deceptive dexterity with the hands.

## SLOW, SLOWLY
(Go slow now.) It is going to surprise some readers to learn that *slow* is a legitimate adverb and has been one since at least 1500. Some words that can be both adjectives and adverbs have two forms as adverbs: *slow* and *slowly, quick* and *quickly, direct* and *directly, sharp* and *sharply, cheap* and *cheaply, right* and *rightly.* The shorter form in each instance is usually confined to short commands ("Drive slow") or to comparisons in an *as . . . as* construction ("Drive as *quick* as you can, but be careful").

## SNUCK
(Sneaky word.) Does the fairly widespread use of *snuck* as the past tense of *sneak* make it correct? Nope. One dictionary lists the word as if it were standard, but the others label it colloquial or dialectal or substandard. The label here would be at least substandard and more probably slang.

## SO LONG
(Bye-bye.) What is the origin of the colloquial phrase *so long?* The Oxford English Dictionary and H. L. Mencken say, without further explanation, that it comes from the German *so lange.* Other authorities suggest it is a shortening of "Don't let it be *so long* until we meet again" or *"So long* as we're apart, good luck" or "God be with you *so long* as we are apart." Another suggestion is that the phrase comes from the Arabic *salaam* and the Hebrew *shalom,* both meaning peace. One text objects to the *shalom* theory on the ground that *shalom* is a greeting, not a farewell as *so long* is. But that objection will not stand up because *shalom* is both a greeting and a farewell. My own wild guess is that *so long* is a contraction of *"So* I'll be getting *along."* The only other piece of evidence that can be offered about the phrase is

that it has been in use since the mid-1800's, for whatever that
is worth. So, so long to *so long* for now.

**SOIL**
  *See* DIRT.

**SOLECISM**
The word *solecism* means a deviation from normal grammar or
idiom. It comes from the Greek *soloikos,* meaning to speak improperly, and that in turn derives from *Soloi,* a city in Asia Minor,
where a corruption of Attic was spoken by Athenian colonists.
(The *o* in *solecism,* by the way, is usually pronounced like the *o*
in *politics,* not like the *o* in *solar system.*)

**SOME**
(No exact some.) Program notes at a symphony concert said of
a composer, "He left behind *some* 22 works." The word *some*
means about, approximately. Therefore it should not be applied
to something specific like the figure 22. You could say the composer left behind *"some* 20" works, but not *"some* 22." (*See* CER-
TAIN.)

**SOMEONE**
  *See* ONE WORD, TWO WORDS.

**SOMETHING ELSE**
When a youngster of today wants to designate something or
someone as remarkable or exceptional he often uses the term
*something else.* A great violinist will be hailed as *something else.*
What else? A drummer? A tuba player? What else? Actually, the
phrase is not as far out as it sounds at first. *Something else* could
be translated into *something different* and that in turn could be
translated into *exceptional,* a commonplace word that means rare,
not ordinary. What is indeed far out is a commercial that calls
a little cigar *something else* and then says, "It's a whole *nother*
smoke." *Nother* is a manufactured word, based on a misapprehension of *an other,* but oddly enough, the misapprehension
dates back to Middle English. Not that its age makes it any more
acceptable.

## SOMETIME, SOME TIME
A letter to the editor of a newspaper contained this sentence: "I was a victim of that demolition plan and *sometime* ago moved my business out of the city." The question is whether that adverb should be one word or two. In defining the single-word adverb Webster's New World Dictionary inadvertently provides a clue to the answer. The definition goes like this: "Sometime. 1. at *some time* not known or specified." The one-word version is used to designate an unspecified point in time, as in, "I'll see you *sometime* soon." The two-word version is used to designate an indefinite period (not point), as in, "I moved my business out of the city *some time* ago." As an adjective meaning former, which is not commonly used, the single-word version is the only proper one: "My *sometime* friend, Joe." (*See* ONE WORD, TWO WORDS.)

## SPEAK VS. TALK
Those two verbs are closely synonymous, as in "I *spoke* to John" or "I *talked* to John," but their "correctness" depends on what kind of communication you have in mind. *Speak* is the stronger of the two, the more formal, the more one-sided. *Talk,* which is softer, implies in the foregoing instance, that you and John engaged in two-sided conversation or even that others joined in. However, as we intended to imply by putting the word "correctness" in quotation marks up above, the distinction between the two words is quite slight and the use of one or the other could hardly be called incorrect.

## SPELLING
(Simplified riting.) George Bernard Shaw, prestigious exponent of simplified spelling, is credited with having been the author of the ancient gag about the spelling of *fish.* He is supposed to have said that the word is spelled *ghoti.* How come? Well, the *gh* is as in enou*gh,* the *o* as in w*o*men and the *ti* as in na*ti*on. Shaw didn't get very far in his campaign for simplified spelling, but he put up a good *gh*eight.

## SPICK-AND-SPAN
The expression *spick-and-span* (sometimes the *k* is dropped) goes far back. It began with the *span* part, which was originally

*span-new,* derived from the Old Norse *span-nyr,* meaning new like a freshly shaved chip. *Span-new* was used by Chaucer. The *spick* part is apparently related to spikes or tenters, which were, and are, frames for stretching newly made cloth. Essentially, then, the expression means new or fresh, but over the years it has been broadened to take in the sense of clean and neat.

## SPIFFLICATED
Surprising, in a way, is the fact that the thought having the most slang synonyms in English is *drunk.* The Dictionary of American Slang, by Wentworth and Flexner, lists well over 300 of them, ranging from *alkied* to *zig-zag,* and including such familiar ones as *blotto, crocked, four sheets to the wind, half seas over, ossified, shikker* and *soused* and such unfamiliar ones as *buzzed, fogmatic, how-come-ye-so, loop-legged, mokus* and *pigeon-eyed.* The vast number of *drunk* words, says the slang dictionary, "does not mean that Americans are obsessed with drinking, though we seem obsessed with talking about it." So maybe we should keep silent next time we *tie one on.*

## SPIT AND IMAGE
According to Webster's Third New International Dictionary, there is "a former popular saying that a child with a great resemblance to its father looks as much like him as if it had been spit out of his mouth." From that saying came the meaning of the word *spit* to denote an almost exact likeness. Usually the word is used in the phrase *spit and image,* which is repetitive, as are several phrases in English—*hard and fast,* for example. To confuse matters, most users of the phrase say *spittin' image.* Images may spit, but when did you last *see* one do it?

## SPOONERISMS
An article of reminiscences about the late Milton Cross recalled that on one occasion the radio announcer, intending to tell listeners to stay tuned for the news, said: "Stay stewed for the nudes." That type of accidental confusion of sounds is called a *spoonerism,* a word derived from the name of the Reverend W. A. Spooner of New College, Oxford, who was famous for such utterances. Here are a few examples of slips of that kind culled from dictionaries: "a well-boiled icicle" for "a well-oiled bicy-

cle"; "Let me sew you to your sheet" for "Let me show you to your seat"; "tons of soil" for "sons of toil"; "half-warmed fish" for "half-formed wish"; "our queer old dean" for "our dear old queen"; "a blushing crow" for "a crushing blow." Enough. Those slips and quips give you the idea. So let's stack the crops —er—let's stop the cracks.

## SUBJUNCTIVE

(Lost in the would's.) A recent supermarket ad in a newspaper read this way: "If you would have utilized all the food coupons in last Wednesday's paper you would have saved $16.64" that is an improper construction. Properly, the first part of the sentence should read, "If you had utilized all the food coupons, etc." The writer probably thought that *had utilized* was just a plain old past tense and that a subjunctive was called for to express the hypothetical condition. What he didn't realize is that *had* can also serve as a subjunctive verb, as can be established here by dropping the *if* and writing, "Had you utilized all the food coupons, etc." As a general rule it is erroneous to have a *would have* in the condition part of the sentence if there is another *would have* in the result part. Now go out and cash in those coupons.

(Differing moods.) Which of these sentences is correct? Number 1 reads: "If I am elected, the first thing I would do would be to clean up crime." Number 2 reads: "If I am elected the first thing I would do is clean up crime." The verdict here is that neither sentence is correct because each begins with a clause in the indicative mood ("If I *am elected*") then switches to the subjunctive ("the first thing I *would do*"). The solution is not to put the first clause into the subjunctive; no condition contrary to fact is suggested. "If" does not need to be followed always by the subjunctive mood. Often it introduces a clause of supposition and in such cases the indicative mood is usual: "If John was in town yesterday, I did not know about it." The sentence above should read: "If I *am elected*, the first thing I *will do will be* (or *is*) to clean up crime." Let it be said here, incidentally but not unimportantly, that the subjunctive is almost a vanishing species in today's English. (*See* IF.)

## SUFFIXES

(-ability.) A political article contained a sentence saying that a poll showed the incumbent ahead "on the basis of greater experience and *electability.*" About the same time, a newspaper sentence said that the sending of messages privately from the White House to reporters to get across to a government official that he has outlived his usefulness was a valuable technique because "it allows for *'deniability.'*" And two days later a reporter wrote about voters who expressed *favorability* toward a candidate. Are we on the verge of a new era of suffixation such as those that gave us *-wise* words (*weatherwise, dollarwise*) and *-ese* words (*Pentagonese, pedaguese*)?

(-ee.) A headline read, "Police Use Dogs, Planes in Hunt for 4 *Escapees.*" The difference between *escaper* and *escapee* seems to be at an end, that is, it looks, alas, as if the improperly formed term *escapee* has just about won out over *escaper*. The suffix *-ee* is properly attached to a verb to make it into a noun indicating a person or thing to which something is done—an *employee* is one who has been hired, who is employed, a *trainee* is one who is being trained. However, several words with the *-ee* improperly attached, such as *standee* and *refugee,* are standard or close to it, and *escapee* now seems to be in that category. *Escaper* does not sound natural and *fugitive* is not appropriate in all instances because of its common association with lawbreakers, which those fleeing from oppression or injustice may not be. The best guide is to use properly formed *-ee* words whenever possible and try to avoid new, improperly formed coinages.

(-er.) In a word game a contestant came up with the word *roarer*. A friend of his challenged that term, and even though no money was at stake, wrote to me for a verdict. He need not have written. The word appears in just about every dictionary, though treated insignificantly. As a matter of fact, the suffix *-er,* in the sense of one who has to do with or who does, can be tacked on to countless words to coin fairly legitimate new words.

(Feminine endings.) Even before feminists got into the act the tendency was to do away with feminine word endings. Who needs words like *usherette* or *farmerette?* There are some feminine words that seem to be too firmly established to be dispensed with—words like *actress, heroine, stewardess* (though *attendant* is battling this one) and *waitress.* But all in all the trend is to avoid the feminine form—in writing, that is.

But I ran across one difficult case. I wrote about the agreement of a restaurant to hire additional women "as waiters and busboys." Then, with the extreme feminists in mind, I wrote, "The waiters become waitresses; no problem. But how about the busboys—busgirls? buswomen? buspersons?" That caused a professor to take typewriter in hand and point out, quite correctly, that "occupational titles that contain the word *man* [and presumably *boy,* too] have long since become neuter nouns and there is no reason to distort the English language into absurdities." Then, in a lighter vein, he wrote, "If you must invent a word for lady busboy, why not busters or bust boys?" In a still lighter vein he added, "And if you run into trouble with bellhop, the solution is easy and obvious: bellehop." A more serious and surprising comment came from another reader. He noted that a term for busboy that appears in Webster's unabridged dictionary is *omnibus.* It's there all right. I checked in the big Oxford dictionary and found it there, too, with the definition "a man or boy who assists a waiter at an hotel, restaurant, etc." The Oxford cited a use of the word *omnibus* in this sense as far back as 1888.

(-ism.) The suffix *-ism* is coming into increasing use. Words like *consumerism, racism* and *sexism* are common these days. but some of them are so new that they have not yet made their way into dictionaries. It's a safe bet that they will achieve recognition, however. The suffix covers a broad field, denoting action, practice, behavior, abnormal condition, doctrine, cult or adherence to a system or principle. It provides a kind of shorthand that is clear and useful. For instance, without the word *consumerism* one would have to resort to some such elaborate phrase as "adherence to the cause of asserting or defending the rights and interests of the consumer." Without *sexism* one would have to fall back on *male chauvinism* (or maybe *female chauvinism*), which isn't so bad, but is, after all, another *-ism.* The language does keep growing.

(-ist.) For some time now we have had with us the word *racist,* one who emphasizes racial differences, finds one race superior to another and seeks to preserve that superiority. It is not the

most perfectly formed word in the language because the suffix
-*ist*, in its applicability here, would mean an adherent of or a
believer in. A believer in what? Race? Not really. But the word
is sufficiently established to appear in new dictionaries, so not
much can be done about it. Now, however, a parallel word has
been appearing: *sexist*. In addition to the meaning of -*ist* given
above the suffix can also denote a person who practices or who
is skilled in. Those meanings may apply to *sexists*, but they are
not what the users of the word have in mind. What *sexist* is
designed to mean is a believer in male superiority, a male chauvinist. So that word, too, is a malformation. A better term—
though not from a headline writer's point of view—would be
*male supremacist*. (And, please, let no one suggest *malefactor*.)
*Sexist* is close to an abomination and should be resisted even
though there is little hope that the tide can be stemmed.

(-ize.) Among the words that have been coined through the use
of the -*ize* suffix probably *finalize* has received the most publicity
and the most sneers. But a far worse one was minted recently
by, of all people, former President Ford. Discussing inflation, he
said: "As of the last report it would *annualize* at about 7.2 percent
contrasted with 12 or 13 percent rate of inflation in 1974." The
odd thing about this invention is that the -*ize* word becomes an
intransitive verb whereas most of the other coinages are transitive—you *hospitalize* a patient or *tenderize* a prune or *moisturize*
your skin. But inflation is not going to *annualize* anything; it's
just going to *annualize*. P.S.—About two minutes later the President said, "We have to *maximize* our effort" against crime. Here's
mud in your -*ize*.

(-ster.) The present suffix -*ster*, as in *prankster* or *punster*, traces
back to Old English, in which it was spelled -*estre*. Before the
fourteenth century it appeared in words that had a feminine
connotation, but after 1300 it had no connotation of gender. It
figured—and still figures—in the coinage of many words, not
infrequently disparaging words such as *trickster* and *gangster*.
And another thing to be noticed about the suffix is that it is not
normally attached to verbs but rather to nouns and occasionally
adjectives; verbs tend to pick up the suffix -*er* (*singer*, *player*), but
nouns often pick up the -*ster* ending (*mobster*, *tipster*, *speedster*).
Two adjectives that come to mind as companions of the -*ster*

suffix are *youngster* and *oldster,* and though the first of those is all right because disparagement of kids is common and is not usually meant seriously, the second one, *oldster,* should be avoided because it is liable to cause resentment.

## SUPERIOR (THAN?)

A Montreal radio station ran a commercial for a reupholstering company that said if you send the company your old couch you will get back "a *superior* one *than* you had before." Is that use of *than* becoming acceptable? The answer is no. In Latin, oddly enough, *superior* is the comparative degree of *superus,* meaning above, but in English it is not a comparative of anything and therefore is not followed by *than.* Maybe the upholsterers got their Latin and their English confused.

## SUPERSEDE

If *precede* and *intercede* are spelled with a *c* in the middle, why is *supersede* spelled with an *s* in the middle? Long, long ago *supersede* did have a *c* in its middle, but it no longer has. Nor should it have because it derives from a different root from those other words and a lot of others like them. *Supersede* comes from the Latin *super-* (above) and *sedere* (sit) and means literally to sit above. The other words have as their main root the Latin *cedere,* meaning go. Or should we say that the other words sprouted from a different cede?

## SUPINE

*See* PRONE.

## SURVEILLANCE, SURVEIL

A Federal judge prohibited the F.B.I. from "attending, *surveiling,* listening to, watching or otherwise monitoring" a Young Socialist Alliance convention. For a long time we have had the word *surveillance* in English, but the verb *surveil,* pronounced sur-vale and meaning to keep a close watch on someone or something, is a stranger that has appeared only in recent years and only occasionally. The verb is a back-formation from the noun. In French, whence *surveillance* comes, there is a verb—*surveiller*—but that is different from the North American coinage. (*See* CONVERSION.)

## SYLLEPSIS

That word is a rhetorical figure in which a single word is used to link two thoughts, each of which gives a different meaning to the linking word. A down-to-earth example: "The star of the Giants smacked a pillar at the airport and a home run at Candlestick Park today." Notice that *smacked* first has the meaning of walked into, then the meaning of hit a baseball. That's *syllepsis*. Sometimes a writer, trying to sound witty, employs it like this: "More than three years and several hundred Vice-Presidential speeches later, Mr. Agnew was still trying to persuade Americans to accept his philosophy." First *later* is used in the literal sense of the passage of time, then it is used in the sense of totaling or counting. That particular type of *syllepsis*, by the way, is so common as to be bromidic. But the figure is sometimes used with telling humorous effect.

## SYNCHRONIZATION
*See* BACK CLIPPING.

## SYNCOPE

Not long ago a columnist used the word *wonderous*. There is no such word, though presumably there was at one time. If there ever was, the present-day word, *wondrous*, arrived through a process known as syncope, the dropping of a letter, a sound or a syllable from the middle of a word. It is that process that gave us *laundress* in place of *launderess*, and *ne'er-do-well* in place of *never-do-well*. Sailors seem to be fond of *syncopation* (same as *syncope*); they take orders from the *bo's'n* in the *fo'c's'le*.

## SYNDROME

It wouldn't be surprising to hear someone say these days, "Joe suffers from the pizza *syndrome;* he ate four for lunch today." Properly, *syndrome* applies to a set of symptoms or signs characteristic of a disease or a disordered condition. But, probably because of its pretentious sound and its scientific flavor, it has been taken over into everyday speech to describe the most commonplace situations or conditions. The only trouble with that is that the word is on its way to losing any precise meaning at all.

# T

## TA

Some Scrabble players asked your host whether there was such a word as *ta*, which one of them had used and defended. Odd as it may seem, there is such a word. It is a British interjection, defined in Webster's New World Dictionary as meaning "thank you; originally a child's term." So what we would like to say to those Scrabble players is *ta*.

## TAKE

(*See* BRING AND TAKE.)

## TAKE (NOTICE)

A radio announcer said, "There is still a major decision to be *taken*." That use of *taken* is correct. One meaning of the verb *take* is to adopt by choice, so it is proper to say one *takes* (i.e., chooses) a decision. Incidentally, *take* is one of the most versatile words in the language. Dictionaries have columns and columns of different meanings for it, ranging all the way from obtaining by conquest to letting a pitched baseball go by without swinging at it.

## TAKE CARE, TAKE HEED

How a slight change in the connotation of a word can lead to an international incident was demonstrated a while ago in the United Nations Security Council. The Soviet representative, Yakov A. Malik, accused Americans of trying to distort Moscow's position on colonial matters and then cautioned them, as the interpreter translated his words, to "take care" in discussing Moscow's policies. That provoked Daniel Patrick Moynihan, then the United States representative, to retort that Americans "don't give a damn" about threats from Moscow. Later Mr. Malik said his words had been mistranslated—he hadn't said "take care," but rather "take heed." Offhand and normally there isn't much difference between "take *care*" and "take *heed*"; both suggest paying close attention to something. But "take *care*" often contains an undertone of caution or watchfulness, and so it could be a warning word. All of which suggests that interpreters and all the rest of us should heed our words and take care in their selection. In short, be precise.

## TALK
*See* SPEAK.

## TARE
You go into a market and you ask for a pound of potato salad. The clerk puts a plastic container on the scales, then spoons potato salad into it until the scales register one pound. Are you then getting a pound of potato salad? No, because the clerk hasn't allowed for the *tare*—the weight of the container. You should have asked him to put the container on the scales first so that you could deduct the *tare*. The word comes from the Arabic *tarhah*, meaning what is rejected. No charge for that marketing tip.

## TAUTOLOGY
The word *tautology* means repetition of the same idea in other words. It comes from the Greek *tauto*, meaning the same, and *-logos*, saying. The *tauto* part of the word has no connection with *taut*, meaning tight. But I might say—nay, will say—that tautology is loose-ology.

(Heard you the first time.) Some folks—and they're usually folksy folks—will occasionally say, "I have a friend of mine who plays a good game of tiddlywinks." They shouldn't say it. That locution *"I have a friend of mine"* is rather low-grade English. The reason is that it says the same thing twice. When you say, "I have a friend," you have at once established possession with the word *have.* Then if you go on to say, "a friend of mine," you are repeating the idea of possession, and tautology is considered a fault by users of good English. So just say, "I have a friend," or "A friend of mine," and go ahead with the tiddlywinks. (*See* REDUNDANCY, PLEONASM.)

## TEACH

(Does she teach college?) In a TV commercial a young woman says, "I teach college." Shouldn't she say that she teaches in college or at a college or at the college level? True, "I teach college" has an unnatural sound about it. Yet, "I teach school" does not. Webster's unabridged dictionary, second edition, gives an example much like "I teach school," but labels it "now chiefly U.S." Webster's third edition also gives a similar example with no label at all. What seems to be called for is an arbitrary decision and here it is: "I teach school" is idiomatic, and acceptable because it is idiomatic; "I teach college" is not at all common, at least not common enough to be acceptable; "I teach seminary" is impossible. (*See* OBJECTS, DIRECT AND INDIRECT.)

## TENSES

(Mostly perfect.) All right, here goes: The *present tense* is used to express something happening now ("He *is waiting* in the living room"), or usual conditions ("It *is* warm in the Virgin Islands") or general truths ("All men *are created* equal"). The *past tense* is used to express something that happened or a condition that was in being in the past ("He *wore* his new jacket yesterday," "Medieval art *was* representational"). The *present perfect tense* is used to refer to things that began in the past and "touch" the present ("For centuries taxes *have supported* governments"). The *past perfect tense* is used to refer to things that happened in the past and were completed earlier than other things that happened in the past ("Caesar *had been* Emperor only a short while before he was assassinated"). (*See* FORECAST.)

(Sequence of tenses.) Two simple sentences will illustrate how the tense of the main verb of a sentence normally governs the tense of the verb in a subordinate clause. Sentence 1: "He *promises* he *will* take the dog out before midnight." Sentence 2: "He *promised* he *would* take the dog out before midnight." The conversion of "He *promises* he *will*" to "He *promised* he *would*" is a conversion to what is called the normal sequence, and the normal sequence is what careful writers employ.

But not infrequently a not-so-careful writer will compose a sentence like this: "The prosecutor *said* last night that if the Senate committee *tries* to subpoena material from his office, he *would* fight the move in court." Obviously there is an inconsistency in those tenses: *said* and *would* are past tense verbs, but *tries* is a present tense verb. It should be *tried.* Some of those same writers sometimes follow the *said* with two present tense verbs, *tries* and *will,* and though the inconsistency is not as glaring as that in the quoted sentence, it is not considered good form. One exception to the normal sequence is what is called the vivid or exceptional sequence, which is used when the subject matter of the subordinate clause involves a timeless truth or something that is habitual. Examples: "The minister *told* the children that dishonesty *does* not pay"; "The child *discovered* that dogs love a bone."

## THAT

There is a tendency among many editors to eliminate the conjunction *that* almost every time it appears. Unfortunately, it is not possible to lay down any rules on when it should be used and when it may be omitted. In most instances its inclusion or exclusion is a matter of idiom—that is, how the sentence sounds to one whose native tongue is English. In general you cannot go wrong if you include it. Here's an example: "My present impression is the statement is correct." It is not wrong, but a *that* would improve the sound of it.

Beyond simple sentences of that sort three guides may be laid down. One is to use *that* when a time element intervenes between the verb and the clause. For instance: "The coach said today his team was in A-1 condition." Aside from the sound of it, which is a little, though not importantly, awkward, the sentence is susceptible to ambiguity: Does the *today* refer to the *said* or to the team's condition? The second guide concerns a sentence in which the verb of the clause is long delayed so that it is not quickly clear that a clause is present at all. Example: "The prosecutor disclosed a document pertaining to the brokerage company swindle was a forgery." A *that* after *disclosed* would certainly make the sentence easier to read. The third guide involves a sentence in which a second *that* clears up confusion about who said or did what: Example: "The coach said *that* the quarterback was not playing his best and the team's morale suffered." If the coach said the morale suffered, a *that* is definitely needed after the *and*.

## THAT AND WHICH

In the best usage there is a distinction between these two pronouns. *That* is used to introduce a restrictive or defining clause —one that defines the noun it is attached to and cannot be omitted. For instance: "The mountain *that* is the highest in the United States is Mt. McKinley." *Which* introduces a nonrestrictive or parenthetical clause—one that adds information but could be omitted without changing the sense of what is being said. For instance: "Mt. McKinley, *which* is in Alaska, is the highest mountain in the United States." If you feel the need for commas around the clause, you can be sure it is a *which* clause. Rarely do people use *that* when the word should be *which,* but quite often they use *which* when the better word would be *that*. It may be because *which* tends to sound more formal and they think they are being more elegant. In everyday speech the *that's* far outnumber the *which's,* and it should be so in written language.

## THAT, WHICH AND WHO

If Miss Thistlebottom taught you that *who* applied to people she was correct, but if she told you that *that* applied only to things, forget it. *Who* applies to people, *which* applies to things and *that* may apply to either. You may say either "the boy *that* lives next door" or "the boy *who* lives next door."

## "THE LATE"

(Better late than . . .). When does one use *the late* in referring to deceased persons? Some say the phrase is limited to those who have been dead for ten years or less, but the general question does not lend itself to a definite answer. At one extreme you would not speak of *the late* Leonardo da Vinci; at the other extreme you would not do what a few newspapers do and refer to a person who was killed by an auto yesterday as *the late* Annie

Body. We may rule out those two extremes. We may rule out also the ten-year limit because it is not accepted in general usage. If the deceased is someone prominent such as Churchill, Roosevelt or de Gaulle, *the late* is so well known as to be superfluous. If the deceased is not prominent, *the late* might be used for twenty-five years or more. But if such a person has just died, perhaps a month or so should be allowed to pass before *the late* is applied, and meanwhile the phrase "who died July 1" could be used. You will find that dictionaries are no help. They all say *the late* means recently dead, but what does "recently" mean?

## THEM AND THOSE

The Lord's Prayer says, "And forgive us our trespasses, as we forgive *those* who trespass against us." The Englishman makes it, ". . . forgive *them* who trespass against us." Which is correct? The answer is that either *those* or *them* is correct. Each word is a pronoun, which is what is required in the quoted passage. Let it be noted irrelevantly that *those* is also an adjective (*"those* roses"), whereas *them* is not (*"them* roses"? Never).

## THERE, THERE

When *there* introduces a series of nouns the first one of which is a plural, the verb is plural. Example: "On his property *there were* three orange trees, two lemon and one grapefruit." But a question arises when a singular noun heads the series. Technically the verb still should be plural because the subject—the series of nouns—is plural. But many writers and readers feel more comfortable with a singular verb in such close contact with a singular noun and so we see sentences like this: *"There was* something about her that was physically attractive and something that was stimulating to one's mind." Or like this: "There was a man standing there and a dog and two children." Without doubt the singular verb is preferable to a plural in each of those sentences. Which proves that there are occasions when one should not be too technical.

A sentence in a magazine read as follows: "There were a yacht, a plane, a motor launch and weekends with Princess Margaret and Lord Snowdon." The *were* is unarguably correct, but, as we said, some writers prefer a singular verb in a series such as that in which the first item is singular, and their preference is not usually disputed. That preference is even more defensible if the first element of the series is somewhat extended, as in, "There *was* in the living room a sofa with a plaid slipcover, a coffee table, a television set and three chairs." And if two or more of the elements in the series constitute a single thought, a singular verb is normal: "There *was* his bed and board still to be paid for."

## THING
(One thing and another.) Some words have a host of meanings that we are often not aware of until someone questions one of them. Here's a dialogue that demonstrates the difficulties of the word *thing.* First speaker: "There is such a *thing* as being too forgiving." Second speaker: "What *thing?* A written pardon may be a *thing,* but to be forgiving is not." From that point, the argument takes off. We could say that the use of *thing* in a context like that is idiomatic, which it is, and let it go at that. But dictionaries contain so many definitions of the word that it becomes clear that the disputed use is quite valid. The definitions range from an inanimate object to a matter of circumstance, an idea, an opinion or a quality. And there are many more, so many that one gets the idea that there is such a *thing* as being too nit-picking. When you delve into the etymology of *thing,* you begin to discover how it came to have so many diverse meanings. Its parents were Old High German, Old Norse, Old Frisian, Middle Dutch, Old English, Indo-European and a couple more languages. Quite a thing, that word!

## THOSE
*See* THEM AND THOSE.

## TIME, QUESTION OF
If you had an appointment with someone for 3 P.M. and desired to change it to 2 P.M., would you ask him to move it *forward* or *back* an hour? Consult Webster's New World Dictionary, under the adverb *back,* and you will find this definition: "to or toward an earlier time." That would seem to solve the problem; you would ask to have the appointment moved *back* an hour. But wait, hold it. If you look under the adverb *forward,* you will find this: "toward the front or a point in front or before; ahead."

That would seem to give *forward* the same standing and footing as *back*. So that's no help. We shall have to be, and will be, arbitrary: *Forward* has a real connotation of bringing something closer or causing something to be earlier, whereas *back* has a connotation of putting something farther away. Therefore changing an appointment from 3 P.M. to 2 P.M. would be moving it *forward*. (To be fair to the dictionary, it should be said that the definition of *back*—"toward an earlier time"—probably is intended to refer to past time, though it doesn't say so.) One other complication should be noted. When you are moving your clock from 3 o'clock to 2, as at the end of daylight saving, you are moving it *back*, not *forward*. Ending the discussion on that note should guarantee you a couple of nights of insomnia. (*See* A.M., P.M.)

## TITLES
(He's entitled.) A silly fad that, if not started by the news magazines, was at least popularized by them is to take descriptive matter about people and turn it into ahead-of-name titles. Thus we might read about "Ground-Floor Cleaner and Mahogany Furniture Duster Blanche Krankheit," to make up a ridiculous example. An actual illustration is this one about the late Anita Louise: "She was married to Academy Award-winning producer and 20th-Century Fox production chief Buddy Adler." If a title like that is to be clapped onto a name, it should be capitalized throughout. But what is gained by coining such a title? Wouldn't it be better and more natural to begin with Buddy Adler and let the rest follow his name? Long titles are at best clumsy, but if you wish to write "Former Secretary of Health, Education and Welfare Caspar W. Weinberger" at least you will be using an actual title, not a ridiculous made-up one.

## TO A DEGREE
(Second degree.) *To a degree* is an interesting phrase because it can mean almost opposite things. For one thing it sometimes means to a large extent, as in, "She has a fine mind and *to a degree* she is beautiful." For a second thing the phrase sometimes means somewhat or to a limited extent, as in, "His book advocates centralized control and *to a degree* is a plea for fascism." Maybe the language should make up its mind.

## TOADY

Once upon a time there were quack doctors who had assistants
to help them sell their quack medicines. At that time toads were
generally believed to be poisonous, so the assistant would pretend to eat some of them, then the medicine man would give him
a dose of his quack medicine and, behold, the assistant would
be cured and the doc would be in business. Logically enough,
such an assistant was called a *toadeater* and the short for that was
*toady*. Today the word *toady* means a fawning flatterer or one
who does dishonest things to win favor. He might even pretend
to have a frog in his throat.

## TO A MAN

"To a man, the Senators on the committee agreed with the
President." We all know what that means: Every Senator on the
committee agreed with the President. But why *to a man?* What
has *to* got to do with it? The word *to* has dozens and dozens of
meanings and one of its meanings as a preposition is indicating
a degree reached or right down to a final position. Thus *to a man*
means reaching and including the final person. Ah, it's quite a
language, this English.

## TOILET

Euphemisms overflow the word *toilet,* which is itself a euphemism. What brings it to attention here is a letter from a woman
whose husband and son are both named John and who says she
is outraged by the use of the term *john* to refer to a toilet. She
wants to know how it originated. The origin of *john* is particularly difficult to trace. H. L. Mencken in *The American Language*
says the term may be related to the English *jakes,* meaning a
privy (and there is another euphemism). The *Oxford English Dictionary* finds that *jakes* was in use as far back as the 1530's. It may
be that the very commonness of the hallowed name John had
something to do with the coining of the word *john.* (Incidentally,
speaking of euphemisms, a Michigan school superintendent, no
less, writing a short article on rules in schools, used the word
*bathrooms* three times. *Lavatories* would be bad enough, but at
least pupils do supposedly wash in school *lavatories,* but do they
take baths in school *bathrooms?*)

The foregoing explanation of the word *john* was challenged in separate letters from two readers who agreed on a different explanation. In England in the time of Queen Victoria, they wrote, a plumbing engineer used a trap, or gooseneck, that changed the flow of water in the toilet. That chap was a resourceful plumbing engineer, later knighted by Queen Victoria, and his name was John Crapper. Shall we go on?

That second explanation was disputed by another reader who wrote that the inventor of the flush toilet was Thomas Crapper. To suggest a different derivation of the word *john*, that reader quoted from a book by Wallace Reyburn as follows: "For many years the British firm Armitage, one of the biggest in sanitary-ware, enjoyed a great advantage over their rivals in export to the United States because they used to trade under the name of their original owner, the Reverend Edward Johns. It appealed to Americans that they could literally buy Johns imported from England." The name of the quoted book? *Flushed With Pride.*

That still did not settle the discussion concerning *john*. Another reader called attention to an Encyclopedia Britannica entry that credits Sir John Harington, who lived two centuries before Crapper, as the inventor. Harington wrote a facetious book on the subject entitled *A New Discourse of a Stale Subject, Called the Metamorphosis of Ajax.* Two things should be noted: first, that *stale* is an old word meaning the urine of livestock; second, that *ajax* is an obsolete jocular term for *jakes*, which in turn is an archaic word for a *privy* and one that we some lines back connected with the word *john.*

Further on the subject of euphemisms, the British have a couple of their own. One is *W. C.*, which stands for water closet, another is the *loo.* Where does *loo* come from? Eric Partridge, the British etymologist, hazards two guesses. One is that the term derives from the French *l'eau*, meaning water. The other is that in some devious way it traces back to *gardy-loo,* which has its origin in the French *gare l'eau*, the slops thrown into the street. A better guess than either of these appears in Webster's unabridged, third edition, which traces the word to the French *lieux d'aisance*, which means literally room of comfort.

A final observation: there are, as I have noted, a flock of euphemisms for *toilet*. But, as I have noted, *toilet* is itself a euphemism. What is the "real word" it is a cover-up for? I have never heard of a "real," down-to-earth word that means what is called *toilet.*

## TO THE NTH DEGREE
(Going to extremes.) We have all heard the expression *to the nth degree,* as in, "The play was boring *to the nth degree.*" A friend inquires about the meaning and origin of the expression. Basically *n* is a mathematical symbol and it refers to the final item in an infinitely increasing or decreasing series of numbers, values or whatnot. *To the nth degree,* therefore, means to an infinite degree or, in common usage, to an extreme.

## TRADITIONAL, USUAL
(No hand-me-down.) *Traditional* is not the same thing as *usual.* Something that is *traditional* is handed down unwritten from generation to generation; something that is *usual* is simply of common occurrence. There is a tendency among some writers to use *traditional* when all they mean is *usual* or *common* or *customary.* Here is an example of the misuse: "The National Stock Exchange is dwarfed in size by both the New York Stock Exchange and the American Stock Exchange. It has *traditionally* traded about as many shares in a full year as the Big Board might handle in one booming session." This misuse almost suggests that the National Exchange was deliberately trying to limit its turnover to abide by some long-established custom.

## TRANSPIRE
(Bad leak.) This word is widely misused. The nontechnical meaning of *transpire* is to be emitted as a vapor, hence, to leak out or become known. But those who tend to reach for the fancy word use it as if it meant to happen or take place. They would be likely to write, "After the opening hit in the fifth inning the downfall of the home team *transpired* rapidly." A truly remarkable misuse was this one concerning a rumor that spread in Rome: "Since little *transpires* that does not leak out, the Vatican itself is somewhat embarrassed." If the word were properly used in that sentence, what it would be saying is that little that leaks out does not leak out. It is quite usual and proper for words to develop new and useful meanings. But what is useful about that misuse of *transpire* when we already have *happen, occur, take place,*

*come about*—and yea, even *come to pass?* Moreover, the misuse is harmful to the language because no other word expresses the proper meaning of *transpire,* a meaning that is endangered.

## TRIAGE
A word that has been broadening as the world moves along is *triage,* meaning to sort or choose and derived from the French *trier,* which means the same thing. At first *triage* referred to the sorting of produce in the market. Then in World War II it was applied by the Allies to the dividing of the wounded into three groups: those likely to die no matter what was done for them, those likely to recover and those who could be saved if cared for promptly. More recently the word has been applied to the starving countries in a clouded attempt to find a system of food priorities.

## TRY TO, TRY AND
(Nice try.) Some people say, "I'm going to *try to* get this job done by three o'clock," and others say, "I'm going to *try and* get this job done by three o'clock." How about it? Strictly speaking the *try to* version is correct, but the *try and* version is rapidly displacing it, at least in spoken language. When you examine it closely the *try and* locution expresses two operations—trying and doing—though that is usually not the intention. Nevertheless, it sometimes has its uses because it conveys a slightly different meaning. *"Try and* bear up" lends a note of encouragement, "I'm going to *try and* make him stop smoking" lends a note of determination and "You just *try and* make me" lends a note of defiance. In the last of these examples *try and* is really the only possible locution. Still, generally speaking, *try to* is the proper literary form.

## TURBID, TURGID
Just as *flaunt* and *flout* are almost sound-alikes, so are *turbid* and *turgid,* but, as is true of the first pair, they mean different things. *Turbid* means muddied or muddled. *Turgid* means bombastic or grandiloquent. Here's a way to remember the distinction: Let the "b" in *turbid* stand for bog (mud) and the "g" in *turgid* for grandiloquent. Think you'll ever forget again? Probably.

## TWO BITS

So you want to know about the term *two bits*. Originally a *bit* referred to a small silver coin that was worth 1/8 of the Spanish peso. Called a *real,* that small coin, used at one time as currency in the southwestern United States, was worth 12 1/2 cents. Therefore two of them—that is *two bits*—were worth 25 cents, four of them were worth half a dollar. Eight *reals* were worth a dollar and the now obsolete Spanish-American dollars were called *pieces of eight.* So now you know about *two bits* and *pieces of eight*—in short, you have two bits of information.

## TYCOON

A powerful businessman is often known as a *tycoon,* a word that has come a long way—all the way from the Far East. It derived from the Chinese *ta,* great, and *kiun,* prince or ruler, and it was picked up in the Occident in the middle of the last century.

# U

## UNAWARE, UNAWARES

(When to change your unaware.) A question that is posed occasionally is whether it is ever proper to use *unawares,* with a final *s.* It is proper when the word is used to mean unexpectedly or suddenly or by surprise as in "to take someone unawares." It is not proper, however, when a phrase or a clause reads out of the word. For instance, you would not—or should not—say, "He was *unawares* of my presence," or, "I was *unawares* that she was married."

## UNCOUTH, COUTH

(Negatives minus positives.) It is true that there are some words in English that appear only in negative forms and make you wonder why they have no positive forms: *uncouth* is one (Who ever describes anyone as *couth?*), others are *inept, inert, unkempt.* Strangely enough, for most of such words a positive form does or did exist or an ancient language had one from which the modern word was derived. There is, for example, the word *kempt,* but who uses it? *Inept* derives from *in-,* meaning not, and *aptus,* meaning apt, which is very much with us in today's language. *Disgruntled?* Well, pigs *gruntle* when they are contented and are *disgruntled* when they are not. However, why the positives of such words are either obsolete or rare is a mystery. Maybe, as the old song said, we should accentuate the positive.

## UNINTERESTED, DISINTERESTED
The prefixes *un-* and *dis-* mean just about the same thing—the opposite of. But when joined to *interested* they produce two words of quite different meanings. *Uninterested* denotes lacking interest, indifferent. *Disinterested* denotes free of personal motive, unprejudiced. A movie critic may or may not be *uninterested* in a picture, but the ethics of his profession demand that he be *disinterested. Disinterested* is often used as if it meant indifferent, but it shouldn't be. It should be confined to its sense of neutrality because no other word quite conveys the same meaning—of neutrality with lack of a selfish motive. Sometimes it looks as if trying to preserve this distinction is a losing battle, but let's stay in there swinging.

## UNIQUE
(One and only.) A New York shop sent out a brochure in which it described itself as "the world's *most unique* toy store." *Unique* means the only one of its kind or unequaled. Since something cannot be more unequaled than something else or the most sole thing in existence, *unique* is what might be called an absolute; there cannot be degrees of uniqueness. A thing could be *more nearly unique* than something else, meaning that it more closely approaches the state of uniqueness, but it cannot be *more unique* or *most unique.*

## UNLIKE
(No like.) The word *unlike* is as troublesome as *like.* Here is an example of its misuse: "No matter how poor the lens, an image of high quality will be formed in holographic reproduction, *unlike* as in conventional photography." In that sentence *unlike* is functioning as a preposition. Therefore it should govern a noun or the equivalent of a noun. Professor James A. Martin of the University of Michigan Law School thinks it would be a good idea if our language had a word such as *unas,* combining *not* and *as,* but, failing that, he suggests making it "unlike the way it is." That requires a few more words than the original, but it gives us acceptable usage. (*See* LIKE.)

## UNTIL, TILL

(Raiding the 'til.) Two perfectly good words are *until* and *till.* But for some people they apparently are not good enough. Thus we see ads that use this variation, "Open Thursday nights *'til* 9 P.M.," or this one, " *'till* 9 P.M." The apostrophized forms are not approved and are indeed quite unnecessary. *Until* and *till* mean the same thing as those forms and the same thing as each other. If there is any distinction between the two, it is that *until* has a slightly more "formal" sound than *till* and is the more frequently used at the opening of a sentence. (*See* APOSTROPHES.)

## UP/DOWN

This one has to do with adverb peculiarities. When you are driving your car down the street and come to a stop light and take your foot off the gas pedal, do you slow *up* or slow *down?* And how do you know if you are driving *down* the street rather than *up* the street? In both instances either adverb will do; idiom allows either. The car might have been loaded *up* or loaded *down* with luggage, and while you were driving, your home might have been burned *up* or burned *down.* Of course, adverbs are not always interchangeable in that way. You can only speed *up,* not *down.* And the situations are quite different when a man is dressed *up* and when he is dressed *down.* Sometimes adverbs are quite meaningless or are mere intensives, as when we say, "I lit *up* a cigarette," or, "Write *down* your name." (*See* BURN UP, BURN DOWN; FILL IN, FILL OUT; VERBS WITH TAILS.)

## UPCOMING

(Ongoing word.) What does *upcoming* say that *coming* does not? Nothing really. But for some mysterious reason it has achieved wide popularity in the last few decades—something that the similarly formed *forthcoming* has not achieved. *Upcoming* is by no means a new word. The Oxford English Dictionary lists uses of it as far back as the 1300's, though the uses that far back were more literal ones, such as one's *upcoming* after he had fallen down. The listing does show, however, that the making of new words by putting together usual ones has been going on since the earliest times of the English tongue. Maybe it also shows that English for centuries has been an up-and-coming language.

**URNING**
  *See* HOMOSEXUAL, MALE.

**USAGE**
  *See* USE.

**USUAL**
  *See* TRADITIONAL.

**USE, UTILIZE, USAGE**
(Everyday use.) The simple word *use* doesn't enjoy the popularity it should. Is there a conspiracy afoot to kick it out of the language? That may be an extreme view, but there can be no doubt that the fanciers of the fancier word—those who, to sound impressive, prefer the long word to the short one—shun it when they shouldn't. They are the ones who would say, "He *utilized* a screwdriver to clean his fingernails." There is a use for *utilize*, but that's not it. The principal meaning of *utilize* is to put to profitable use, as in, "The city will *utilize* its garbage as landfill."

Then there is the struggle between *use* and *usage*. The longer-word fanciers will say, "The authorities have no reliable data on the effects of marijuana *usage*," when they mean simply *use*. The meaning of *usage* is customary or traditional practice. The word also has the specialized meaning of the way in which words are employed in a language.

In both instances it's not merely a matter of using the simpler word; it's also a matter of using the precise word and avoiding the imprecise word.

**USED TO**
(An item of use.) Here is a pretty common solecism: "When Preacher Roe *use to* throw the spitball, everyone complained except Stan Musial." The verb *use* in the sense of habitually or accustomed sometimes takes a final *d* and sometimes not. In the regular past tense, as in the sentence cited, the word should be *used.* If, however, the auxiliary *did* appears, the verb should be *use:* "Preacher Roe *did use* to throw the spitball." The *did* takes care of providing the past tense. The similarity of the sounds between the two forms *use* and *used* often tends to throw writers off so that they produce a sentence like this: "We are getting sex

films today such as we *didn't used* to get a decade ago." That is as illogical as to write, "In former days girls *didn't went* to bars." It should be added that although *use* in the sense cited is common in conversation, it is considered quite graceless in writing.

**UTILIZE**
   *See* USE.

# V

## VAMP

A *vamp* is the upper part of a shoe. The word comes from the French *avant,* before, and *pied,* foot. The verb originally meant to provide a shoe with a new *vamp,* then it came to mean to patch up or refurbish. That *vamp* who lives down the block may be as comfortable and friendly as an old shoe, but there's no etymological connection between her and shoes. She is a shortening of *vampire.*

## VENAL, VENIAL

A pair of words that sometimes puzzle people are *venal* and *venial.* A *venal* official is one who is corrupt, who can be bought off. *Venial* does not have nearly as bad a meaning, though its meaning is not good either. It refers to something that is forgivable. A *venial* sin is one that can be excused or overlooked. If you think of the word as rhyming with genial, you won't have the meaning of it, but you will have at least a clue to how it contrasts with *venal.* And you might also keep in mind that *venal* rhymes with penal.

## VERBS WITH -ED

Many verbs in English change their forms for the past tense and participial categories; for example, *know, knew, known.* But there are verbs that retain one form for the present, past and future tenses and participial version. A few that come to mind quickly are *bet, wet, wed* and *quit.* Early in this century Ambrose Bierce, a columnist and short-story writer, insisted in his book *Write It*

*Right* that *-ed* has to be tacked on to verbs of that sort. He did not have his way then and is not likely to have it. Given a choice, Americans usually seem to prefer the shorter of two forms (unless they are trying to sound scientific or are being pretentious). A minor exception in verbs of this kind is *fit.* Although in ordinary conversation it might be all right to say, "The jacket *fit* him perfectly," in careful writing the preferred form is *fitted.* (*See* TENSES.)

## VERBS, SPLIT

The practice of some copy editors of unsplitting every split verb is questionable. No English rule says that an adverb must not be positioned between parts of a compound verb. In fact, more often than not that is the natural place for it. Example: "Science *is* gradually *learning* what causes earthquakes." In some instances the superstition about not splitting a compound verb can lead to ambiguity: "A plan for reducing unemployment slowly *has been evolving* in Congress." Placing *slowly* ahead of *evolving* would clarify the intent of the sentence. The opposition to the split verb seems to be related to the opposition to the split infinitive. Both splits were in acceptable use until some grammarians condemned them, for an unknown reason, in the eighteenth and nineteenth centuries. But those grammarians are steadily losing ground these days, and that is all to the good. (Did you note the split in the preceding sentence? Did it bother you?)

## VERBS WITH TAILS

A modern tendency in language is to tack adverbs or prepositions onto verbs, often unnecessarily. Nobody *heads* a committee any more; he *heads up* a committee. *Check,* in the sense of confirm or verify, has attracted almost half a dozen tails, none of which modify the meaning in the slightest: *check into, check on, check out, check over* and *check up.* In another category, however, are tails that do modify the meaning of the verb and are necessary. The verb *break,* for instance, means something different when it is followed by *in, out, away, down, up, apart, even, off* or *in on.* There are other necessary combinations, such as *bottle up, beat down, up* or *off,* and *check in* or *out* (at a hotel). There are many other examples in both categories, but they seem to multiply most in the unnecessary category, probably for faddish reasons. Perhaps language, particularly colloquial language, needs to change to keep alive. (*See* BURN UP; FILL IN.)

## VERBAL
*See* ORAL.

## VERY (GOOD ADVICE)
As a matter of style in writing, the word *very* is a good one to avoid most of the time. The word it modifies usually is stronger standing alone. Not long ago a columnist recalled that shortly after he joined *The Emporia Gazette* its noted editor, William Allen White, summoned him to criticize one of his stories. " 'Very tired,' it says here," White declared. "Remember this: Whenever you write the word *very* in a news story, scratch it out and substitute the word *damn*. Then scratch out the *damn*."

## VIABLE
(Fad word.) A district attorney in New York decided not to prosecute a case because, he said, he had found "no *viable* criminal offense." The word *viable*, possibly because it is important-sounding, has been subjected to considerable use—and misuse —in recent times. Basically and primarily it means able to live or capable of taking root and growing. Beyond that it has been extended to mean workable, and still further to mean real in the sense of alive. But none of those meanings would fit what the district attorney had in mind. He wasn't thinking that the offense would not be able to survive, but rather that a prosecution would not be able to. What he intended to say, perhaps, was that he had found no prosecutable offense. And if he was determined to use an important-sounding word, why not *prosecutable?* It's five syllables whereas *viable* is a mere three.

## VIRTUALLY
*See* PRACTICALLY.

## VOICE, ACTIVE
(Stylist turns seer.) In a book, *Newsman's English* (copyrighted 1972), Harold Evans, editor of *The Sunday Times* of London, gives some sound advice to the effect that in writing it is prefera-

ble to use the active voice of verbs because it is stronger and
more economical than the passive voice. Then comes this passage: "Of course, there are occasions when the passive voice
must be used. Some particular word, usually a proper noun in
news reports, must be made the subject of the sentence, and that
may legitimately demand the passive voice. For instance: 'A
rhinoceros ran over Richard M. Nixon today.' That is active (and
news). But it would be better in the passive voice so that Mr.
Nixon has precedence over the rhino: 'Richard M. Nixon was
run over by a rhinoceros today.' "

## VOICE, "FALSE PASSIVE"

(Was given.) Almost 70 years ago Ambrose Bierce in *Write It
Right* said: " 'The soldier was given a rifle.' What was given is
the rifle, not the soldier. 'The house was given a coat (coating)
of paint.' Nothing can be given anything." His dictum, concerning what came to be known as the *false passive,* was picked up by
newspaper editors, who turned it into a rule for reporters and
editors, and some of them may be clinging to it to this day. It
also appeared in some nineteenth-century grammar books. But
there is no substance to the objection. When the fancy label
"retained object" was applied to the construction to explain it,
the objections to it began to vanish and today they are as invalid
as Bierce's idea that "coat of paint" should be changed to "coating of paint." So in this instance not only may a bad mark be
given to Bierce, but also Bierce may be given a bad mark.

# W

## WAKE, AWAKE

These two verbs mean the same thing and there are no hard and fast rules about their use. *Wake* is the common, everyday word: "*Wake* me at seven," "The fire engines *woke* the baby." *Awake* is used in poetic senses ("He will *awake* no more") or in figurative senses ("The fuel shortage is *awakening* the public to the energy crisis"). There is little to be said beyond that except that *wake* is often followed by up, but *awake* never is.

## WELL (AND GOOD)

What distinction, if any, is there between "I feel *well*" and "I feel *good*"? Used that way, *well* relates to health and means there is nothing wrong physically. *Good* could mean the same thing, but could also mean pleasant or happy. Of course, if *feel* in those sentences is intended to refer to the sense of touch, the adverb *well* would be the word to use, not the adjective *good*.

In his book *Strictly Speaking,* Edwin Newman points out that people in sports as well as sports reporters and commentators often say, "The team is playing *good* right now." That misuse of the adjective *good* as if it were an adverb grates on him, and properly so. A team doesn't play *good;* it plays *well.* And if you want to speak *well,* you won't say you are speaking *good.* (*See* ADJECTIVES AND ADVERBS.)

## WHAT'S THE PROBLEM

A sentence that points up the difficulty with the word *what* is this one: "What makes these man-made monsters of the deep particularly vulnerable are their huge size and the special properties of their buoyancy." The verbs *makes* and *are* do not agree in number as they should because they have the same subject. Two common misunderstandings are illustrated by the sentence. One is a vague notion that *what* is singular. Actually it is sometimes plural: *"What look* like diamonds are not always the real thing." The other fault is being unduly influenced by the noun or nouns that come immediately after the main verb; this influence is known as attraction. The point to remember is that *what* may stand for either *the thing (or element) that* or *the things (or elements) that* and, whichever way you decide it, the two verbs must agree. Therefore in the sentence quoted the verbs should be either *makes* and *is* or *make* and *are.* In that sentence it could go either way. Here, however, is a sentence that is one-way: "What is most striking about Paris is the beauty of its buildings and the way that beauty is preserved." Because of the two nouns, *beauty* and *way,* there would be a temptation to use the verb *are* after *Paris,* but it must be resisted.

## WHENCE, WHITHER
(A couple of old words.) John Kenneth Galbraith has written a book entitled *Money: Whence It Came, Where It Goes.* If the first part of the title begins with *whence,* shouldn't the second part begin with *whither?* It could, of course, but it need not. Both *whence* and *whither* are used poetically and both have a slightly archaic sound, but *whence* occurs more commonly than *whither,* which for some obscure reason is often replaced by its more modern equivalent *where.* Caution: If you use *whence,* don't put a *from* ahead of it; the *from* idea is built into the word.

## WHETHER (OR NOT)
Often the *or not* after *whether* is a space waster. If you say, "It is not known *whether* the defendant will testify," you most certainly do not need an *or not* after the *whether.* On the other hand, if you say, "The parade will be held *whether* it rains," you most certainly do need an *or not.* When the intention is to give equal emphasis to the alternatives the *or not* is mandatory. And a good test of this is to try substituting an *if* for the *whether.* If that produces a change in meaning (as it would if you were to say, "The parade will be held if it rains"), then *or not* must be sup-

plied. In the first sentence cited above changing the *whether* to *if* ("It is not known *if* the defendant will testify") produces no altered meaning; therefore the *or not* is better omitted.

## WHICH
*See* THAT, WHICH (AND WHO)

## WHITHER
*See* WHENCE, WHITHER

## WHOEVER, WHOMEVER
(Wrong objective.) A fellow from N.B.C. called up, obviously to get a bet settled, and asked about a sentence that went something like this: "The pay should be adequate for whomever is doing the job." His question was, "Should it be *whomever* or *whoever?*" The answer is *whoever.* The pronoun is not the object of the preposition *for;* the entire following clause is the object. And within that clause the pronoun is the subject. Therefore, *whoever.* That should settle it for whoever is interested.

## WHO
*See* THAT, WHO, WHICH.

## WHOM'S DOOM
*The following article, which I wrote in 1975, appeared in The New York Times Magazine.*

If I have anything to say about it, the pronoun *whom* will be dropped from the English language except in one context. And I do have something to say about it in what follows.

It all began in my nationally syndicated newspaper column. In a slightly abbreviated form, the argument went like this:

"When a newspaperman writes, 'Five families told *who* they wanted for Mayor,' we have to assume either that he is not letter-perfect in grammar or that he is defying a centuries-old rule of syntax. Anyone who knows his English could tell him that the pronoun is the object of the verb *wanted* and therefore should be *whom.* That's what it says in the book, but it's not what is said by the vast majority in the streets, in the homes or even in the classrooms.

"It is not only because *whom* is useless and senseless; the word is in addition a complicated nuisance. Think, for example, of the puz-

zle-solving needed to determine the proper pronoun to use in each
of these sentences:

"'A suspect *whom* the police identified as John Jones was arrested.'

"'A suspect *who* the police said was John Jones was arrested.'

"'*Whomever (whoever?)* she marries will not be the boss in her
home.'

"The pronoun in the objective case form serves no purpose in the
language and should be banished, except when it follows immediately after a preposition and 'sounds natural' even to the masses, as
in 'To *whom* it may concern' or 'He married the girl for *whom* he had
risked his life.' Except for such post-prepositional uses of *whom*,
forget it."

Dropping *whom* will be neither radical nor unprecedented. The
wiping out of case declensions of pronouns has been going on for
centuries. The seven Indo-European cases were reduced to four,
then by the time of the Middle English period the four were cut
down to three with the disappearance of the distinction between the
dative and the accusative.

More than a century and a half ago Noah Webster denounced
*whom* as useless and argued that common sense was on the side of
"*Who* did he marry?" And half a century ago H. L. Mencken in *The
American Language* said, "Although the schoolma'am continues the
heroic task of trying to teach the difference between *who* and *whom*,
*whom* is fast vanishing from Standard American; in the vulgar language it is virtually extinct." He went on to note that "even in
England, says the Oxford English Dictionary, and on the highest
levels, *whom* is 'no longer current in natural colloquial speech.'"

Mencken made a valid point when he said that *whom* was fast
vanishing, but the real point is the vanishing point: How can we
speed its arrival? How can we escape from this pedagogical perplexity?

It seemed to me that the first step was to find out what experts
on English thought about *whom's* doom. So I drew up a list of a
couple of dozen teachers, consultants on dictionaries, writers and
knowledgeable linguists, striving, so far as I was able, to achieve a
balance between liberals and conservatives. A copy of the foregoing
argument was sent to each of them along with a letter asking each
to indicate agreement or disagreement with it by a vote of "yea" or
"nay" and inviting any comments the recipient cared to make. Not
to keep you in suspense, the results were 6 "nays," 15 "yeas" and
4 in-betweens, most of which leaned more to the "yea" side than the
"nay" side.

The comments ranged from interesting to fascinating. Space restrictions, alas, permit no more than brief excerpts from them. But here goes:

## Nays (6)

**Prof. Lionel Trilling,** Columbia University—"Difficult though the correct use of *whom* often is, it seems to me that the difficulty it entails is of a kind the confrontation of which tends to build character, and in our cultural situation we need all the character we can get."

**Russell Baker,** New York Times columnist—"I am in favor of having less said better right now. Having to pause at the thorn patch of *whom* assists the cause. I don't think we need any more encouragements than we already have to unthinking expression."

**Herbert Brucker,** former Hartford Courant editor—"Granted the academicians can never control the language of ye lower middle classes, ye tradesmen and ye masses. Language remains a living flux, whether Miss Thistlebottom likes it or not. But it seems to me the policemen of the King's English should squawk when common speech has the effect of chalk squeaking on a blackboard."

**Walter W. (Red) Smith,** New York Times sports columnist—"Is ignorance of grammar or the rules of syntax to be the criterion for accepted usage? Because Oom the Omnipotent can't manage the Omnipotent Whom, are we to let the infidel have his way? Not if you ask I."

**Rudolf Flesch,** writer on English style—"I'm afraid I can't quite bring myself to vote the poor little word *whom* out of the language. True it has almost vanished from where it once was firmly ensconced, but it has returned by the back door."

**Marya Mannes,** author and critic—"Anyone who says 'to who should I send this letter' should be shot. [Miss Mannes apparently overlooked the after-a-preposition exception.] The dropping of *whom* from the language is the direct equivalent of substituting *like* for *as,* along with the spastic stutterings of *yu'know's* as a prelude to all statements."

## Yeas (15)

**Prof. Jacques Barzun,** Columbia University—Flat vote; no comment.

**Dwight Macdonald,** author and critic—"YES, a thousand times YES on your proposal to deep-six *whom.* One of the practical beauties of English is its delightful poverty of inflection (ditto its confining of gender to sex). English has replaced French as the world's second language precisely because of its lack of such archaic frills. So do let's excise this vermiform appendix."

**Prof. Sheridan Baker,** University of Michigan—Flat vote; no comment.

**Prof. Robert L. Allen,** Teachers College, Columbia University— "I definitely agree with you that there is practically no need for the objective form *whom:* I feel that it would have passed out of the language long before this if only English teachers would ignore it."

**William F. Buckley Jr.,** editor of National Review—"Your distinction is exactly correct. Where *who* sounds right, it should be retained. . . . You are aware of the Leo Durocher answer to a tough question at a banquet speech? (Pause) 'Whom knows.' "

**Jessica Mitford,** author—"Or how about this one: You have rung a friend's doorbell late at night. He calls out, "Who is it?" Do you answer, "It is only I," or "It's only me"?

**Prof. S. I. Hayakawa,** President Emeritus, San Francisco State College—Flat vote; no comment.

**Margaret M. Bryant,** Professor of English Emeritus, City University of New York—"Jespersen long ago pointed out that *who* has become so generalized that it is practically the only form used in colloquial speech. In fact, those who have been made conscious of the form *whom* often employ it in the wrong place —a symptom of the decadence of the form. Since there is so much confusion and ample evidence on the use of *who,* I vote for the caseless use of *who.* "

**Eric Partridge,** English lexicographer—Flat comment "yes" in margin.

**William Morris,** editor of the American Heritage Dictionary— "You will recall that for many years The New Yorker used to cite misuses of *whom* under the standing head The Omnipotent Whom. About ten years ago I asked Hobie Weekes why I no longer found these items in the magazine. 'We ran a survey,' replied Hobie, 'and discovered that our readers didn't know what the things were all about.' "

**Roy H. Copperud,** Editor & Publisher columnist—"As for comment, I held forth at length on this subject on pages 436–7 of my Dictionary of Usage and Style."

**Prof. Mario Pei,** Columbia University—"One thought occurs to me on the negative side. Once the reform goes through, where will it be applied? In works of grammar and the better forms of writing, of course. But what about colloquial usage, particularly among journalists and politicians? Will they accept the simplification, or go on mixing the two forms in accordance with their delightful present habits?"

**Prof. Bergen Evans,** Northwestern University—"In my opinion a small fault lies in *whom,* a big one in ought." (A Dictionary of Contemporary American Usage, by Bergen and Cornelia Evans, discusses *whom* at some length.)

**Prof. Maxwell Nurnberg,** New York University—"If you look at page 35 of 'Questions You Always Wanted to Ask About English,' you will see that I agree 100 per cent with you."

**Vermont Royster,** Wall Street Journal contributing editor— "While my Yea vote is on principle, I must add that I am too cowardly to act upon it in practice. Furthermore, I foresee small success for this worthy enterprise. Who are we to succeed where Mencken and Noah Webster have failed?"

## In-Betweens (4)

**Norman Cousins,** editor of Saturday Review/World—"Admittedly, there are cases when insistence on correct usage is stuffy and pedantic; I see no reason why *who* shouldn't suffice. But if you abolish *whom,* as you propose, will you not therefore be judging those who use the word correctly? In this case, you are abolishing sin for the sinner but superimposing it on the virtuous. Why not simply call off the hounds in both cases?"

**David B. Guralnik,** editor of Webster's New World Dictionary— He voted by putting a question mark after Yea and making this comment: "The uncertain reply reflects my belief that advocacy of any linguistic change does not properly fall within my professional responsibilities. I do, of course, have personal reactions to a number of usages. I agree that the use of *whom* in the objective case (except where it immediately follows a preposition) seems to be on its way out of the language. My ear readily accepts either 'Whom did you see at the fair?' or 'Who did you see at the fair?' with equanimity. I am jarred only by such hyperurbanisms as 'He is the one whom it is believed will be nominated.' If the demise of *whom* were to result in the disappearance of that grotesquerie, I would be personally grateful."

**Jess Stein,** editor of the Random House Dictionary—He checked both Yea and Nay and wrote a "but" in between, then commented: "I simply don't think this is the kind of thing one determines in English. The language has an ornery quality that keeps it from yielding to logic, convenience or fiat. I can't argue in favor of continuing to teach *whom* and *who* in textbooks, but to whom shall we turn? to who?"

**Prof. Albert H. Marckwardt—** "Naturally I agree with the general purport of your treatment of *whom,* but your approach to the problem leaves me with mixed feelings. On the one hand, it is tantamount to announcing the death of Queen Anne; on the other, it suggests a kind of French Academy stance toward language change, a naive belief in the force of post hoc linguistic legislation. I doubt that advocacy, in the form of a solemn pronouncement that *whom* is dead or should die, will have much effect one way or the other."

As you see, there is little defense of *whom* on the ground of "correctness" or necessity. There is some on the ground of discipline and building of character. But most interesting to me is the feeling suggested in two or three of the responses that the banishing of *whom* is not the kind of thing that can be legislated. It is true that changes in the language in the past have come about by themselves without anyone's doing anything about them. But does that mean that nothing can be done? Has anyone—including Mencken and Webster—ever attempted to do anything beyond commenting on the need for a change?

I propose a course of action. To begin with, I propose that teachers of English drop the obviously futile attempt to drill into pupils' minds the senseless rules about *whom.* I suggest that such bodies as the National Council of Teachers of English and the Council for Basic Education decide that such rules are null, void, useless, trouble-making and from now on to be ignored. For the present the existing textbooks can remain in use with the teachers pointing out that what the books say about *whom* is in the same class as what some of them say about the split infinitive or about ending a sentence with a preposition. But from now on the textbooks should note that those rules are archaic.

But what about the grown-up who agrees that *whom* should go, but shrinks from doing anything about the matter himself for fear the "purists" will think him ignorant? For you who feel that way I have a gimmicky solution. No matter who you are writing to don't use a *whom* except after a preposition and, so he won't think you are ignorant, write at the bottom of the letter "I favor Whom's Doom except after a preposition." Better yet, get yourself a rubber stamp (cost about one dollar) and stamp that declaration on your stationery. It would look like this:

## I FAVOR WHOM'S DOOM
## EXCEPT AFTER A PREPOSITION

Who knows, after enough of us use such a stamp maybe the bumper-sticker people will grab the idea, spread it far and wide and our cause will be whom free.

### Who vs. Whom—Test Yourself

Score each of the following seven passages right or wrong. The answers given below are the way Miss Thistlebottom and her fellow traditionalists would score them.

1. If you can't trust Jones the Clothiers, who can you trust?
2. Now I see who he laughed at.
3. He was angry with whoever opposed him.
4. Instinctively apprehensive of her father, whom she supposed it was, she stopped in the dark.
5. Arthur, whom they say is kill'ed tonight . . .
6. The man whom they saw emerge from the car fired two shots.
7. The man who they say emerged from the car fired two shots.

Answers

1. wrong. 2. wrong (by Ben Johnson). 3. right. 4. wrong (by Charles Dickens). 5. wrong (by William Shakespeare). 6. right. 7. right.

## WILL
*See* SHALL.

## WINDFALL
The fad word *shortfall* brings to mind *windfall,* which is about four centuries older. William and Mary Morris in their *Dictionary of Word and Phrase Origins* say that in medieval England commoners were forbidden to chop down trees for fuel, but if a strong wind broke off branches or blew down trees, the debris was a lucky and legitimate find. Other sources suggest that the same conditions applied to fruit and even flowers. Today the word designates any unexpected advantage or piece of good luck.

# WORD DIVISION

Let it be said at once that there are no unanimously accepted rules about how to divide words at the ends of lines. Recently, in a newspaper the word *misused* was divided after the second *s* with the *ed* on the next line. One hesitates to say it is incorrect, but at least two books on usage in publishing frown on carrying over to a second line a terminating syllable of only two letters. Incidentally, but not irrelevantly, one of the most amusing word divisions, which crops up in newspapers constantly, is splitting the word *sources* after *sour*. Needless to say, that is a division that is improper as well as sour. One of the troubles that newspapers are encountering these days is that the automated type-setting systems never learned how to divide a word or when not to divide a word at the end of a line. One of those droll accidents happened in the Ann Arbor *News*. A sentence about anagrams spoke of "the fun of rear-" (end of line) *"ranging* the letters of a word." No comment.

# WORD CHANGES (FRONT AND BACK)

(Corned beef awry.) Writing about a political candidate's visit to the lower East Side in New York, a reporter wrote that "he ate a *corn beef* sandwich on rye bread with mustard." The meat being referred to is, of course, *corned beef* and that is the way it normally appears on menus. But there is a tendency among American plain people, as Mencken points out in *The American Language,* to drop the *d* sound when it appears before a consonant in the following word. Thus we have *ice cream* rather than *iced cream* (in both written and spoken language) and in American speech we also have *mash potatoes, hash brown potatoes, whip cream, old-fashion root-beer, bran new,* and *French fry potatoes,* which sometimes go a step further and become *French fries.* How many of these slurs will become legitimatized is unpredictable, but it can be said that the slicing of *corned beef* has not made it yet.

The dropping of the last letter or syllable of a word is called *apocope.*

(A napple?) Just as children often speak of a *napple* when they mean an apple, so our forefathers not infrequently did just that. Today's *newt* originally was an *ewt.* That kind of change is termed *prothesis.* On the other hand if a word began with an *n,* people sometimes assumed that letter was part of the article *an* and dropped it from the word. For instance, through a process known as *aphaeresis* the Middle English word *napron* became *apron*, the Middle English snake *nadder* became *adder* and the Arabic *naranj* became *orange*. Thus did the names of some commonplace things get perverted. But after all what's in a name?

## WOULD HAVE (OF)

(We've had enough of *of*.) What bothers Miss Thistlebottom and me is the use of *would of* instead of *would have*. When people speak, the contraction *would've* often sounds like *would of*, so you can't blame some schoolkids for writing it that way—once. But if teachers are doing their job properly, that first time should be the last time. *Hadn't of* is something quite different because *hadn't have* is not good English to begin with.

## WRACK, RACK

One doesn't *wrack* one's brains; one *racks* them. The verb *wrack*, as its spelling suggests, is related to *wreck*. The verb *rack*, on the other hand, is related to the noun *rack*, which in one sense was an instrument of torture. *Wrack*, therefore, means to wreck or ruin, and that isn't something you'd be likely to do to your brains. *Rack* means to torture or torment or stretch or strain, and that you might well do to your brains. It should be clear by now that this discussion has not been *nerve-wracking* (it hasn't wrecked your nerves, one likes to think), but it may have been *nerve-racking* (that is, it may have strained your nerves).

## WRONG, WRONGLY

(A wrong that's right.) The expression "don't get me wrong" has a slangy sound to it and it has been questioned by some people. One thing that gives it a colloquial feel is the use of *get* in the sense of understand. But that is a proper use of the word; indeed, it is related to the Indo-European base *ghend-*, from which came the Latin *prehendere*, meaning to grasp, understand. And then there is a feeling that *wrong* is wrong. You may think that it should be *wrongly*. But *wrong* is an adverb, too, and *wrongly* would sound stilted. All of this is not to say that "don't get me wrong" is the most dignified expression in the language, but rather to say that it is not an indictable offense.

## WROUGHT

A common misuse of a word is illustrated by this sentence from
a news dispatch: "The rains wrought havoc in parts of central
Korea." What the writer probably had in mind was the verb
*wreak* and he thought the past tense of it was *wrought.* But no.
*Wrought* is an alternative past tense of *work,* and its meaning is
shaped or molded or fashioned. The word the reporter wanted
was *wreaked,* which means, among other things, inflicted or
afflicted.

# X

## X-TIMES

(Problem of the times.) A question in a physics test that was reprinted in a newspaper recently raised a question of usage. In essence the question began, "If that distance is made three times larger than it now is . . ." Some argue that "three times larger than" means "four times as large as," which is not what the test meant to say. They contend that "three times larger than" one is four since three times one is three, and that amount added to one—i.e., producing a "larger than" total—would make four. They maintain that the wording should have been "three times as large as." Something that is three times as large as one is three. Certainly as far as common usage is concerned and perhaps also as far as technical mathematical usage is concerned that contention is correct. It's a tricky question, but obviously there is a difference between the two wordings that should be kept in mind.

A similar error is involved in the phrase *five times smaller than*. What is usually meant when that phrase appears is *one-fifth smaller than*. If you thirst for precision, drink up that fifth.

# Y

## Y'ALL

To avoid the idea of gender in the salutations of letters—such as "Dear Sir" or "Dear Madame"—a reader of Dear Abby's column suggested "Dear Y'all." Whereupon sweet Abby replied, "Y'all's entitled to Y'all's opinion; but I doubt that it will play in Peoria." Needless to say, she received letters declaring that she was in error in using *y'all* as a singular, that it is always used as a plural. H. L. Mencken, in *The American Language*, devotes a considerable piece of space to this question. He concedes that 99 times out of 100 the term is used as a plural, but then summarizes a running argument over that 100th time. If you want to be safe and sound, you will use *y'all* only as a plural.

## YE GODS

Here and there and now and again one encounters a restaurant called Ye Olde Chop House or something like that. The odds are at least 10 to 1 that the encounterer will pronounce the first letter of that name like the *y* in *yes*. Yes? No, that is not the way to pronounce it. The proper way to pronounce the word is *the*. It seems that in Old and Middle English the first letter of that word was a character called the thorn, which looked somewhat like the small-letter *p* and was pronounced *th*. But early printers erroneously substituted the letter *y* for the thorn and that introduced the present-day confusion. Of course, there is an archaic pronoun spelled *ye* and in that word *y* is properly pronounced like the *y* in *yes*.

## YET, AS YET

(Another problem—yet.) Are there rules about the use of *as yet* versus *yet*? In almost all contexts the use of *as* with *yet* is optional. You may say either, "He has not arrived *yet,*" or, "He has not arrived *as yet,*" as your little heart desires. There is one exception: When *yet,* meaning up to now, stands at the head of a sentence the *as* is just about mandatory. You would say, *"As yet* he has not arrived," but not, *"Yet* he has not arrived."

A peculiarity about that little rascal *yet* has apparently attracted no attention among authorities on usage but is most interesting. Take a look at this sentence: "The Dwarfs football team has *yet* to win a game." Everybody understands the sentence, but what do the words actually mean? You cannot omit the *yet,* nor can you move it to another position. You could do either of those things if the sentence read, "The Dwarfs have not *yet* won a game." So *yet* in the original sentence is the crucial word. But no dictionary definition explains it as used there. The word as so used, together with that construction, must be set down as a baffling idiom.